NORTHWEST SHORE DIVES

Second Edition

NORTHWEST SHORE DIVES

Second Edition

Stephen Fischnaller

Bio-Marine Images

Olympia, Washington

First Printing: August 1986
Second Edition: August 1990
Second Edition, Second Printing: March 1993

Published by Bio-Marine Images
2315 Muirhead Avenue NW
Olympia, Washington 98502

Library of Congress Catalog Card Number: 90-81452
Fischnaller, Stephen
Northwest Shore Dives

336 p., 21.5 cm
Bibliography: p 311-313
Includes Index
ISBN 0-9617106-1-6

All photos by the author
Printed and bound in the United States of America

ART CREDITS: By Figure Number

Animal drawings by Rae Dixon-Heinlein:

Animal drawings by Kevin Kelln:

Animal drawings by Siri Tuttle:

Map screens by Joy Vanderwerff

ACKNOWLEDGEMENTS

While growing up I was fortunate to have a father who took time from his busy schedule to introduce me to the biological world. He patiently showed my brothers and me a variety of animals, while pointing out behavior patterns and encouraging us to understand their life cycles. My first "wet" exposure to the underwater world occurred on the shallow edge of a freshwater lake in eastern Washington. I still remember the small sculpins that caught my attention as they scurried across the bottom. Without this early guidance, my interest in biology would be considerably less and this book would not have been written. A special thanks to my father and friend, Joseph Fischnaller, for this wonderful introduction to the biological world and, more recently, for the time he contributed while helping to proofread text.

Many friends have generously contributed to this project by participating with dives and providing encouragement and suggestions which helped make this book a reality. I would like to thank Sharon Rose, Bill Vincent, Helen Martin, Stuart Westmorland, Craig Pierce, and Carl Baird for the help that they gave as dive partners while collecting field information for the first edition. I would also like to thank Doyla Doty, Dan Doty, Dana Dean, Dan Duel, Barbara Duel, Gary Bower, Francine Harmeson, Keith Wyatt, Jolene Usitalo, Karen Trangmar, and Bruce Woods for their help as dive partners during the revision process.

A special acknowledgement goes to Joy Vanderwerff for her cheerful and enthusiastic support throughout the revision process, and for the many hours that she contributed as a dive partner. She made suggestions on diving safety, helped with animal identification, assisted with current mapping and photography, and made repeated dives at some sites to help determine times of plankton flow reversal (slack water). She patiently modeled for the cover photograph showing a diver beneath the Lime Kiln Point Lighthouse, as well as the photos of a diver feeding wolf-eels and an octopus. In addition to helping with field work, Joy also contributed her editing skills toward making suggestions as to how rough areas of text could be improved.

Many other individuals working in the sport diving industry have generously provided encouragement and suggestions throughout the project. I appreciate their interest in this book, and valuable input as divers and dive store owners. I would also like to thank those who provided air fills and assistance with equipment. A special thanks goes to Dan Eason for suggesting dive sites in the south sound area, and for his encouragement while I was learning to dive. Several people generously shared maps that they had made of dive sites. While these maps are not included in this book, the information was a helpful addition to my own observations while writing the respective dive site descriptions. A sincere thanks to Darrell Turner, Don Peterson and Heidi Lund for sharing their map of the Edmonds Underwater Park; to Rick Hiney and John Shields who mapped the bottom in front of the Ed Munro Seahurst Park; and to Ben Jackson and Karla Reece for their map of Saltwater State Park.

Ben Jackson also helped by reviewing the Current Table Section for clarity. Dave and Patti Jones reviewed the Non-Diver Activity section for each dive site and made suggestions for activities that could be added to the text. Jeff Christiansen shared bottom and structure depths for one of his favorite dive sites in south Puget Sound. Roland Anderson helped by answering questions about marine animals. Their help with this project is greatly appreciated.

I also would like to thank Rae Dixon-Heinlein, Kevin Kelln and Siri Tuttle for creatively combining their artistic ideas with the biological details needed to produce accurate pen and ink drawings.

As with any publication, errors seem to have a way of hiding during the editing process. Any errors remaining in the text are my responsibility. I welcome all suggestions or corrections that readers may have.

TABLE OF CONTENTS

The Greater Puget Sound Area

Figure 1

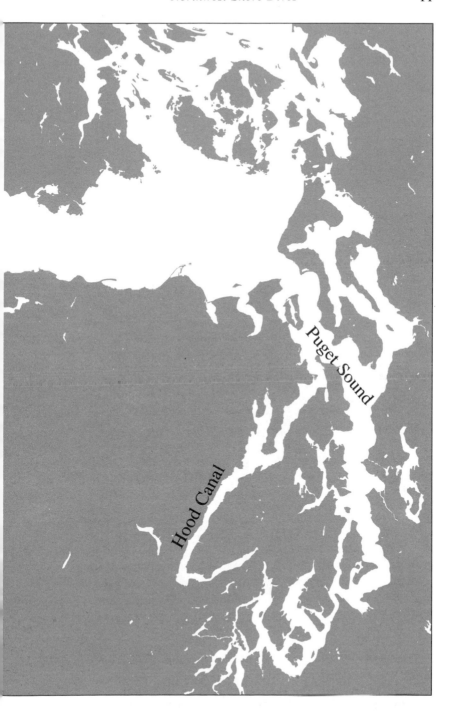

*If there is magic
on this planet,
it is contained in water.*

Loren Eisely

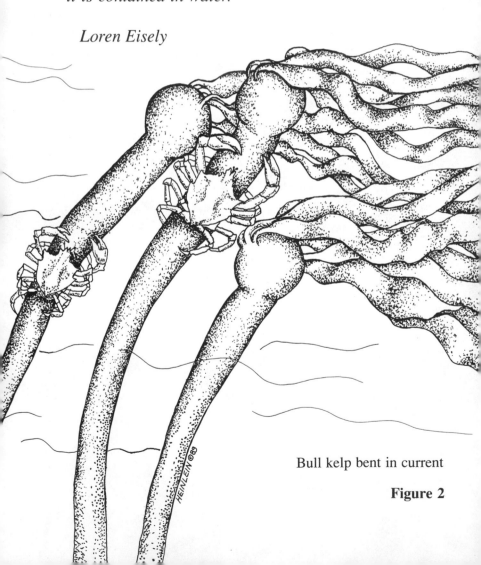

Bull kelp bent in current

Figure 2

PART 1. INTRODUCTION

Puget Sound, the Strait of Juan de Fuca and the San Juan Islands are beautiful and wonderful places to explore. They are unique areas where long inland passages provide an environment that is protected from the heavy surge so common along the Washington coastline. Many animal species found in the deep protected waters along this coastline are also found in the shallower protected areas of inland passages where they are visible to divers. Here, hidden from surface view, are the struggles for life and reproduction that go on twenty-four hours a day. The underwater world is a highly competitive jungle where animals constantly compete for living space, food, mates and life itself. The surviving animals remain alive because they are able to successfully compete in this environment by swimming rapidly, camouflaging themselves efficiently, growing large enough to discourage predators, or using an effective defense mechanism. As divers, we have the exciting opportunity to visit this beautiful and fragile marine world.

Survival requirements for plants and animals include nutrients, water, oxygen, sunlight and living space. If any one of these factors is missing or limited in a biological system, plant and animal growth also will be limited or stop altogether. Deep, nutrient laden water is constantly upwelling as water passes back and forth over nine major submerged ridges in the Puget Sound region. This constant supply of nutrients provides food for the bacteria and planktonic plants that form the base of the food chain. With all other growth factors present except sunlight, the biological stage is set. With the increased hours of sunlight during the months of early spring through summer, the waters literally explode with life. Huge masses of brown algae and kelp grow in just a few weeks, transforming exposed bottom configurations into jungle-like vistas. Plankton populations increase dramatically during this time and, in turn, serve as a major food source for many filter feeding animals.

Other seasonal changes in the marine environment can be just as dramatic. The huge growth of kelp present after each summer is torn from the rocks by pounding winter storm waves and tossed onto the beaches to rot. Due to the decreased hours of sunlight during fall and winter, plankton slowly die off. By early spring, when plankton populations have decreased to a minimum, visibility may reach 60 or more feet. Then, as spring daylight hours continue to lengthen, plankton populations suddenly increase (or bloom), and the cycle begins over. The kelp beds regrow and visibility again drops to the 8 to 20 foot range. Many people never have the opportunity to see these natural changes that occur beneath the surface. The same people probably will never experience the sensations of swimming for extended periods while submerged in a fluid that is eight hundred and twenty times denser than air. Divers have this opportunity, but, with it comes the responsibility of conservation and pollution control. As our population continues to increase, we must all learn to protect our environment. Some take excessive numbers of fish and shellfish that are eventually discarded without being eaten. These people either forget or don't care that the animals they have taken will be gone the next time they dive in the same area. Plankton populations bloom seasonally, but it takes eight to ten years for a lingcod to attain a length of 36 inches and a weight of 30 pounds. Only one-tenth of one percent of newly hatched fish survive to reach adult size. Life is too precious to kill just for the thrill of the hunt. We can all help by taking only the food needed for our immediate and personal use, and then by being sure to eat it before it spoils. For an increasing number of divers, successful dives are no longer contingent upon making a catch, but instead are dependent upon the ability to enter and exit the water safely, and to enjoy diving for the pleasure of watching marine animals interact in their natural environment.

When the revision process began for this book, it was not intended to be as extensive as it turned out. The original idea was to add about 10 new dive sites, plus inshore slack current correction factors for the East Wall of Toy Point (Fox Island). Once the correction factors had been determined for Fox Island, we continued diving to identify and collect information for potential new dive sites. This diving soon expanded to include many sites that were previously listed in the first edition. By the time the revision was completed, eight sites had been identified where times of inshore slack currents were significantly different from mid-channel slack currents. Correction factors for these sites were determined from field observations of plankton flow reversal, and are included in this edition. Additionally, ebb and flood current patterns were mapped at sites where directional flows were found to be different from main channel flows. This information is described in the Hazard Section of each respective dive site description.

Two dive sites, Sund Rock and the Fox Island Abandoned Ferry Pier, have been removed from this edition of Northwest Shore Dives (twelve were added). Conflicts have developed between divers and residents at these sites, at least partially because of misuse by divers and dive instructors. Since the purpose of this book is to provide readers with a list of dive sites available for public use, sites with contested public access are not included. When diving at any site, be considerate of residents living on adjacent property, as well as other divers who will visit the site later. Always make it your goal to leave a dive site in the same or better condition than when you found it.

In sharing these dive sites and animals with you, I hope that your visits to this beautiful and fragile marine environment will be as enjoyable as my visits have been. I also hope that you will have the opportunity to experience the thrill of watching an animal's natural feeding or hunting behavior. Discovering how marine animals compete for survival goes hand-in-hand with learning to appreciate and protect them.

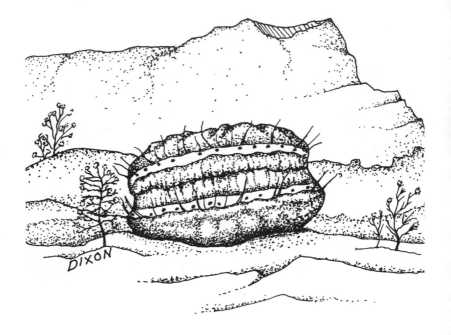

Figure 3   Pink Scallop

PART 2. CONTINUING TO DIVE AFTER CERTIFICATION

SAFETY AND EQUIPMENT

Learning to dive safely begins with professional instruction from a qualified instructor. During a basic SCUBA class, students are introduced to sport diving equipment, personal diving skills, and the fundamental relationships between compressed air, water pressure and human physiology. Yet learning to dive does not stop with the completion of a basic class, but is a continual process of improving and maintaining personal water skills. Once these skills are developed, an individual must dive regularly to maintain them and to continue to develop a level of personal comfort. The combination of personal comfort in the water, good physical condition, properly fitting equipment in good repair, and adequate planning for each dive promotes diving safety.

If you take care of your equipment, you can rely on it to function properly when you need it. This means washing your equipment in fresh water after each day's use. While washing it, inspect it for damage, then make repairs as needed. Your regulator deserves special care; soak it in fresh water for a few minutes instead of just rinsing it. The regulator is the most important piece of equipment a diver uses. Have it overhauled annually by a qualified service technician to insure that it will continue to function properly.

Before beginning each dive, calculate when slack current will occur. Make a final check of surface conditions for current and surge. Before entering the water, identify alternate exit points on either side of the area that you will be diving and discuss these with your buddy. Plan your entry and exit points so that you will not be swimming against the current when returning to shore. Always dive within the range of your ability and be willing to abort a dive if you are not comfortable with any aspect of it. Enjoy your dives.

CURRENTS, CURRENT TABLES and TIDE TABLES

Except for a few seconds each day, marine waters are constantly flowing through the many intriguing inland passages of the Pacific Northwest. Every four to eight hours, this water slows to a stop (slack current). During the following few seconds, billions of planktonic plant and animals, which have been constantly streaming in one direction for the past several hours, hang in the water column nearly motionless. Then, as if by magic, they begin to move in the opposite direction.

In reality, periods of slack current do not occur at the same time throughout the Puget Sound region. It takes time for this huge volume of water to move through the long passages. There are even some locations where the water never does stop moving, but continues to move in one direction during both flood and ebb exchanges. In these areas, periods of minimal current occur during the times when slack currents would otherwise be expected.

Pacific Northwest divers soon learn that most dives are more comfortable, more enjoyable, and safer when timed with the occurrence of slack currents. Actual slack lasts only seconds; however, from a practical standpoint, apparent slack will last from 10 to 30 minutes on either side of true slack. This gives a time window of 20 to 60 minutes every six to eight hours when the current will be minimal. Current tables are used to predict when these windows will occur.

Both current tables and tide tables are organized in a similar manner; yet one major distinction, often overlooked by sport divers, is that *current tables predict the horizontal movement of water and tide tables predict the vertical movement of water.*

Contrary to expectation, slack current often does not coincide with the occurrence of high or low tide in the Pacific Northwest. The time separation between a slack current and extreme tidal height is variable. This difference changes from day to day, being as much as two hours apart at some locations. Tide tables may appear to estimate times of slack water accurately, but only when apparent slack coincides with the occurrence of a high or low tide.

Tide tables are used to estimate times of maximum and minimum tidal heights, not times of slack current. *When planning dives, use current tables to estimate times of minimal current, and tide tables to estimate tidal height.*

CURRENT REFERENCE STATIONS

The brief period of minimal current flow is referred to as "slack before flood" (near low tide) when followed by a flooding current, or "slack before ebb" (near high tide) when followed by an ebbing current. The term "flood current" is used to refer to the movement of water into inland passages, while the term "ebb current" refers to the movement of water out of inland passages.

The following seven current reference stations are located in the Puget Sound, Strait of Juan de Fuca, Rosario Strait, and San Juan Island areas:

Admiralty Inlet
The Narrows
Deception Pass
Strait of Juan de Fuca
Race Rocks
Rosario Strait
San Juan Channel

Current tables list the following types of information for each reference station:

1. Daily predictions for times of minimum current
2. Daily predictions for times of maximum current
3. Daily predictions for maximum velocity of current
4. Direction of current flow
5. Velocity of current at any time
6. Duration of slack

Located in the same areas, with the above seven current reference stations, are 124 current substations for which slack current time correction factors are available. These correction factors represent time differences between the occurrence of slack water at reference stations and their substations. There are four correction factors for each substation; two for slack water times (flood and ebb) and two for times of maximum current (flood and ebb). To estimate when slack water will occur at a substation, time correction factors are either added or subtracted to/from the daily slack current predictions for a reference station. To find the time of maximum current, do the same type of calculation using the time correction factors for maximum current. Substation correction factors remain constant from year to year, while predictions for reference stations change daily.

Current tables and tide tables are published annually in two volumes by the National Ocean Service. These volumes cover the Pacific Coast of North America and Asia; one for currents and one for tides. A handy single volume, containing current and tide tables just for the Pacific Northwest, is published by Island Canoe, Incorporated. Island Canoe, Inc. also publishes two spiral bound books of current maps, entitled *Puget Sound Current Guide* and *San Juan Current Guide*. This information is extremely helpful in visualizing directions of current flow and locations of current stations. Current tables and tide tables must be purchased annually, while information in current maps remains constant and need be purchased only once. Island Canoe publications are concise, easy to use and available from many dive stores, marine supply stores and western Washington book stores.

PREDICTING TIMES OF SLACK CURRENT FOR SITES IN *NORTHWEST SHORE DIVES*

Current tables provide estimates of when slack currents will occur in mid-channel. When planning a dive, it is important to realize that currents often change direction in shallower inshore areas before changing direction in mid-channel. Knowing this, generally plan to enter the water 20 to 30 minutes ahead of predicted slack unless otherwise directed (additional current information is listed in the Hazards Section of each dive site description). Actual times of slack water also may be significantly influenced by weather conditions. Each dive site description in *Northwest Shore Dives*, except Crescent Lake, contains a "Current Table" section listing the name of a reference station and time correction factors that are to be used when calculating slack current. Inshore slack current correction factors are listed in this edition of *Northwest Shore Dives* for eight sites that have significant differences between mid-channel and inshore flows. These inshore slack current correction factors were determined from field observations of plankton flow reversals for dive sites at Rosario Beach, Edmonds Marina Beach, Warren Avenue Bridge, Titlow Beach, the Fox Island Bridge, Toy Point on Fox Island, Sunrise Beach, and the Hood Canal Bridge. They are listed by site name only, and do not have substation numbers. All other correction factors represent mid-channel flows, and are listed by substation numbers.

To figure out times of minimal current for a dive site listed in this book, follow the steps below:

1. Choose a dive site listed in this book and locate the "Current Table" section found in the dive site description. Find the name of the current reference station and the listed time correction factors for slack current.

2. Using a current table, turn to the section for this reference station. Find the times of slack water for the day that you will be diving. Write these down in a vertical column with the direction of flow that will follow slack. To avoid confusion between times of slack water and times of maximum flow, a "sF" can be used to designate slack before flood, and a "sE" for slack before ebb. In a column to the right, write down the correction factors opposite the respective sF or sE designation. Your columns would look like this if you were planning a dive at Titlow Beach, on August 10, 1990:

| The Narrows | Titlow Beach | |
Slack Water Time	Time Corrections	Predicted Times of Slack Water
02:18 sF	−0:05	
07:53 sE	+0:33	
14:16 sF	−0:05	
20:23 sE	+0:33	

Figure 4

3. Add or subtract the time correction factors identified in step one, to or from the daily current predictions for the reference station. Your columns will now look something like this:

| The Narrows | Titlow Beach | |
Slack Water Time	Time Corrections	Predicted Times of Slack Water
02:18 sF	−0:05	02:13 sF
07:53 sE	+0:33	08:26 sE
14:16 sF	−0:05	14:11 sF
20:23 sE	+0:33	20:56 sE

Figure 5

4. Daily current predictions are in standard time; add one hour to the slack current times during daylight saving time.

ADJUSTING BOTTOM DEPTHS TO COMPENSATE FOR TIDAL HEIGHT

Most bottom and structure depths listed in *Northwest Shore Dives* have been adjusted to represent depths that occur during tidal heights of 10 feet.

Perhaps you want to visit the west wall of Fox Island, but do not want to dive deeper than 80 feet. You would like to know what the depth will be along the bottom of this wall during your dive. From the dive site description in this book, you find that the rock ledge is crescent shaped with the end closest to the dive site entry at 56 feet (10 foot tide). The other end of the rock ledge is at 64 feet (10 foot tide).

To figure out what the actual depths along the base of this wall will be, the first step is to use a tide table to find out what the tidal height will be during your dive (excellent directions for determining the height of tide at any time are available in tide tables). Next, find the difference between the predicted tidal height and the ten foot reference tidal height used in *Northwest Shore Dives*. If the tidal height is lower than 10 feet, subtract the difference from the bottom depths listed for the base of the ledge. Conversely, if the predicted tidal height is higher than 10 feet, add the difference to the listed bottom depths. The resulting depths represent the height of water predicted to occur over the base of the ledge during your dive.

SELECTING A DIVE SITE

Each dive site description is divided into ten sections. The first nine contain information often used by divers when selecting and planning their dives. The tenth section consists of a drawing and biological description of a marine animal that divers may see while diving. These ten sections are described as follows:

Habitat and Depth:
This section provides a brief summary of what divers may find at a dive site in the way of structures, habitats, animal species and depths. Submerged structures include rock and clay ledges, bridge supports, rock jetties, tire reefs, concrete reefs, barges, boats, cars, a dry dock, wharf pilings, and the undersides of floating docks.

There are at least six different types of habitats in Puget Sound. These include rock formations, kelp beds, eelgrass beds, sand flats, mud flats and wharf pilings. The boundaries between habitats are not always clear, and may overlap each other. Eelgrass beds typically grow from sand and mud bottoms between the 19 and 24 foot depths (10 foot tide). Because bull kelp holdfasts require hard structures for attachment, the bottom beneath kelp beds will usually be rocky and no deeper than 40 feet (12 meters), although stipe lengths of up to 66 feet (20 meters) may occur by late summer.

Since animal populations are constantly changing, divers may not see the same animals as are reported in this section. Instead, they may see some of the animals listed, along with additional ones.

Most bottom and structural depths listed have been adjusted to represent depths that are expected to occur during 10 foot tidal heights. Depths for sites in the San Juan Islands and Strait of Juan de Fuca have been adjusted to Port Townsend tides. Depths for all other sites have been adjusted to Seattle tides.

Site Description:
This section provides suggested entry and exit points, locations of underwater structures, and alternate dives that can be made at the respective site.

Skill level:

A skill level has been assigned to each dive site. Dives classified for "All Divers" are located in sheltered areas requiring only basic skills to dive safely; "Intermediate" dives have two or three prominent hazards that a diver must consider when planning a dive; and "Advanced" dives have multiple hazards requiring accurate planning and advanced skills to dive safely.

Hazards:

Prominent hazards which divers may encounter are listed for each respective dive site. When present, they include currents, kelp, surge, small boats, and fishing line. Directions of flood and ebb current flows arc also included in this section, along with inshore current patterns if different from the main channel flow.

Facilities:

This section lists the facilities available at (or near) each respective dive site. Facilities may include dry changing areas, rest rooms or outhouses, hot showers, equipment showers, barbecue stands, picnic benches, covered eating areas, play structures, camping, hiking trails, fishing piers, parking, and closing hours. The closest air fill stations are also listed.

Travel Distance and Directions:

Mileages from Bellingham, Seattle and Olympia are listed in this section, along with driving directions.

Current Table:

This section names a current reference station and slack current correction factors for each respective site. This information is used when estimating slack current times. The preceding section on Currents, Current Tables and Tide Tables explains how to use these correction factors in greater detail (see pages 18-22).

Telephone Location: Contains directions to the closest phone.

Non-Diver Activities:
This section is for those choosing to stay above water. Many dive sites are located in (or near) public parks that are fun to explore, especially for those who enjoy being outdoors. Suggested non-diver activities include beach walks, picnicking with friends, fishing from public piers, volleyball, frisbee, baseball, hiking, bicycling, and exploring local communities.

Marine Animals:
I encourage divers to learn about the fascinating marine world they see while diving. Divers doing this will discover an increased appreciation for diving and the marine animals and environment that they see. They will begin to recognize animals and behavior patterns that might have been missed during earlier dives. They may even find that later, when others have lost interest in diving and have dropped out of the sport, they still eagerly look forward to their next dive. To encourage readers in this learning process, each dive site description includes a pen and ink drawing of an animal they may see at the site. The biological description with each drawing provides an introduction to the animal and its behavior characteristics.

Many excellent books are available on marine biology. Please invest in a few that interest you, and use them to identify the animals you see when diving. It may take more than one dive to recognize the distinguishing features for a specific animal, but this is an intriguing and rewarding process of discovery. To help you get started, a list of books on marine biology topics can be found in the appendix.

PART 3. SAN JUAN ISLAND

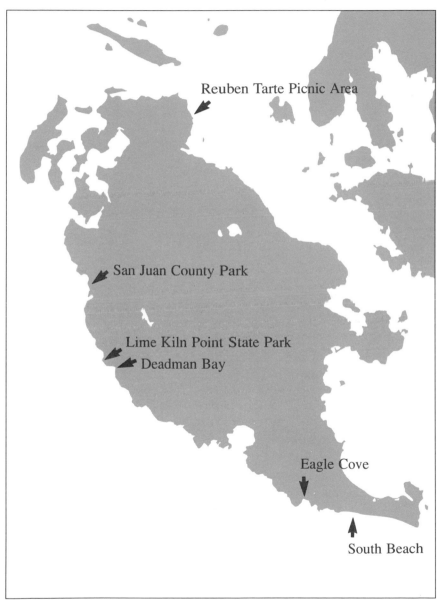

Reuben Tarte Picnic Area

San Juan County Park

Lime Kiln Point State Park
Deadman Bay

Eagle Cove

South Beach

Figure 6   San Juan Island

REUBEN TARTE PICNIC AREA

Habitat and Depth: With a little imagination and the right light, divers can sometimes see a dark stone lion sitting on the silty-sand bottom in Reuben Tarte Cove. The lion never seems to sleep, but instead is constantly guarding the entrance to this narrow cove, occasionally attacking boats that pass too close to the tip of the short rocky knoll.

Rocky shorelines reach out from each side of Reuben Tarte Cove. The longer rock ledge, forming the western side of the bay, extends into the water to 32 feet (10 foot tide) at the mouth of the bay. Beyond the inshore rock formations, on the west side of the bay, large boulders and underwater ledges extend down to 50 feet.

A few of the animals you may see when diving at this site include perch, painted greenling, stalked and red sea squirts, sea urchins, nudibranchs, blackeye gobies, chitons, red and green Christmas anemones and colorful sea stars.

Site Description: To explore the rock ledges and boulders located near the mouth of the bay, swim to the western rocky cliff, and submerge. Continue to swim outward, past the base of the cliff, until reaching the 50 foot depth. At this point, you can either turn to the northwest to explore the rocky shoreline, or to the southeast to swim an arc back inshore. Divers swimming this arc will find large rocks across the mouth of the bay and around the small rocky knoll forming the east side of the bay. If the light is right, you may even see the lion quietly resting in its favorite spot beneath the northwest tip of this knoll.

A second dive can be made by swimming along the rocky shoreline southeast of the rocky knoll. Have fun and enjoy your visit with the lion!

Skill Level: Intermediate.

Hazards: Current, bull kelp and wind-generated swells.

Localized current in Reuben Tarte Cove moves in a counter-clockwise direction during both flood and ebb exchanges.

A pebble beach provides an easy entry area

When wind-generated swells create rough surface conditions at this
site, dive sites located on the opposite side of the island may be flat
calm and good alternate dive sites (Deadman Bay, Eagle Cove and
San Juan County Park).

Current flow near Reuben Tarte Cove is affected by water
movement through President Channel, Spieden Channel and San
Juan Channel. The channels converge at the northeast tip of San
Juan Island, near Reuben Tarte Cove.

Flood currents move west-northwest through San Juan Channel
(past O'Neal Island and Reuben Tarte Cove) toward Limestone
Point, changing direction at the east end of Spieden Channel to flow
north-northeast into President Channel (see map on page 30).
When diving this area during slack before a flood current, explore
the shoreline southeast of Reuben Tarte Cove so that your return
swim will be with the flooding current.

Ebb currents move south-southwest through President Channel,
driving onto the shoreline between Limestone Point and Rocky Bay.
Current striking this shoreline, a short distance west-northwest of
Reuben Tarte Cove, divides into two directional flow segments.
One segment moves away from Reuben Tarte Cove, rounding

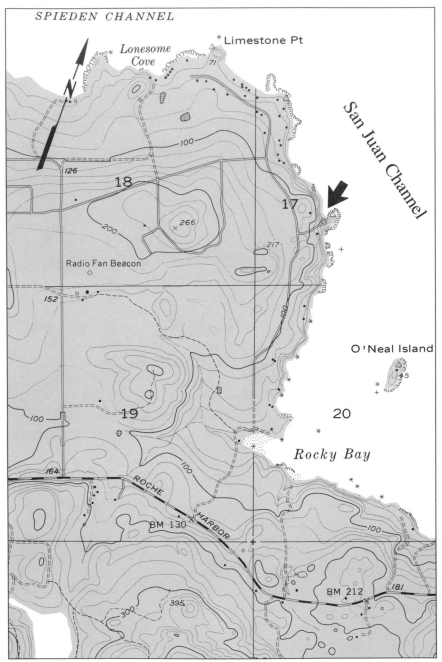

SPIEDEN CHANNEL

Lonesome Cove

*Limestone Pt

71

San Juan Channel

100

126

18

266

200

17

217

Radio Fan Beacon

152

100

O'Neal Island

45

19

100

20

100

164

Rocky Bay

ROCHE HARBOR

100

BM 130

0

300 395

BM 212

181

Figure 7

Not Intended For Navigational Use

Limestone Point into Spieden Channel. The other segment moves south-southeast past Reuben Tarte Cove, through Rocky Bay, and into San Juan Channel. When diving during slack before an ebb current, swim out along the shoreline north-northwest of Reuben Tarte Cove so that your return swim will be with the ebbing current. Divers venturing far enough along this shoreline will swim into a quiet silted area. Northwest of this area, ebb currents flow away from Reuben Tarte Cove, toward Limestone Point and Spieden Channel. Southeast of the silted area, ebb currents flow toward Reuben Tarte Cove.

Facilities: None at the immediate site. San Juan County Park has camping facilities and rest rooms. Hot showers are available at either Roche Harbor Marina or Friday Harbor Marina. Air tanks can be filled in Friday Harbor, either at the local dive store or on a commercial dive boat moored at Friday Harbor Marina.

Travel Distance and Directions: Reuben Tarte Picnic Area is located on San Juan Island, 10 miles northwest of Friday Harbor.

Mileage from Bellingham = 54 miles
Mileage from Seattle = 86 miles
Mileage from Olympia = 155 miles

Drive to Anacortes and follow the signs to the Washington State Ferry. Board the ferry for Friday Harbor and enjoy a two hour scenic ride through the San Juan Islands.

After leaving the ferry in Friday Harbor, take the first left-hand turn uphill onto Spring Street. In two blocks, turn right onto Second Avenue. In 0.3 mile, turn right onto Tucker Avenue (becomes Roche Harbor Road at fork) and follow for 7.3 miles to the intersection of Roche Harbor Road and Rouleau Road, just past Mile Marker 7. Turn right onto Rouleau Road and follow for 1.0 mile before turning right onto Limestone Point Road. In 0.8 mile, turn right onto San Juan Drive and follow for 0.3 mile before turning left into a gravel parking area. Drive down a steep gravel road 0.1 mile and park.

Current Table: San Juan Channel.
Look up the daily current predictions for San Juan Channel. Apply the following time corrections to calculate slack current times:

> Time corrections for subordinate station 1695:
> Minimum current before flood: +23 minutes
> Minimum current before ebb: –60 minutes

Telephone Location: None at the immediate site. Drive either to Roche Harbor or Friday Harbor. In Friday Harbor, you will find a phone on Second Street between the Town Of Friday Harbor Business Office and the Inter-Island Telephone Company buildings.

Non-Diver Activities: Reuben Tarte Cove's beach is covered with dark gray pebbles that glisten in the sunlight when wet. Visitors to this small bay can enjoy the mingling smells of fir trees and salt water while catching some sunshine on this short, secluded beach. There is also a prominent rocky knoll with a wonderful view across San Juan Channel to Jones, Orcas and Shaw islands.

Spending the weekend on San Juan Island can be fun. Overnight accommodations include several comfortable and romantic bed-and-breakfast establishments, waterfront cabins, motels, a hostel, and camping facilities (reservations recommended). Visitors can easily spend the better part of a day roaming around Friday Harbor. They quickly learn that the passage of time in town coincides with the docking and sailing of ferry boats.

Friday Harbor is the largest community in the San Juan Islands. It contains many different and interesting shops, including restaurants, book stores, art galleries, a whale museum and the San Juan Historical Museum. The Friday Harbor Marina is another interesting part of the community.

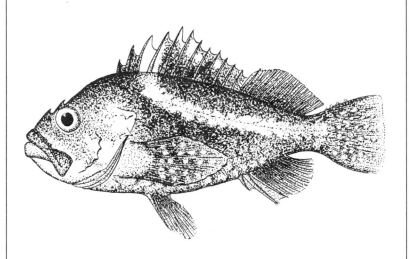

China Rockfish

The china rockfish, *Sebastes nebulosus*, has a beautifully striking black and yellow coloration. Its body is blue-black with yellow speckles and a prominent yellow stripe. The stripe extends downward between the third and forth dorsal fin rays to the lateral linc and then back to the base of the tail.

The lateral line, used to sense pressure changes created by the movement of other animals, is a collection of nerve endings along a fish's side. With this sensory system, fish can "feel" a diver's approach well before making visual contact.

Divers often see China rockfish in the Strait of Juan de Fuca and the San Juan Islands. They commonly live in rocky habitats between 40 and 70 feet in depth, yet have been recorded as deep as 420 feet (128 meters). China rockfish are territorial and may grow to a length of 17 inches (43 cm).

Figure 8

SAN JUAN COUNTY PARK

Habitat and Depth: Wonderful feelings accompany the act of crawling out of a tent in the morning, knowing that only a few steps away there is a diving experience waiting.

The rocky shoreline in San Juan County Park extends from Smallpox Bay to North Bay. Submerged rocks and a maze of bull kelp attract a variety of colorful animals. This is an interesting dive because of the bright colors, rock formations to swim around, and the sheer mass of animals that live here.

Animals living in this rocky habitat include blackeye gobies, turban snails, chitons, limpets, sea cucumbers, sea urchins, sharp-nosed crabs, small colorful tube worms, yellow cup corals, sea anemones, nudibranchs, giant barnacles, yellow sponges, blood stars, sun stars and sunflower sea stars.

Depth of the sandy-cobblestone bottom, between the shore and Low Island, ranges from 10 to 60 feet. North-northwest of Low Island, rock ledges drop past 108 feet.

Site Description: Four different dives are possible at San Juan County Park. All are great dives, each having a slightly different bottom terrain.

South of the park viewpoint and boat launch, divers can swim out along the southern shore of Smallpox Bay (opposite side of the bay from the boat launch) to avoid most of the small boat traffic. Rock structures along this shoreline extend downward 30 to 40 feet to the silty-sand bottom of Smallpox Bay.

A second entry point is located below and to the left of the park viewpoint. Entering from this point will place divers along a rocky shoreline between North Bay and Smallpox Bay. There are interesting animals and rocks all along this shoreline.

The third entry point is located in North Bay, immediately north of the large grass field in the park. This is a good entry choice for divers planning to explore the sandy bottom of North Bay or the rocky shoreline stretching northwest of San Juan County Park.

A madrona tree grows on the viewpoint at San Juan County Park

A fourth dive is possible by entering the water, either below the viewpoint or from North Beach, and swimming offshore toward Low Island. A kelp bed and series of rock steps surround this small island. The maximum depth between Low Island and the shoreline is 60 feet (10 foot tide). Swimming north-northwest from the north end of Low Island, divers will find a rocky bottom sloping to approximately 70 feet before dropping vertically to 110 feet. The south end of the island is shallower, reaching a depth of only 36 feet (10 foot tide).

Skill Level: Intermediate.

Hazards: Strong current, kelp and small boats.

Strong rip currents develop between the park shoreline and Low Island. Because of these currents, the swim to Low Island should be attempted only during slack current periods that will be followed by low exchanges. Before beginning a dive at this site, check the daily slack current predictions for Admiralty Inlet. Apply the appropriate flood or ebb correction factor (listed below) to find the

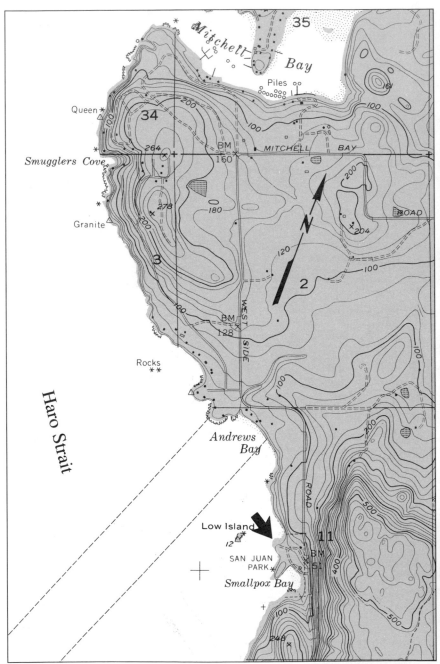

Figure 9

estimated time of slack water. Be sure to look at the water surface before entering to confirm that current has slowed and is near slack.

Facilities: Campsites, rest rooms, fire pits, picnic tables and a boat launch. Hot showers are not available in the park, but are available at both Roche Harbor and Friday Harbor marinas. Air fills are available in Friday Harbor at a local dive store or on a commercial dive boat moored in the marina.

Travel Distance and Directions: San Juan County Park is located on San Juan Island, 14 miles west of Friday Harbor. Friday Harbor is a two hour ferry ride from Anacortes.

Mileage from Bellingham = 58 miles
Mileage from Seattle = 90 miles
Mileage from Olympia = 159 miles

Drive to Anacortes and follow signs to the Washington State Ferry. Board the ferry for Friday Harbor and enjoy the ride through the San Juan Islands. After leaving the ferry, take the first left hand turn uphill onto Spring Street. In two blocks turn right onto Second Avenue and follow the main road for 7 miles (Second Avenue will become Guard Street and then Beaverton Valley Road). Turn left onto Mitchell Bay Road. Drive 3.1 miles to San Juan County Park (Mitchell Bay Road will curve to the right, then left, and left again to become West Side Road). The park entrance will be on your right-hand (west) side.

Current Table: Admiralty Inlet.
Look up the daily current predictions for Admiralty Inlet. Apply the following time corrections to calculate slack current times:

Time corrections for subordinate station 1725:
Minimum current before flood: +01 minutes
Minimum current before ebb: +36 minutes

Telephone Location: On the outside back wall of the San Juan County Park Office.

Non-Diver Activities: Visitors looking across the clearing in the park often become spellbound by the dramatic view of Haro Strait and Vancouver Island. Low Island is part of this view. Located a short distance from shore, it is surrounded by kelp that often glistens in the sunlight. Sea gulls soar overhead, dipping and turning as they search for food. Beyond the island, ships and whales pass through the channel, almost within touching distance. Haro Strait is alive. It is a magical place where the sound of water lapping on rocks blends with the twinkle of lights from Vancouver Island. Other activities in the park include camping, picnicking, fishing and photography.

San Juan Island has several historical landmarks that are fun to visit, such as Roche Harbor, the Afterglow Vista Mausoleum, English Camp and American Camp.

Roche Harbor Resort was originally a limestone mining town owned by the McMillin family. The unusual Afterglow Vista Mausoleum, nestled away in trees, is a quiet reminder of this past life on San Juan Island. The main structure of the mausoleum was built from stone by John McMillin, and now serves as a family tomb. A raised platform supports several columns that reach upward to a stone ring. Beneath this ring, and encircled by the columns, is a stone replica of the McMillin Family table, surrounded by chairs. Engraved in the back of each stone chair is the name of the family member whose ashes are enclosed beneath the seat.

American Camp and English Camp, now part of the San Juan National Historical Park, represent opposing military camps that were built when England and the United States were on the threshold of war over a territorial boundary dispute. The dispute climaxed when a Hudson Bay's pig was shot by an American settler in 1859 after the pig repeatedly returned to root in his potato patch. English and American ships began to land men and weapons as they prepared for war. War was diverted when both sides agreed to jointly occupy the island until the dispute could be settled.

American camp is located at the south-east end of San Juan Island. English Camp is located on West Valley Road, 4.6 miles from San Juan County Park.

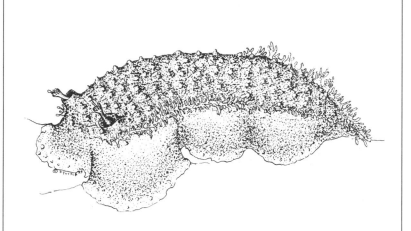

Orange Peel Nudibranch

The orange peel nudibranch, *Tochuina tetraquetra*, is one of the world's largest nudibranchs. Its bumpy, orange-yellow body is bordered on each side with a row of white branchial plumes that serve as respiratory structures. Two retractable sensory organs, called rhinophores, are located on the frontal area of this animal (see background of Plate 20). It lives in the subtidal zone, where it feeds on sea pens, growing to reach a length of 12 inches (30 cm).

Figure 10

LIME KILN POINT STATE PARK

Habitat and Depth: Hidden away beneath the Lime Kiln Lighthouse is a magnificent watery world. Bull kelp grows in its shallower inshore area, forming a kelp canopy over the surface that reduces light to a twilight. Below the kelp, a series of deep rock ledges and walls are covered with pink coralline algae and thousands of small animals. Rock structures extend from the surface to below 110 feet in depth.

Colorful invertebrates compete for living space as they thickly cover almost every rock surface. Orange tentacles of the burrowing sea cucumber protrude from cracks in rocks, while giant acorn barnacles sweep their feet in and out of their large calcareous shells as they feed. Red and green sea urchins graze on kelp with small sharp teeth, slowly pulling kelp stipes down from the surface with their tube feet and body weight. Solitary glassy sea squirts stand sentry duty over rocks. Seemingly delicate and out of place, these beautiful translucent animals feed on plankton filtered from the water. Small orange cup corals cover many rocks, competing for living space with chitons, snails and limpets. A variety of sea anemones display their tentacles as they wait for their next meal to blunder into their stinging grasp. Hundreds of brittle stars live beneath rocks and barnacles, while reaching their arms into the surrounding water to collect food particles. Sponges, octopuses, and hydroids contribute still more color and variety to this rocky habitat.

Site Description: Marine animals are protected from collection in Lime Kiln Point State Park. Please respect this marine sanctuary by leaving the animals in the water so other visitors may also enjoy the area's natural beauty.

From the northwest end of the parking area, walk along a service road that passes to the left of a wooden water tank and winds downhill to the water and lighthouse.

Immediately to the left of the lighthouse is a cleft in the rocks, forming an easy entry and exit point. Walk down through the rocky cleft, enter the water, and duck in under the kelp canopy to begin your descent along the rock ledges.

The Lime Kiln Point Lighthouse

Skill Level: Intermediate

Hazards: Kelp and strong current.

Current moves through Haro Strait in a northwest direction during flood cycles, and in a southeast direction during ebb cycles. Inshore from the main channel flow, in the small bay immediately south of the lighthouse, the current direction is reversed, moving in a clockwise direction during flood and counterclockwise during ebb. Plan your dive around slack current times.

Facilities: Picnic tables are located along the rocky shoreline south of the lighthouse. Rest rooms are in the parking area near the entrance to the park. Lime Kiln Point State Park is open from 8 A.M. to dusk. Air fills are available in Friday Harbor or Anacortes.

Travel Distance and Directions: Lime Kiln Point State Park is located on the west side of San Juan Island, 2 miles south of San Juan County Park.

> Mileage from Bellingham = 60 miles
> Mileage from Seattle = 92 miles
> Mileage from Olympia = 162 miles

Drive to Anacortes, follow signs to the Washington State Ferry, then board the ferry for Friday Harbor and enjoy a two hour ride through the San Juan Islands.

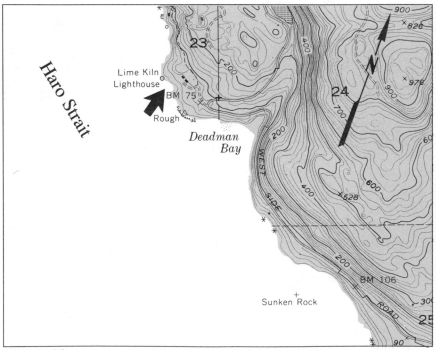

Figure 11   Not Intended For Navigational Use

After leaving the ferry, take the first left hand turn uphill onto Spring Street. Go two blocks and turn right onto Second Avenue. Follow the main road for 7 miles (Second Avenue becomes Guard Street and then Beaverton Valley Road). Turn left onto Mitchell Bay Road. Drive 3.1 miles to San Juan County Park (Mitchell Bay Road curves to the right, then left, and left again to become West Side Road). The entrance to the park will be on the right side of the road. Continue past the entrance to San Juan County Park for 2.5 miles, then turn right into Lime Kiln Point State Park, just before a sharp curve in the road.

Current Table: Admiralty Inlet
Look up the daily current predictions for Admiralty Inlet. Apply the following time corrections to calculate slack current times.

Time corrections for subordinate station 1720:
Minimum current before flood: +76 minutes
Minimum current before ebb: +59 minutes

Telephone Location: Turn left as you leave Lime Kiln Point State Park and drive 2.7 miles back to San Juan County Park. A public phone is located on the outside back wall of the San Juan County Park Office.

Non-Diver Activities: Lime Kiln Lighthouse is perched on a low, rocky bluff. It is closed to the public, but visitors can walk to the shoreline to see this picturesque lighthouse and enjoy the dramatic view across Haro Strait. A whale watching platform, located on a rocky bluff near the lighthouse, provides a good vantage point for the view.

This rocky habitat is also a good area for snorkeling. From the surface, one can glimpse the countless numbers of small animals that live beneath a kelp canopy.

Deadman Bay is located a short walk from Lime Kiln Point State Park. To reach it, follow West Side Road southward for 0.2 mile to where an open hillside slopes to a sandy beach and Deadman Bay.

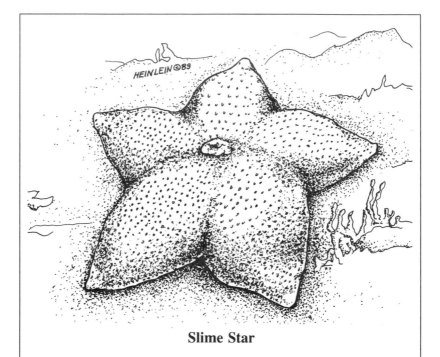

Slime Star

The slime star (or cushion star), *Pteraster tesselatus*, gets its name from the animal's ability to produce large amounts of mucus when stressed. If placed in a bucket with other animals, this seemingly innocent sea star will produce enough mucus to smother the other animals.

The slime star has a thick, puffy central disk with five thick arms. It ranges in color from a mottled brown and yellow to uniform shades of light or deep yellow. A central opening at the top of the central disc is used for respiration. Slime stars feed primarily on sponges, but are also reported to eat bryozoans, anemones, and hydroids. They reach a diameter of 7 inches (18 cm).

As is common with many sea stars, scale worms live in association with the slime star. One or two worms can often be seen imbedded between spines on the underside of the this animal.

Figure 12

DEADMAN BAY

Habitat and Depth: Unless you arrive by boat or airplane, your first view of Deadman Bay will be from the roadway. An open, grassy field slopes downward to a small pebblestone beach and the dark rock formations and kelp beds that border each side of this picturesque bay.

A long rocky shoreline forms the east side of the Deadman Bay (left side when looking out from shore), rising vertically above the water and stretching to the south. Rock formations along the south end of this wall extend down to 47 feet in depth (10 foot tide). On the opposite side of the bay and west end of the beach, a low rock structure juts out into the bay a short distance. Past this rock formation, a long rocky shoreline continues to extend outward while rounding to the west-southwest.

Animals you may see while diving along the rocks include octopuses, perch, tube snouts, blackeye gobies, nudibranchs, sharp-nosed crabs, hermit crabs, chitons, limpets, sea stars, Christmas anemones, sea squirts, sea urchins, sea cucumbers and shrimp.

This shallow bay has a silty-sand bottom that reaches a maximum depth of 52 feet (10 foot tide).

Site Description: During the summer and fall, both rocky shorelines in Deadman Bay have extensive kelp beds that are fun to swim through. When diving in thick kelp, a light is often useful to brighten the holes and crevices in the rock formations and enhance the brilliant reds and yellows of the animals living on the rocks.

Along the east side of the bay, divers can explore a long rock ledge that rounds outward to the south-southwest for 0.2 nautical mile. Discovering the types of animals that live in a partially protected rocky habitat can be exciting.

The west side of the bay also extends outward for 0.2 nautical mile, but to the west-southwest. This shoreline offers a series of submerged rock formations and walls that are covered with communities of red, purple and green sea urchins. While the inner bay is rich with animal life, an even richer abundance lives on the rock faces outside the bay.

A canoe passes over a kelp bed on the east side of Deadman Bay

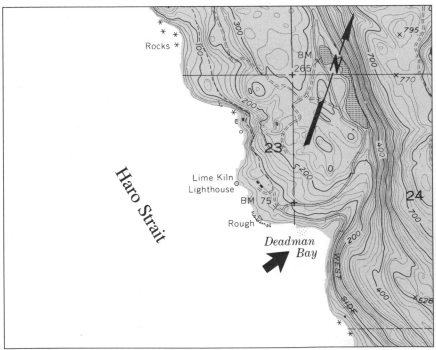

Figure 13

Not Intended For Navigational Use

Skill Level: All divers (in the inner bay) to advanced (when swimming to the mouth of the bay).

Hazards: Strong currents with variable direction, thick bull kelp, and wind generated surge. At least three circular current patterns occur in Deadman Bay during flood and ebb cycles. Divers will find that the current changes direction and becomes stronger as they swim out along either side of the bay. It is best to dive this site during a slack period before a low exchange.

During a flood cycle, divers swimming out along the east side of the bay will at first be swimming into current. As they continue to swim outward, they will pass through a seemingly slack area, and then will find themselves swimming with current.

Conversely, divers swimming out along the west side of the inshore area during a flood cycle will initially be swimming with current. A short distance from the beach the current reverses. Beyond this point, divers will be swimming against an inbound current, until, further out along the rocky shoreline, the current reverses again and flows outward.

When diving during an ebb current, divers swimming out along the eastern shoreline will at first be swimming with an outbound current. Continuing to swim outward, they will reach an inbound current. Finally, near the mouth of the bay, the current will shift again and divers will be swimming with an outbound current.

Divers swimming out along the western side of Deadman Bay during an ebb current cycle, will at first be swimming against an inbound current. Continuing outward, they will pass through an quiet area before swimming into an outbound current. Finally, near the mouth of the bay, they will again be swimming against an inbound current.

Facilities: None at the immediate site. Outhouses are located at Lime Kiln State Park. San Juan County Park has camping facilities and rest rooms. Hot showers are available at both Friday Harbor Marina and Roche Harbor Marina. Fill your air tanks before leaving Anacortes, or in Friday Harbor at the dive store or on a commercial dive boat moored in Friday Harbor Marina.

Travel Distance and Directions: Deadman Bay is located on San Juan Island, 17 miles west of Friday Harbor.

> Mileage from Bellingham = 61 miles
> Mileage from Seattle = 93 miles
> Mileage from Olympia = 162 miles

Drive to Anacortes and follow the signs to the Washington State Ferry. Board the ferry for Friday Harbor and enjoy the two hour ride through the San Juan Islands. After leaving the ferry, take the first left hand turn uphill onto Spring Street. In two blocks turn right onto Second Avenue and follow the main road for 7 miles (Second Avenue becomes Guard Street and then Beaverton Valley Road). Turn left onto Mitchell Bay Road. Drive 3.1 miles to San Juan County Park (Mitchell Bay Road becomes West Side Road). Continue past the entrance to San Juan County Park for 2.5 miles. From a sharp curve in the roadway (at the entrance to Lime Kiln State Park), drive an additional 0.2 mile to a turn-out on the right side of the road. Park and walk down the hill to Deadman Bay.

Current Table: Admiralty Inlet.

Look up the daily current predictions for Admiralty Inlet. Apply the following time corrections to calculate slack current times:

> Time corrections for subordinate station 1720:
> Minimum current before flood: +76 minutes
> Minimum current before ebb: +59 minutes

Telephone Location: Follow West Side Road northwest for 2.9 miles to San Juan County Park. A phone is located on an outside wall of the park office.

Non-Diver Activities: Lime Kiln Point State Park is a 0.2 mile walk northwest along the road above Deadman Bay. In Lime Kiln Point State Park, a narrow service road leads past a wooden water tank, then downhill to an observation platform and the Lime Kiln Point Lighthouse. From the viewing platform beside the lighthouse, visitors are able to look across Haro Strait to Vancouver Island.

Sun Star

The sun star, *Solaster stimpsoni*, is easily recognized by the blue-gray stripes radiating outward from the top center of its central disc to the tip of each ray. The sides of each ray are usually a contrasting yellowish-orange color or, occasionally, a light red. This colorful sea star frequently has ten rays; however, individuals with up to fourteen rays may be seen. Growing to a diameter of 10 to 14 inches (25-36 cm), it is commonly seen in subtidal areas of Puget Sound, the Strait of Juan de Fuca and the San Juan Islands. This colorful sea star feeds primarily on sea cucumbers.

Figure 14

EAGLE COVE

Habitat and Depth: Eagle Cove is a wide secluded bay which divers can easily spend the day exploring. The cove has a log-strewn sandy beach, bordered at each end by wind and wave swept rocky shorelines. Sand, eelgrass, kelp and rocky habitats merge in Eagle Cove, resulting in a beautiful and rich environment that is home to many small animals.

Swimming through the kelp forest and around the large rocks provides only a brief glimpse of the tremendous natural beauty, which is part of this fragile environment. During the summer months, bull kelp grows along each side of the bay to form a heavy kelp canopy that reduces the underwater light to twilight. Within this dimly lit world, countless numbers of animals move about as they compete for survival.

A few of the animals you may see when diving include painted greenlings, octopuses, tube-snouts, perch, white sea cucumbers, red sea urchins, white plumose anemones, and a variety of colorful sea stars.

Inside Eagle Point (see map on page 51), submerged boulders and ledges extend downward to 56 feet (10 foot tide) in depth, where they disappear into a smooth sandy bottom.

Site Description: Along the west side of the shallow inner bay, divers can enjoy exploring the rocks and kelp that are only a short swim from shore. Divers up to a longer swim can continue past the first rocky point (visible from the beach) and out along the shoreline toward Eagle Point.

Swimming out along the east side of the bay, the shoreline rounds an unnamed point (still in the inner bay) into another small and shallow rocky bay. The bottom along this side of the cove does not deepen as quickly as on the west side. Please leave the site and animals as you would like to see them on a return visit.

Skill Level: Intermediate.

Looking southwest across Eagle Cove to Eagle Point

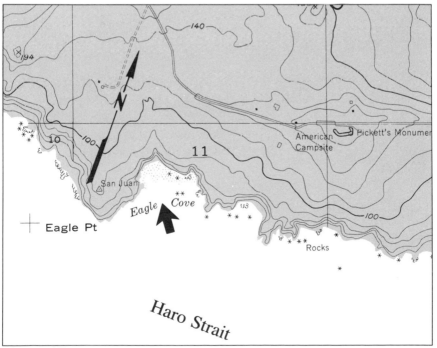

Figure 15

Not Intended For Navigational Use

Hazards: Thick bull kelp, moderate current and wind generated swells.

Flood current flows westward into Eagle Cove, where it is driven onto the western shoreline between Eagle Point and the small unnamed point that is visible from the beach. After striking the shoreline, current flow turns south-southwest and flows out along the rocky shoreline before rounding Eagle Point and flowing west-northwest with the main flow of Haro Strait. Inside the unnamed inner point, flooding currents flow in along the shoreline, turning in a clockwise pattern across the beach and then flowing out along the rocky shoreline on the eastern side of Eagle Cove.

Divers swimming out along the western shoreline during a flooding current will at first be swimming against current. After rounding the inner point, where the current flow reverses, they will be swimming with an outbound current.

Directional flow for ebb current is variable in Eagle Cove, depending on the size of exchange. During ebb exchanges of six feet or less, current flow resembles the previously described flood pattern. During larger exchanges, ebb current flows past the mouth of Eagle Cove, from Eagle Point to the east-northeast. At these times, divers will experience only light current inside Eagle Cove.

Facilities: None at the immediate site. Hot showers are available at the Friday Harbor Marina and Roche Harbor Marina. San Juan County Park has camping facilities with rest rooms, but no hot showers. Air fills are available in Friday Harbor on a commercial dive boat moored in the Friday Harbor Marina or at the local dive store.

Travel Distance and Directions: Eagle Cove is located on San Juan Island, 6 miles south of Friday Harbor. Friday Harbor is a two hour ferry ride from Anacortes.

Mileage from Bellingham = 50 miles
Mileage from Seattle = 82 miles
Mileage from Olympia = 151 miles

Drive to Anacortes and follow signs to the Washington State Ferry. Board the ferry for Friday Harbor and enjoy the two hour trip through the islands.

After leaving the ferry, take the first left hand turn uphill onto Spring Street. Follow Spring Street for 1.4 miles, turn left onto Douglas Road, and drive another 1.4 miles before turning left onto Little Road. In 0.4 mile, turn right onto Cattle Point Road and follow for 2.7 miles. Just before entering American Camp, turn right onto Eagle Cove Road and follow for 0.4 mile to a small public access parking area. Park and walk down a wooded trail to Eagle Cove.

Current Table: Admiralty Inlet.

Look up the daily current predictions for Admiralty Inlet. Apply the following time corrections to calculate slack current times:

Time corrections for subordinate station 890:
Minimum current before flood: −77 minutes
Minimum current before ebb: +64 minutes

Telephone Location: San Juan County Park Office.

Non-Diver Activities: Individuals interested in watching or photographing wildlife will enjoy their visit to Eagle Cove and the surrounding countryside. Hundreds of rabbits live in burrows throughout the soft fields around American Camp. During the spring, the rabbit population seems to explode as young rabbits appear at the burrow openings to sun themselves. They provide a source of food for hawks and eagles, which are commonly seen flying overhead while hunting for their next meal.

Tiger Rockfish

If any fish were to remind a diver of a swimming bandit, it probably would be the tiger rockfish, or *Sebastes nigrocinctus* (magnificent black belt). This fish is easily recognized by five dark red bars extending vertically across its pale red side. Two smaller dark bars radiate back from the eyes to the edge of the operculum. Another smaller bar radiates from each eye to the top of the head.

When not out foraging for food, this striking fish frequently retreats into hiding in rock crevices. It is a territorial and solitary fish, growing to 24 inches in length (61 cm), and living at depths between 50 and 900 feet (15-274 meters). Divers are more likely see this fish north of Puget Sound.

Figure 16

SOUTH BEACH

Habitat and Depth: While the dive at South Beach is not for big game hunters, it is a wonderful dive for those interested in looking at small animals in a sandy habitat. The shallow bottom slopes gradually downward, and although seemingly flat and open, is full of life. The bottom in the inshore intertidal zone is cobble, changing to smaller size particles, coarse sand, and then fine sand as you move offshore.

As you swim over the bottom, especially during the summer months, you may see countless numbers of sand lances erupting in waves from the sandy bottom. These little silver fish seem to emerge from nowhere, popping out of the bottom part way, pausing briefly as if stuck, and then wiggling free to swim away. Enormous schools of sand lances may surround you during your dive.

Gunnels hide in the eelgrass and kelp, using their diet determined yellow-green or red-brown colors for camouflage. Decorator crabs disguise their backs with sponges and plants. Pacific spiny dogfish cruise this shallow area looking for food. Hermit crabs scurry about on the bottom, and hooded nudibranchs cling to eelgrass while collecting passing plankton from the water.

Two species of eelgrass form wide bands between the 17 and 26 foot depths. Beyond the eelgrass, there are a few isolated rocks scattered over the bottom at depths greater than 35 feet. The maximum depth for a shore dive in front of South Beach is approximately 45 feet (10 foot tide).

Site Description: South Beach is a long sandy shoreline that extends eastward for two miles to the southeastern tip of San Juan Island. This stretch of shoreline is part of a national park beach, and thus a marine preserve. It is illegal to collect animals of any kind at this site.

South Beach has an easy access; as you can drive to within a few feet of the water. Enter from any point along the beach and swim out over the shallow, gently sloping bottom while looking for the small animals that live in this habitat.

South Beach stretches to Cattle Point

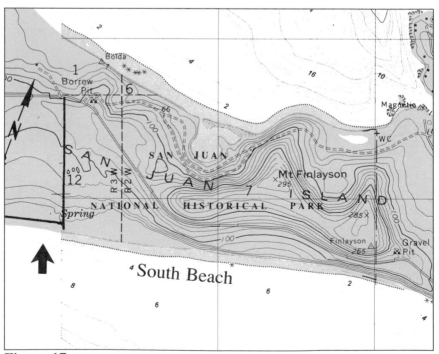

Figure 17   Not Intended For Navigational Use

Skill Level: All divers

Hazards: Moderate current and wind generated swells. Both ebb and flood currents move parallel to shore, in an eastward direction toward Cattle Point.

Facilities: Outhouses and picnic tables. Air fills are available in Friday Harbor.

Travel Distance and Directions: South Beach is located on the south side of San Juan Island, 2 miles west of Cattle Point.

Mileage from Bellingham = 52 miles
Mileage from Seattle = 153 miles
Mileage from Olympia = 84 miles

Drive to Anacortes and ride the Washington State ferry to Friday Harbor on San Juan Island.

The first left turn after leaving the Friday Harbor Ferry Dock will put you on Spring Street. To drive directly to South Beach from Friday Harbor, follow Spring Street for 1.6 miles, through town and past the airport, before turning left onto Douglas Road. Then follow Douglas Road for 1.5 miles and turn left onto Little Road. Take the next right turn onto Cattle Point Road, drive for 4.3 miles and turn right onto Picketts Lane. Picketts Lane will end at South Beach in 0.5 mile.

When driving to South Beach from the west side of San Juan Island, follow West Side Road past San Juan County Park, Lime Kiln Point State Park, and Deadman Bay (see pages 37, 42-43, and 48 for directions to these dive sites). After passing Deadman Bay, West Side Road becomes Bailer Hill Road. Follow Bailer Hill Road through a 90 degree left turn onto Douglas Road. After making this turn, take the next right-hand turn onto Little Road and follow the above directions.

Current Table: Admiralty Inlet
Look up the daily current predictions for Admiralty Inlet. Apply the following time corrections to calculate slack current times:

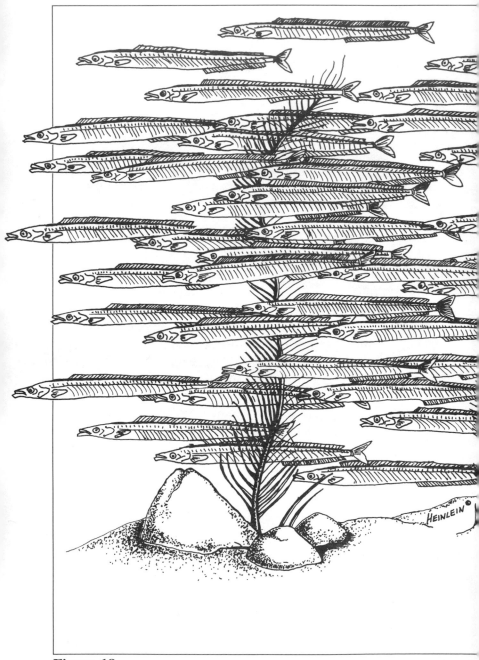

Figure 18

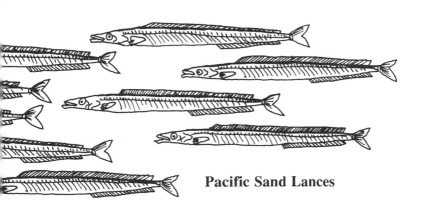

Pacific Sand Lances

Divers often see large schools of the Pacific sand lance, *Ammodytes hexapterus*, gliding silently through shallow, inshore areas. These dense groups of small silver-gray fish contribute to the magic of the underwater world. The fish move in unison as one large flexible entity that is constantly changing shape. Schools of both the Pacific sand lance and Pacific herring move into intertidal and high subtidal areas to feed on copepods, amphipods and mysids. In turn, birds and larger fish feed on Pacific sand lances and Pacific herring.

Coloration is similar in the two species, each having a gray upper body and silvery sides. Both species of fish have a forked caudal fin, but can be easily differentiated by distinctive differences in body shape and the length of their fins.

Pacific sand lances have long, slender bodies with long dorsal and anal fins. The dorsal fin extends over two-thirds of the body length, while the anal fin is slightly longer than one-quarter of the body length. In contrast, Pacific herring have thicker bodies with very nearly the same proportions that salmon have. Additionally, its dorsal and anal fins are short in length.

The Pacific sand lance has an interesting habit of burrowing into the sand, presumably for protection. This fish grows to 8 inches in length (20 cm).

Time corrections for subordinate station 890:
Minimum current before flood: –77 minutes
Minimum current before ebb: +64 minutes

Telephone Location: None at site. Drive 8.3 miles to Friday Harbor. A phone is located on Second Street between the Town Of Friday Harbor Business Office and the Inter-Island Telephone Company buildings.

Non-Diver Activities: The shallow depths along this long sandy beach provide an area easily accessible to snorkelers. A mask, snorkel, fins and wetsuit are the only equipment needed for a person to see the hundreds of interesting animals that live here. A brief swim without a wetsuit is possible too, especially during the summer months when the sunshine slightly warms the shallow water along the shoreline.

Looking eastward over the long sandy stretch of South Beach, Cattle Point Lighthouse can be seen perched on a bluff at the southeast tip of San Juan Island. South Beach stretches for 2 miles, from Picketts Lane at the South Beach day use area, to the Cattle Point Lighthouse. This long stretch of beach is accessible from land only at each end. Weather and tide permitting, people can walk the beach from the South Beach day use area to the lighthouse and Cattle Point Interpretive Area (a good place to meet a ride or have a picnic).

To reach the Cattle Point Interpretive Area from the beach, walk past the lighthouse on the southeast tip of San Juan Island. Continue around Cattle Point and then across a sandy bay to a trail leading to the Cattle Point picnic area at the top of the bluff and the eastern end of Cattle Point Road. The picnic area is situated above a narrow passage that separates San Juan Island from Lopez Island, at the south end of San Juan Channel.

Other activities include visiting nearby American Camp, watching the rabbits that live in the surrounding fields, kite flying from the sandy beach, or building a fire (in designated fire pits only) while enjoying a wonderful view across Haro Strait to Vancouver Island, the Strait of Juan de Fuca and the Olympic Mountains.

PART 4. **ORCAS ISLAND**

Figure 19   Orcas Island

BROWN ROCK / OBSTRUCTION PASS

Habitat and Depth: The potential for a remarkable dive at Brown Rock provides incentive for making this long surface swim from shore. Divers making the swim will not only have an adventure in current, but, after reaching the rock, will find an intriguing formation to explore. Thousands of colorful animals cover the outer side of Brown Rock. Orange sea cucumbers, white sea cucumbers, red sea urchins and giant acorn barnacles are the dominant species. In addition, delicate golden staghorn bryozoans, orange cup corals and chunks of white sponge are attached to the rocks. Other animals include gumboot chitons, smaller chitons (such as the beautifully marked lined chiton), limpets, purple sea stars, sun stars, large sunflower sea stars, blood stars, six-rayed stars, green urchins, nudibranchs and hermit crabs.

The outside base of Brown Rock is at 44 feet (10 foot tide). Beyond this point, a moderate slope continues downward to a depth of 67 feet (10 foot tide) where the bottom becomes a mixture of shale, sand and mud.

Site Description: Enter the water from the beach between the county pier and boat launch. Swim out from shore toward the rock (see the Hazard section below for current information). After reaching Brown Rock, submerge and begin to explore the angular rock formations and wide variety of animals. Outside the rock, a series of ledges drop in jagged steps to the bottom. Inside the rocky formation is an intriguing, narrow and shallow channel that is fun to swim through. Limpets and chitons cover the smooth sides of this channel.

Skill Level: Intermediate divers who are comfortable swimming in current.

Hazards: Current and small boats. Do not attempt this swim during tidal exchanges greater than 5.5 feet or if you are not comfortable in current.

Looking toward Brown Rocks and Obstruction Pass

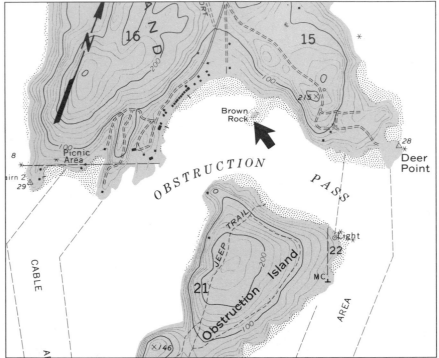

Figure 20   Not Intended For Navigational Use

During both flood and ebb exchanges, inshore currents move counterclockwise from Brown Rock toward the county pier and boat ramp. Slack current periods followed by current reversal do not occur along this shoreline. Instead, inshore current slows when mid-channel slack occurs in Obstruction Pass, then picks up speed again in the same direction.

During an ebb exchange, water enters Obstruction Pass at the east end of the channel and flows counterclockwise along the Orcas shoreline, moving past Brown Rock, the county pier, boat ramp and out along the south-southwest shoreline of the bay.

During a flood exchange, water flows into Obstruction Pass at the south end of the channel and drives onto Brown Rock where it splits into two segments. Inshore from the rock, flooding current turns counterclockwise and flows back along the shoreline toward the boat ramp.

Divers can use the main channel flow during a flood exchange to help with this long surface swim by heading directly out from the county pier, through the inshore current moving away from the rock, and into the main channel flow moving toward the rock. The remainder of the swim to the rock will be with the current. A direct swim to the rock is difficult, but can be made during a low exchange, beginning about 20 minutes before slack. Pick out a mooring buoy in your near path and swim toward it, so that it can be used as a rest stop if needed.

After completing your dive and beginning your return swim, move inside the rock to take advantage of the inshore current moving toward the county pier.

Facilities: A county boat pier and boat ramp.

A rest room is available next door at the Lieber Haven Marina Resort. This resort also offers cabins, a small grocery store, and a restaurant specializing in fresh seafood and French and German pastries (the Lieber Schwann Inn). Air fills are available on the west side of the island at West Beach Resort.

Travel Distance and Directions: Obstruction Pass is located between Obstruction Island and the southeast tip of Orcas Island, 18 miles from the Orcas Ferry Pier.

Mileage from Bellingham = 62 miles
Mileage from Seattle = 94 miles
Mileage from Olympia = 163 miles

Drive to Anacortes, follow signs to the Washington State Ferry, and board the ferry for Orcas Island. After leaving the ferry at Orcas Island, immediately turn left and follow the Orcas-To-Olga Road for 8.1 miles. Turn right into Eastsound and drive 1.3 miles to a tee. Turn right again and follow the Orcas-To-Olga Road for 6.5 miles, past the turnoff to Rosario and through Moran State Park (past the turnoff to Mount Constitution). Turn left at Cafe Olga onto the Olga-Point Lawrence Road. Drive 0.6 miles, turn right at a fork onto Obstruction Pass Road, and drive the remaining 1.9 miles to a parking area beside the Lieber Haven Marina Resort.

Current Table: Rosario Strait.
Look up the daily current predictions for Rosario Strait. Apply the following time corrections to calculate slack current times:

> Time corrections for subordinate station 1535:
> Minimum current before flood: −59 minutes
> Minimum current before ebb: −38 minutes

Telephone Location: Outside the marina office.

Non-Diver Activities: The Orcas Island Artworks is a cooperative gallery where local artists display their art and craft work. Located in Olga, it shares a building with Cafe Olga. Visitors can see the work of local artists while tasting the highly recommended homemade pie served at the cafe.

Nearby Moran State Park offers camping, swimming and hiking. The park has 26 miles of foot trails, ranging from a level 2.5 mile walk around Cascade Lake to a 4.3 mile hike with a 2027 foot elevation gain to Cold Springs. Visitors can also drive to a stone observation tower at the top of Mount Constitution for a panoramic view of Rosario Strait and Bellingham Bay. Islands visible from this vantage point include Patos, Sucia, Matia, Barnes, Clark, Lummi, Sinclair and Cypress.

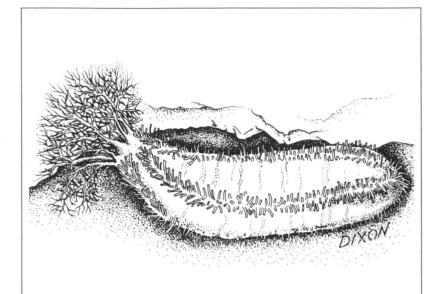

Orange Sea Cucumber

The orange sea cucumber, *Cucumaria miniata*, uses five rows of tube feet to attach its body in place, usually inside rock fissures or lodged between closely spaced rocks. Its colorful oral tentacles are often the only visible part of this striking animal. Tentacle coloration varies, being orange, yellow, bright red or brown. Cucumbers feed by capturing plankton and floating detritus on their sticky tentacles, which are then inserted one at a time into the central mouth to remove the food particles. Orange sea cucumbers grow to 10 inches (25 cm) in length.

Figure 21

DOE BAY

Habitat and Depth: Contorted rocky shorelines form both sides of Doe Bay, bending sharply inward in many places to form intriguing small coves and blind pockets that are fun to peer into. There is minimal inshore current and an easy entry over a narrow, sandy cobblestone beach in front of Doe Bay Village Resort.

Perhaps due to the silt that dusts every structure, animal life is not abundant at this site, although there is a wide variety of animals to see. Animals living on the mud bottom in the mouth of the estuary include hermit crabs, kelp crabs, hooded nudibranchs, flounder and tube dwelling anemones. When diving along the rocky shoreline you may see orange sea cucumbers, frosted nudibranchs, purple sea stars, Christmas anemones, gumboot chitons, sunflower sea stars, California sea cucumbers, red sea squirts, snails, limpets, chitons, shrimp, small sculpins, sea urchins, rockfish, perch, sand lances, kelp greenling and blackeye gobies.

On the east side of Doe Bay, the rocky shoreline drops 15 feet (10 foot tide) to a sandy-cobblestone bottom covered with shell fragments. On the west side of the bay, the rocks meet a silty sand bottom at a depth of 20 feet (10 foot tide). Beyond the rocks, in slightly deeper water (22 feet), is a large eelgrass bed. By 29 feet (10 foot tide), the bottom has changed to a silty-mud.

Site Description: Entry at Doe Bay can be made from a narrow sandy-cobblestone beach in front of the Library/Assembly Hall. From here you can swim out along either the southeast or southwest rocky shoreline.

Along the southeastern shoreline, a submerged rock ledge and wall is located immediately east of the inlet. To reach it, swim across the estuary mouth to the second outcropping of rock, just past the estuary opening, and submerge. The top of the ledge is at 27 feet, while the base of the rock drops to 40 feet (10 foot tide). Large red sea urchins and other colorful invertebrates live along this rock wall.

A wooden lion looks out onto Doe Bay

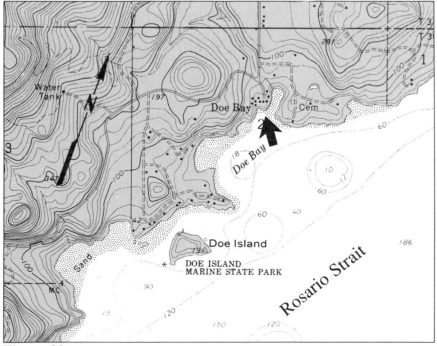

Figure 22   Not Intended For Navigational Use

The shallower rock formations along the southwestern shoreline are also great to explore. Carrying a dive light on this dive will help you see into the many holes and crevices used by animals for shelter.

Skill Level: All divers.

Hazards: Current and occasional small boats. Flooding currents move to the northeast. Ebbing currents move to the southwest.

Facilities: Doe Bay Village Resort has both camping facilities and small rustic cabins. There is also a community kitchen, restaurant, health food and convenience store, sauna, mineral baths (clothing optional), hot showers and even a garden hose for washing equipment. Day use privileges are available for a small fee. Be sure to check in with the office when arriving. Air fills are available on the west side of the island at West Beach Resort.

Travel Distance and Directions: Doe Bay Resort is located on Orcas Island, 19 miles from the Orcas ferry landing. Orcas Island is a 65 minute ferry ride from Anacortes.

Mileage from Bellingham = 63 miles
Mileage from Seattle = 95 miles
Mileage from Olympia = 164 miles

Drive to Anacortes, follow signs to the Washington State Ferry, and board the ferry for Orcas Island. After leaving the ferry, immediately turn left and follow the Orcas-To-Olga Road for 8.1 miles. Turn right into Eastsound and drive 1.3 miles to a tee. Turn right again and follow the Orcas-To-Olga Road for 6.5 miles, past the turnoff to Rosario and through Moran State Park (past the turnoff to Mount Constitution). Turn left at Cafe Olga onto the Olga-Point Lawrence Road. Drive the remaining 3.3 miles to Doe Bay Resort.

Current Table: Rosario Strait
Look up the daily current predictions for Rosario Strait. Apply the following time corrections to calculate slack current times:

Time corrections for subordinate station 1540:
Minimum current before flood: +08 minutes
Minimum current before ebb: +49 minutes

Telephone Location: In front of the Doe Bay Resort restaurant.

Non-Diver Activities: The quiet surroundings of Doe Bay Resort are ideal for enjoying the natural beauty of the northwest while socializing with friends. Canoe rentals and guided kayak tours to the Peapod Wildlife Sanctuary are available at Doe Bay.

The small towns of Olga, Eastsound, Orcas and Deer Harbor have restaurants and interesting shops to explore.

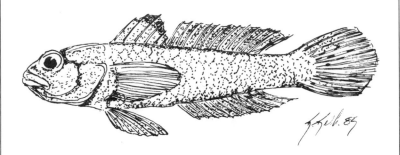

Blackeye Goby

The blackeye goby, *Coryphopterus nicholsi*, grows to 6 inches (15 cm) in length and lives in protected areas where there are rocks to hide under. It has a pale yellow coloration with large black eyes. Other characteristics include a rounded anterior dorsal fin crested in black (the pelvic fins of breeding males are also black), large scales and a rounded caudal fin (tail). This little fish exhibits an interesting territorial behavior. Divers often see it disappearing into a burrow, which it has scooped out beneath a rock, then reappearing at the entrance to peer out. During the nesting season between April and October, the males compete for mates. They swim off the bottom to display their black pelvic fins, then turn and dart back into their dens. This behavior is repeated until eventually a female follows and lays eggs. The male fertilizes the eggs and then guards them until they hatch.

Figure 23

PART 5. LOPEZ ISLAND

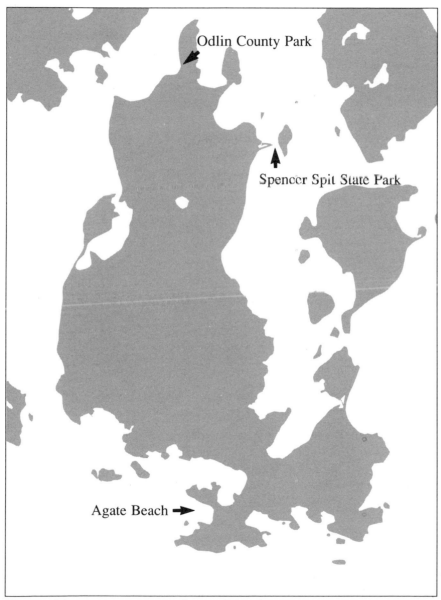

Figure 24   Lopez Island

ODLIN COUNTY PARK

Habitat and Depth: Odlin County Park is a wonderful place to spend the day while playing on a sandy beach. The beach is bordered on each end by a low rocky shoreline, with a short pier extending out at the north end of the park. The bottom depth at the end of the pier is 35 feet (10 foot tide). Tube-dwelling anemones live on the soft bottom in front of the beach. They eat small animals that come into contact with their long, graceful tentacles. When a small hermit crab is dropped onto the anemone, the crab may or may not be eaten. If the crab is fully retracted into its shell when contact is made with the anemone's tentacles, it may not be recognized as food and be rejected. If the crab is only partially retracted, the tentacles may recognize it as food and pass it to the mouth.

Other animals living in this area include California sea cucumbers, sunflower sea stars, hermit crabs, geoducks, orange sea pens, brown and white striped nudibranchs, orange sea cucumbers, sun stars, purple stars, red-orange blood stars, leather stars, slender pipe fish, delicate comb jellies, kelp crabs and sharp-nosed crabs.

A sandy bottom slopes gently downward to a depth of 25 feet, where the bottom then changes to mud. The maximum bottom depth inside the bay is 67 feet (10 foot tide), but continues to deepen outside the bay.

Site Description: There are three dive sites to choose from at Odlin County Park; the bay, the northern rocky shoreline and the southern rocky shoreline.

Entering the water from the beach, divers can swim out into the bay, through the eelgrass and across an open bottom. Both tube-dwelling anemones and large orange sea pens live in the bay. Try feeding a tube-dwelling anemone by dropping a small animal onto the anemone's oral disc and then quietly watching as the animal bends its graceful tentacles inward to contact and capture its prey.

A totally different dive is possible by entering the water near the fishing pier and swimming north along the rocky shoreline. By drifting for a short time beneath the pier, divers may find them

The Odlin County Park fishing and boat pier

selves surrounded by curious fish, perhaps even a school of slender pipefish. Continue swimming north from the pier along the rocky shoreline while exploring the submerged boulders and rock crevices. Look for orange, yellow, and purple ochre sea stars.

A third dive can be made along the rocky shoreline and through a kelp bed on the south side of the bay.

Skill Level: Intermediate.

Hazards: Kelp, small boats, fishing line and moderate current with a variable ebb pattern.

Current moves northward past Odlin County Park during both flood and ebb tidal cycles for exchanges of 3.9 feet (1.2 meters) or less. During larger exchanges, the directional flow of ebb current moves first to the south and then reverses to flow northward. The timing of current reversal during an ebb cycle is variable, being dependent upon the range of tidal exchange, and occurring up to 3 hours into an ebb cycle. Flood currents always flow northward.

Current reversal in Upright Channel occurs during an ebb cycle when current flowing east through San Juan Channel drives onto the west shore of Lopez Island and is deflected into the south end of Upright Channel. As this current increases to equal the force of the opposing current flowing into Upright Channel from the north, a second slack occurs. When an ebb current entering Upright Channel from the south becomes stronger than current entering from the north, the flow reverses. Current then moves northward through the channel while still ebbing.

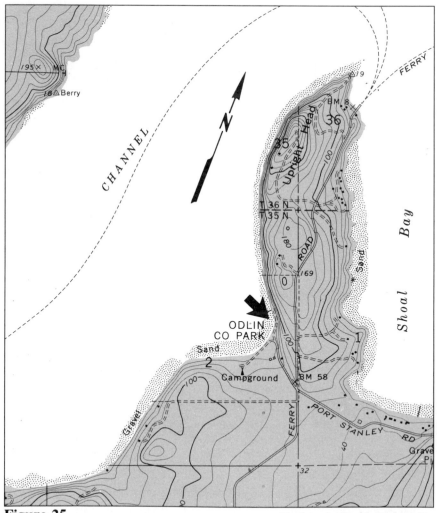

Figure 25

Slack current before a flood cycle does not occur at this site. Instead, the already northern bound ebb current only slows during times of minimum current before picking up speed again as a flood current.

Facilities: Camping, picnic tables, a covered eating area, fire pits, pit toilets, a small fishing pier, softball field, volleyball net and a boat launch. Air fills are not available on Lopez Island. The closest air fill stations are located in Friday Harbor and Anacortes.

Travel Distance and Directions: Odlin County Park is located on Lopez Island, 1.5 miles south of the ferry landing. Lopez Island is a 40 minute ferry ride from Anacortes.

> Mileage from Bellingham = 45 miles
> Mileage from Seattle = 77 miles
> Mileage from Olympia = 147 miles

Drive to Anacortes, follow signs to the Washington State Ferry, and board the ferry for Lopez Island. After reaching the ferry dock at the north end of Lopez Island, drive south for 1.1 miles on Ferry Road before turning right into Odlin County Park. Drive to the water's edge and park.

Current Table: San Juan Channel.
Look up the daily current predictions for San Juan Channel. Apply the following time corrections to calculate slack current times:

> Time corrections for subordinate station 1705:
> Minimum current before flood: +15 minutes
> Minimum current before ebb: +11 minutes

Telephone Location: Beside the park roadway near the office.

Non-Diver Activities: A family can easily spend an active day at this isolated county park. An old rowboat, partially filled with sand, is a great beach-side sandbox for young visitors wishing to take an imaginary trip to sea. For other visitors remaining on shore, there is a grass field with a baseball diamond and a volleyball net. Organize a baseball or volleyball game, toss a frisbee, walk along the sandy beach, fish from the pier or dig for clams.

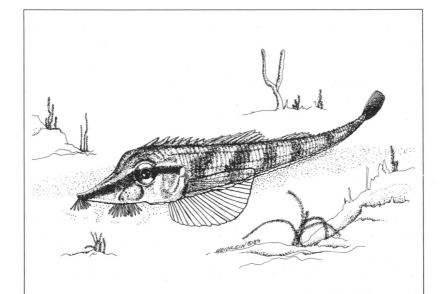

Sturgeon Poacher

The sturgeon poacher, *Agonus acipenserinus*, has an impressive set of whiskers protruding downward from the lower jaw and tip of its triangular shaped snout. Covered with plates instead of scales, this fish is easily recognized by its pointed snout, whiskers, large bony head and slender tapering body. It commonly grows to 9 inches (23 cm) in length, although longer individuals reaching 12 inches (30 cm) have been reported. Sturgeon poachers frequent depths of 60 to 180 feet, but may also be seen in shallower water on sandy and muddy bottoms. It feeds primarily on worms and small crustaceans.

Figure 26

SPENCER SPIT STATE PARK

Habitat and Depth: This dive offers an adventure that is worth the long walk out onto Spencer Spit. A narrow channel at the end of the spit separates the end of Spencer Spit from Frost Island. This is where the dive site is located. Admittedly, it is easier to dive Frost Island from a boat, but boatless divers who walk the spit will be rewarded with a colorful dive along a rock wall.

The bottom in the channel, between Spencer Spit and Frost Island, is sandy with a maximum depth of 64 feet (10 foot tide). The bottom slopes upward from the center of the channel to the base of a rock wall on the west side of Frost Island. North of the spit, this wall reaches a maximum depth of 67 feet (10 foot tide).

Orange tentacles belonging to burrowing sea cucumbers protrude from cracks in rock ledges and walls. Occasional glassy tunicates and small groups of plump, waxy red tunicates stand out against the dark rocks. Hairy yellow helmet crabs, octopuses, grunt sculpins, penpoint gunnels, painted greenlings, decorated warbonnets and orange-spotted nudibranchs are a few of the animals that live here.

When diving below 33 feet, a dive light can be used like a paint brush to restore the red, orange and yellow colors. Sweeping this light across rock surfaces, and the attached animals and plants, returns and brightens the full color spectrum. Pink coralline algae, yellow cup corals and bright red colonies of colonial tunicates burst into view. Sunflower sea stars, blood stars, leather stars, sun stars and slime stars add still more color to the array of animal life covering the rocks.

Site Description: Pulling a red wagon with you, as you walk out onto Spencer Spit, is a convenient way of carrying heavy weight belts and tanks on this long walk of approximately 500 yards. One-third of the way out onto the spit is a picnic table that can be your first rest stop. Closer to the point (two-thirds of the way out onto the spit) is an old cabin with another picnic table. The cabin is open, and provides a second convenient rest stop. From the cabin, you can enter the water on either side of Spencer Spit to cool off, then walk or swim the remaining distance to the sandy point.

Spencer Spit stretches toward Frost Island

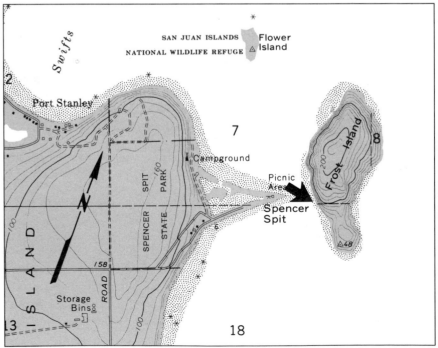

Figure 27   Not Intended For Navigational Use

Enter the water from the end of the spit, submerge and cross the narrow channel toward Frost Island. By following the bottom contour down the sandy slope and across the channel, divers will remain beneath overhead boat traffic. As you ascend along the sandy bottom, now on the opposite side of the channel from Spencer Spit, dark shapes begin to materialize in front of you as you near the rock base of Frost Island. The rock ledges and walls can be explored in either direction around the base of Frost Island, however, there is less sediment along the wall to the north of the spit. Enjoy your dive; it is definitely worth the walk.

Skill Level: Intermediate.

Hazards: Strong current and small boats.

Frequent boat traffic passes through the narrow channel between the end of Spencer Spit and Frost Island. Cross this channel on the bottom to avoid overhead boat traffic.

Currents flow northwest through the channel during flood cycles, and to the southeast during ebb cycles. Plan your dive so that you will be diving during a slack current period and returning along the wall with the current.

Facilities: Rest rooms are located in the upper parking area, between the beach and upper campground. The upper campground has campsites with fire pits, plus a large covered eating area with barbecue stands. The lower campground has wilderness campsites and designated fire pits along the beach. Located at the base of Spencer Spit is a charming day use picnic area with a small rock shelter. Air fills are not available on Lopez Island, but tanks can be filled in Friday Harbor on San Juan Island, or in Anacortes.

Travel Distance and Directions: Spencer Spit State Park is located on the northeast side of Lopez Island, 3 miles south of the ferry landing.

> Mileage from Bellingham = 48 miles
> Mileage from Seattle = 80 miles
> Mileage from Olympia = 150 miles

Drive to Anacortes, follow signs to the Washington State Ferry, and board the ferry for Lopez Island. After arriving on Lopez Island, drive south for 2.0 miles before turning left onto Center Road. Follow Center Road for 0.7 miles and turn left onto Cross Road. Then, in 0.5 mile, turn right onto Port Stanley Road. Now drive 0.2 mile, turn left onto Baker View Road, and drive the remaining 0.6 mile to the outer gate of Spencer Spit State Park.

After passing through a second gate, the first roadway on the right leads to the Ranger Office and a steep gravel access road that winds down to the beach. Due to the limited parking at the bottom of this road (for handicapped and load/unload uses only), plus erosion problems, use of the road is restricted. Before proceeding down the hill, stop at the Ranger Office and ask permission to use the access roadway to transport diving equipment to the base of Spencer Spit. After securing permission, drive your equipment down the hill, unload, and move your car back to the parking area above Spencer Spit. The short walk down to the beach from the parking area is much easier without an exposure suit and gear.

Current Table: Rosario Strait.

Look up the daily current predictions for Rosario Strait. Apply the following time corrections to calculate slack current times:

> Time corrections for subordinate station 1520:
> Minimum current before flood: +46 minutes
> Minimum current before ebb: +19 minutes

Telephone Location: Alongside the park roadway, just inside the inner gate.

Non-Diver Activities: The long sandy beach that forms Spencer Spit is a great place to catch some sun while enjoying a great view. Visitors can go for a walk along the shoreline or through the trees. They can venture out for a swim in the shallow water along Spencer Spit or, with a kayak or canoe, can paddle around Frost Island. Frost Island is privately owned, so do not go ashore.

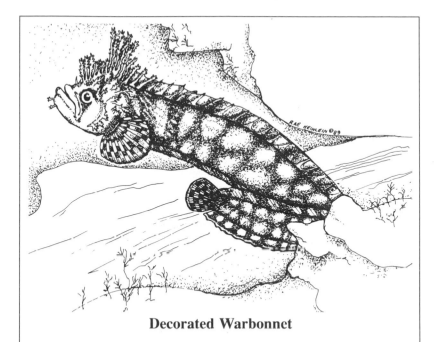

Decorated Warbonnet

Both the decorated warbonnet, *Chirolophis decoratus*, and mosshead warbonnet, *Chirolophis nugator*, belong to the prickleback family. These long slender bottom fishes are often confused with each other, but are easily distinguished. Both fish have a single long dorsal fin, a rounded caudal fin and a single long anal fin. The mosshead warbonnet has an even mat of cirri on top of its head, extending to the front edge of the dorsal fin, but not onto the fin. In comparison, the decorated warbonnet (shown above) also has cirri on top of its head, but of prominently different sizes extending onto the front section of the dorsal fin. The mosshead warbonnet has 13 dark spots marking its dorsal fin, while the decorated warbonnet has a dorsal fin marked with dark bars.

The mosshead warbonnet grows to 5 inches (13 cm) in length and lives in both the intertidal and subtidal areas. The decorated warbonnet grows to 17 inches (43 cm) in length and lives subtidally from 60 to 300 feet (18 to 91 meters).

Figure 28

AGATE BEACH COUNTY PARK

Habitat and Depth: While looking out across this beautiful wide bay, it is easy to imagine two or three tall wooden ships lying at anchor, with a work party rowing ashore to gather supplies. Outer Bay has a long sandy-cobblestone beach that is bordered on either end by a rocky shoreline. At the north end of the beach, a long stretch of rock cliffs drops vertically to the water. A lower and shorter rocky shoreline forms the south side of the bay. Kelp beds and submerged rocks are found beneath the rock bluffs bordering each side of this bay, and also around two rock structures that project above the water line in the center of the bay.

A few of the animals you may see while diving in this area include Christmas anemones, hermit crabs, kelp crabs, gumboot chitons, tube snouts, flounder, urchins, cucumbers, perch, shrimp, blood stars, sun stars, sunflower stars, comb jellies and nudibranchs.

The bottom of the bay is primarily a silty-sand that supports the growth of a large eelgrass bed. Maximum depth in the bay reaches 35 feet (10 foot tide).

Site Description: Walk down the stairs to the beach and swim to the large rock near shore. Its outer side is inhabited by a few sea anemones, hermit crabs and kelp crabs. Try feeding one of the anemones a small kelp crab. You may be surprised with the outcome. Kelp crabs can be very persuasive!

Looking offshore from Agate Beach, "Outer Rock" is located between "Shark Fin Rock" and the northern rocky bluff. After exploring the inshore sandy bay, if you are up to a long swim, turn west-northwest and swim to "Shark Fin Rock" or the adjacent "Outer Rock". You may want to make this swim on the surface to conserve tank air, thus allowing for maximum bottom time.

Located on the outside of "Outer Rock" is a wide rock face that is home to many sea urchins. "Urchin Wall" would be an appropriate name for this piece of the rock. Do not attempt the long swim to this rock if you have not been swimming regularly and are not in good physical shape.

"Shark Fin Rock" and "Outer Rock" can be seen in the distance.

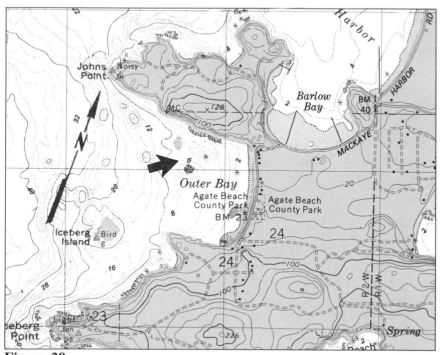

Figure 29

Not Intended For Navigational Use

Skill Level: Intermediate.

Hazards: Current, kelp and a long swim.
Flooding current moves across the mouth of Outer Bay from the south. It is driven onto the northern rocky face, dividing into two directional flow segments at a point where the rock bluff rounds to the north just outside "Outer Rock." Inshore from this point, flood current moves along the rocky bluff toward the beach. It turns in a clockwise pattern along the beach, then moves back out along the southern rocky shoreline.

Ebbing current is almost nonexistent in Outer Bay during tidal exchanges of up to seven feet. During larger exchanges, divers may experience weak ebb currents moving inshore.

This site can be safely dived during either a flood or ebb tidal exchange, but the long swim to "Shark Fin Rock" and "Outer Rock" is easiest when attempted during a slack period prior to a flood current. After exploring these two rocks, divers can make the short swim to the northern rock face and catch the inbound flooding current back to the beach.

Facilities: This is an undeveloped county park. Facilities include a limited parking area along the side of the road, a few picnic tables and two pit toilets. Air fills are not available on Lopez Island. Fill your tanks before leaving Anacortes.

Travel Distance and Directions: Agate Beach is located on Lopez Island, 14 miles south of the ferry landing. Lopez Island is a 40 minute ferry ride from Anacortes.

> Mileage from Bellingham = 56 miles
> Mileage from Seattle = 88 miles
> Mileage from Olympia = 157 miles

Drive to Anacortes and follow signs to the Washington State Ferry. Board the ferry for Lopez Island.

After reaching Lopez Island, drive south for 2.0 miles on Ferry Road before turning left onto Center Road. Continue to follow Center Road for 5.7 miles. Turn left at a tee onto Mud Bay Road.

Drive 2.8 miles and turn right onto Mackaye Harbor Road. Drive the remaining 1.7 miles, past Barlow Bay, to Outer Bay and Agate Beach County Park.

Current Table: San Juan Channel.

Look up the daily current predictions for San Juan Channel. Apply the following time corrections to calculate slack current times:

Time corrections for subordinate station 1655:
Minimum current before flood: +11 minutes
Minimum current before ebb: +34 minutes

Telephone Location: None at the immediate site. Drive 1.7 miles back to the intersection of Mackaye Harbor Road and Mud Bay Road. A phone is located in the Bike Rest Area next to the Lopez Fire Department.

Non-Diver Activities: Outer Bay is especially captivating when the sun is out and light is reflecting between the vertical rock cliffs and the surface of the water. Agate Beach is worth the trip just to look at the rock formations and glistening water while watching the gulls glide from rock to rock.

Go for a walk along the beach, sit in the sun and read a book, photograph sea gulls, and share a meal with friends. Visitors also can stop at the local museum (watch for road signs) or drive back into the town of Lopez to enjoy a meal while looking out over Fisherman Bay and the Lopez Marina.

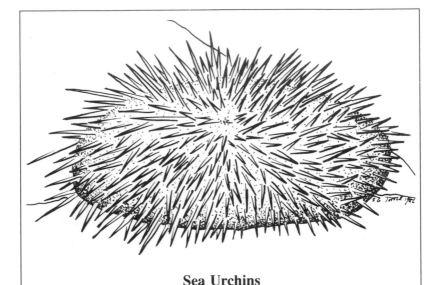

Sea Urchins

Three species of sea urchin live in the rocky intertidal and subtidal areas of the Pacific Northwest. They graze on algae and kelp with 5 sharp teeth which are part of a unique structure called Aristotle's lantern (sand dollars have a similar structure).

The calcium carbonate skeleton of an urchin, called a test, is covered with bumps that function as pivot points for the animal's defensive spines. An urchin can rotate its spines to concentrate the sharp points at an area of intrusion. It also can move the spines apart to make room for the extension of defensive pedicellariae, which are jaw-like structures containing a poison gland. Tube feet are extended through small holes in the test. They are used for attachment, locomotion and to catch floating pieces of algae that are then passed to the mouth.

The small green sea urchin, *Strongylocentrotus droebachiensis*, prefers the protected waters of bays. It has short, needle-like spines, and moves slowly across the bottom while feeding. Test diameter reaches 3 inches (8 cm).

Figure 30

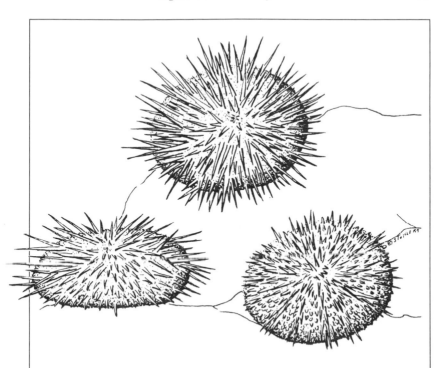

The purple sea urchin, *Strongylocentrotus purpuratus*, is not usually found in the protected waters of Puget Sound, as it prefers the aerated water along exposed rocky shorelines. The purple urchin has about the same test diameter as that of the green sea urchin, but is differentiated by its color and spines, which are slightly longer and thicker. Divers may also find this urchin burrowed into the face of rocks for protection from surge and predators.

The red sea urchin, *Strongylocentrotus franciscanus*, is the largest of the three species of Northwest urchins, with test diameters reaching 5 inches (13 cm). Although called the "red sea urchin," some individuals of this species have purple instead of red spines. Thus, a red urchin cannot be distinguished from a purple urchin by the color of its spines. Instead, the long spine length of the red sea urchin separates this species from the shorter spined purple sea urchin.

PART 6. **ROSARIO STRAIT**

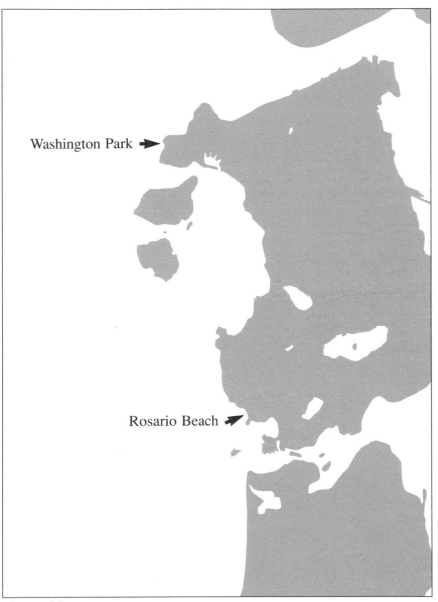

Figure 31

WASHINGTON PARK

Habitat and Depth: At a sharp bend in Washington Park Loop Road, concrete stairs lead down from a parking area onto the flat rocks of Green Point. Stretching to the southeast, from Green Point to the rocky shoreline of Fidalgo Head, is a sandy cobblestone beach. The rock formations at each end of this beach are intriguing and easily accessible.

Divers will find more animal life along the rocky shoreline and kelp bed of Fidalgo Head than on the muddy bottom of this bay. Animals living in this area include moon snails, kelp crabs, sharp-nosed crabs, brooding sea stars, leather sea stars, sun stars, sea squirts, small white sea cucumbers, gumboot chitons, dark yellow and purple ochre sea stars (on the outside of Fidalgo Head), multi-rayed sunflower sea stars, slime stars, small spider crabs, hermit crabs, both red and green sea urchins, flounder, great sculpins, snails and nudibranchs.

Fidalgo Head forms the south side of this bay. Inside the bay, along the base of the inner two-thirds of the rocky shoreline, the bottom is a mixture of gravel and mud. Due to strong current striking the exposed outer third section of Fidalgo Head, the bottom along the base of this section is sand. Extending beneath the surface a short distance, the outer rock structure disappears into the sandy bottom at a depth of 27 to 37 feet (10 foot tide).

Site Description: Divers have a choice of either exploring Green Point or swimming across the bay to dive the shoreline of Fidalgo Head. To explore Green Point, enter the water near the base of the stairs and swim northward (north-northeast) along the low rocky shoreline. To dive Fidalgo Head, swim south-southeast across the shallow bay to the distant rocky shoreline. This swim takes about 10 minutes during slack current periods.

Skill Level: Advanced

Hazards: Strong current, frequent low visibility, kelp, small boats and a long swim for divers venturing out to Fidalgo Head.

Strong currents flow past Green Point

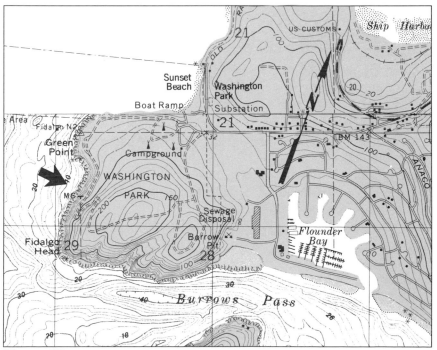

Figure 32 Not Intended For Navigational Use

Due to the high exchange of water occurring in this area, dive only during periods of minimal current. Stay within the bay or along the rocky shoreline to avoid the main channel flow.

Flood currents flow westward through Burrows Pass into Rosario Strait (see map), then turn northward around Fidalgo Head and move inshore along the rocky shoreline. The flow turns counterclockwise in the shallows, flowing across the beach and out past Green Point.

Ebb currents flow southward past Green Point, bend into the bay and collide with the rocky shoreline of Fidalgo Head. The flow then divides, with the stronger segment turning southward and flowing out along the outer third of the shoreline. The other segment moves northward, toward the beach. As this inbound flow reaches the shallows, it turns counter-clockwise in front of West Beach and flows toward Green Point. At Green Point, the current again turns counter-clockwise, moving into the main channel and flowing back toward Fidalgo Head.

To swim to Fidalgo Head, enter the water 20 to 30 minutes before the estimated time of slack water. During this time, your swim out will be against minimal current. When returning from the outside of Fidalgo Head during an ebb current, your return swim along the shoreline may at first be against the current. Once you have moved approximately one-third of the way in from the rocky headland, you will reach a quiet area. Inside this point (the current divide) you will be swimming with an inbound current. When returning from Fidalgo Head during a flood current, your swim will be with the current.

Visibility is often low in this area, presumably due to suspended silt from the Stillaguamish, Skagit, Samish and Nooksack rivers. It usually improves during flood cycles.

Carry a knife and enjoy your dive. Listen for small boat engine noise before ascending.

Facilities: Facilities available in Washington Park include camping, hot showers, rest rooms, changing areas, a covered picnic area, picnic tables, barbecue stands, a play ground and a boat launch. Air fills are available in Anacortes and Oak Harbor.

Travel Distance and Directions: Washington Park is located 3.8 miles west of Commercial Avenue in Anacortes.

Mileage from Bellingham = 46 miles
Mileage from Seattle = 78 miles
Mileage from Olympia = 147 miles

Follow I-5 to Exit 230 and exit onto Highway 20 West toward Whidbey Island and Anacortes. Drive into Anacortes and turn left from Commercial Avenue toward the Washington State ferry. Continue on Sunset Avenue for 3.8 miles, past the turn to the ferry landing, to Washington Park. After driving into the park, turn left onto Loop Road. Follow this one lane road through the trees and along the water for 0.6 mile to a sharp turn. Park and walk down the concrete stairs to Green Point and West Beach.

Current Table: Rosario Strait
Look up the daily current predictions for Rosario Strait. Apply the following time corrections to calculate slack current times:

Time corrections for subordinate station 1500:
Minimum current before flood: −55 minutes
Minimum current before ebb: −08 minutes

Telephone Location: Located by the home in the main camp area, near the end of Loop Road.

Non-Diver Activities: Family and friends will enjoy this woodsy 220 acre marine park while divers are out swimming. Visitors can hike along the rocky shoreline and through the trees from Sunset Beach to West Beach. The trail continues around Fidalgo Head and across a rock bluff that looks down a steep, grassy slope above Burrows Pass. This slope is a great place to stop for lunch and watch the boat traffic far below in Burrows Pass. Other activities include fishing from the rocky shore, visiting the small community of rabbits that live in the boat trailer parking area, playing on the grass, and enjoying the fantastic views of Rosario Strait, Burrows Island, Decatur Island and Lopez Island.

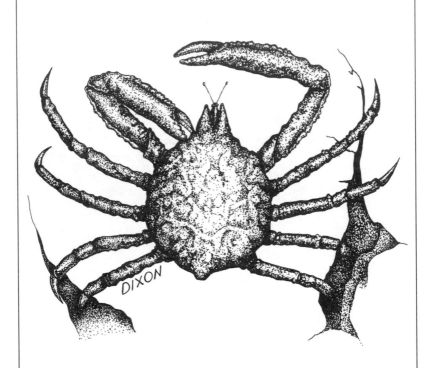

Sharp-nosed Crab

A common crab, often seen in eelgrass and kelp beds by divers, is the sharp-nosed crab, *Scyra acutifrons.* It is one of the spider crabs. This small crab is also known as the masking crab because of its habit of deliberately planting algae and small animals on its roughened body for camouflage. The unadorned carapace width of this crab reaches 2 inches (5 cm).

Both the sharp-nosed crab and the similar decorator crab, *Oregonia gracilis,* have long pointed noses, but are easily distinguished by the shorter and thicker legs of the sharp-nosed crab. The decorator crab has spindly legs and a narrower rostrum.

Figure 33

ROSARIO BEACH

Habitat and Depth: Stretching between two distinct rocky shores within Deception Pass State Park, lies the long pebblestone expanse of Rosario Beach. Rock cliffs plunge into the water along the north side of Rosario Bay, while Rosario Head forms the lower rocky side to the south. A small group of rocks, called "Urchin Rocks," are clustered beside Rosario Head. Northwest Island sits just outside this sandy bay, 0.2 mile from the beach. As a protected marine sanctuary, the area is rich with life and exciting to visit. Rock, kelp and sandy habitats overlap in Rosario Bay, providing shelter for many kinds of animals. Red, green and purple urchins cling to rocks while grazing on kelp. Hermit crabs scurry about on the bottom, carefully staying clear of the colorful sea anemones that patiently wait for their next meal.

Other animals divers may see when diving in this rich area include California sea cucumbers, orange sea cucumbers, sea squirts, nudibranchs, brooding stars, leather stars, giant barnacles, chitons, and limpets.

Bottom depths between the northwest point and south side of Urchin Rocks range from 37 feet to 39 feet. Along the outer face of Rosario Head, depths range from 35 to 40 feet (10 foot tide).

Site Description: Four different dives are possible at this site. To dive either Urchin Rocks or Rosario Head, begin your dive by swimming out from the south end of Rosario Beach toward Urchin Rocks. An entire dive can easily be spent exploring Urchin Rocks. If you are comfortable with a longer swim, continue past Urchin Rocks, following the rocky shoreline around Rosario Head and into Sharpe Cove. Exit from Sharpe Cove and walk the short distance back to Rosario Beach (see map of Rosario Head).

A convenient entry point for the other two dives is at the north end of Rosario Beach. From here, divers can swim out from shore to explore the base of the rock cliffs that form the northern boundary of Rosario Bay. Continuing past this rocky shoreline, divers also can swim to Northwest Island. When diving Northwest Island be prepared for a long swim.

Urchin Rocks are fun to explore.

Skill Level: Advanced.

Hazards: Strong currents, low visibility, kelp and small boats. Suspended silt from the Stillaguamish, Skagit, Samish and Nooksack rivers reduce visibility in Rosario Strait, especially during ebb exchanges when sediment flushes past Rosario Head from Padilla Bay and Guemes Channel.

Flooding current moves northwest past Rosario Head, Urchin Rocks and Northwest Island. A directional segment of this current rounds Urchin Rocks toward Rosario Beach. It flows through the bay in a counter-clockwise direction, moving in front of the beach, then out along the northwestern rocky shore.

Ebbing current moves southeast past Northwest Island, Urchin Rocks and the outer face of Rosario Head. A segment of the main channel flow moves inshore along the northwestern shoreline toward Rosario Beach. It turns past the beach in a clockwise direction and flows out past Urchin Rocks, turning across the face of Rosario Head. Part of this flow rounds the southeast tip of Rosario Head, then turns northward into Sharpe Cove. Plan your dive so that the return swim will be with the current.

When diving Urchin Rocks, begin your swim slightly before slack water prior to a flood exchange. You will be swimming out with an ebbing current, and returning to Rosario Beach with a flooding current. When swimming from Rosario Beach around Rosario Head and into Sharp Cove, dive during an ebb current. You will then be swimming with the current all the way around Rosario Head and into Sharpe Cove. To avoid the possibility of being swept past the end of Rosario Head, be sure to keep the Rosario Head

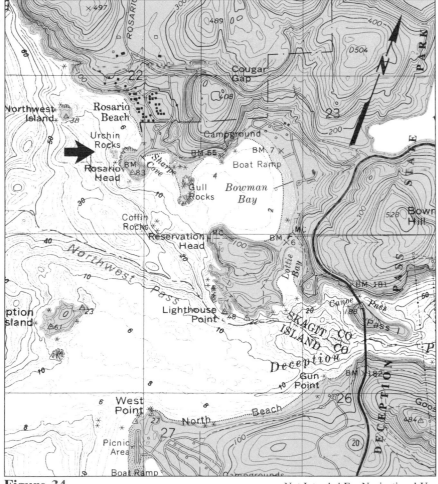

Figure 34   Not Intended For Navigational Use

wall in sight throughout this dive. When diving Northwest Island, swim to the island during slack before an ebb current. Your return swim, along the northern rocky shoreline, will then be with the ebbing current.

Facilities: Camping, picnic tables, a covered eating area with a stone fireplace, rest rooms, hot showers, changing areas, an outside cold shower for equipment, barbecue stands, a grass lawn and play area. Air fills are available in Anacortes and Oak Harbor.

Travel Distance and Directions: Rosario Beach is located in Deception Pass State Park, 10 miles south of Anacortes.

Mileage from Bellingham = 42 miles
Mileage from Seattle = 74 miles
Mileage from Olympia = 144 miles

Follow I-5 to Exit 230 and exit onto Highway 20 West toward Whidbey Island and Anacortes. Drive for 12 miles before turning left toward Oak Harbor and Coupeville (still Highway 20 West). Continue on Highway 20 West for 5.1 miles. Turn right onto Rosario Road (immediately past Pass Lake), and follow the signs to Rosario Beach.

Current Table: Rosario Strait.
Look up the daily current predictions for Rosario Strait. Apply the following time corrections to calculate slack current times:

Time corrections for Rosario Head:
Minimum inshore current before flood: +38 minutes
Minimum inshore current before ebb: +38 minutes

Telephone Location: None at the immediate site. The closest phone is located in the Bowman Bay section of Deception Pass State Park, 1.5 miles from Rosario Beach. To find the phone, drive back toward the main highway, staying to the right where the park road forks. Just before reaching Highway 20, turn right to Bowman Bay. The phone is in the campground at the bottom of the hill.

Non-Diver Activities: The Maiden of Deception Pass Interpretive Display tells visitors an interesting Indian legend about a maiden who went to live with a sea god beneath the waves. A trail leads past this display and out onto the rock cliffs of Rosario Head. From this vantage point, there is a dramatic view of Rosario Strait and of the rocks and kelp below.

A longer trail curves from the base of Rosario Head, near Sharpe Cove, to the northwest end of the Bowman Bay Campground road. The trail then picks up again near the beach at the southwest end of the campground road, heads south-southeast a short distance and then forks. The right fork leads out onto Reservation Head, while the left fork leads to the east of Lottie Bay toward the Deception Pass Bridge. The total round trip to the Deception Pass Bridge and back is only 2.6 miles.

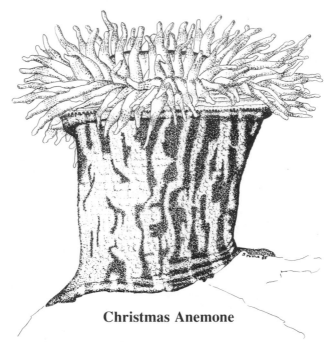

Christmas Anemone

The Christmas anemone, *Urticina crassicornis*, is named for its brightly colored green column that is vividly streaked with red. This colorful anemone attaches to rocks in subtidal and low intertidal areas. Attachment surfaces are not always visible, as individuals attached to a rock on the bottom may eventually become partially buried, leaving only their oral disc and tentacles exposed. Extending from the olive green oral disc are lightly banded, innocent-looking stubby tentacles. These are actually deadly structures, used to capture small animals that bump into them. Each tentacle contains many specialized stinging cells, called nematocysts, which discharge poisonous barbs on contact with prey. The nematocysts are used to paralyze a struggling animal prior to ingestion. *Urticina* has a life span of 60 to 80 years, reaching a disc diameter of 6 to 10 inches (15-25 cm) during this time.

Figure 35

PART 7.   THE STRAIT OF JUAN DE FUCA

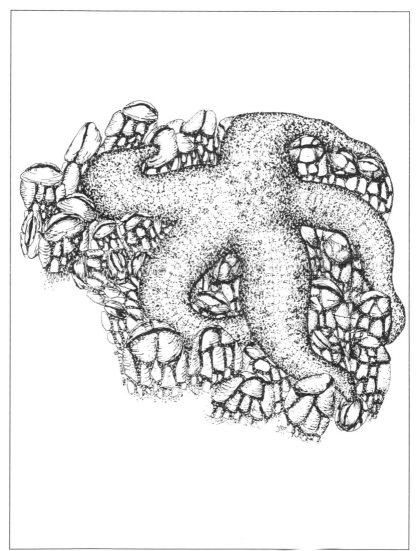

Figure 36   Purple sea stars feed aggressively on clams, mussels and barnacles.

Figure 37   Strait of Juan de Fuca

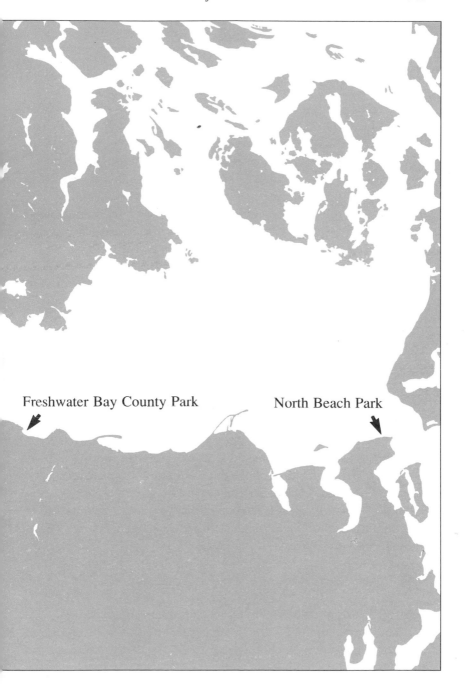

Freshwater Bay County Park

North Beach Park

NORTH BEACH PARK

Habitat and Depth: Sunlight somehow penetrates the thick mass of kelp that grows in front of North Beach. The light passes down through the green water to reach the thousands of small fish and invertebrates that move about through sand channels and pocket-like open areas in the kelp. Though much of the kelp is torn out by winter storms, the growth present by mid-summer is impressive.

Divers who take the time to look at the small animals will find that animal life in this area is incredibly rich and beautiful. A few of the animals living here include ratfish, huge schools of sand lances, skates, kelp greenling, moon snails, flounder, sea urchins, sea stars, sea anemones, perch, nudibranchs and shrimp.

The bottom in front of North Beach is sandy with occasional rocks and thick seasonal bull kelp. Some parts of the bottom are large sheets of hard and slippery clay. Bottom depth is approximately 35 feet (10 foot tide) on the outside of the kelp canopy.

Site Description: Bull kelp beds stretch in both directions along this shoreline. In addition to many submerged rocks, two large rocks protrude from the water a short distance offshore; one east of North Beach Park; the other one west of the park.

Swim out to the kelp and drop down under its canopy. At this point, you have a choice of either skirting the inside edge of the kelp bed or moving through the kelp mass to explore the outside perimeter. When passing through thick kelp, relax and move slowly. Expect to become entangled occasionally. Be willing to back up and untangle yourself instead of struggling to move forward. It is usually easier to untangle by hand than to cut yourself free of the kelp. Enjoy your dive.

Skill Level: Advanced.

Hazards: Strong current, surge, and seasonally thick kelp.

The large volume of water that passes through the Strait of Juan de Fuca with each tidal exchange creates a swift current along the shoreline. Because both flood and ebb currents move parallel to the

North Beach with Point Wilson Lighthouse in the distance

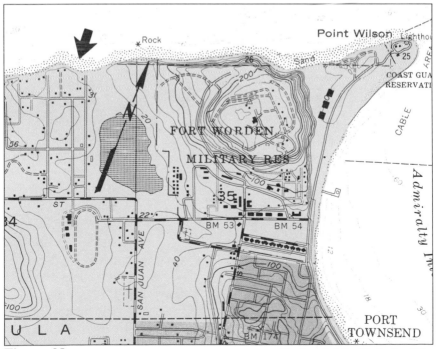

Figure 38   Not Intended For Navigational Use

beach, this site can be dived either during slack current times or during exchanges. If you choose to dive during an exchange, plan your dive as a drift dive. Remember to swim with the current or perpendicular to it, but not against it. When diving during a flooding current, be careful not to drift east of Point Wilson, into Admiralty Inlet. Stay with your buddy and help each other with kelp tangles.

Facilities: Rest rooms, picnic tables and a grass lawn. Air fills are available in Port Townsend, Hadlock and Port Angeles.

Travel Distance and Directions: North Beach is located on the northeast corner of the Olympic Peninsula, between McCurdy Point and Point Wilson.

> Mileage from Bellingham = 69 miles
> Mileage from Seattle = 49 miles
> Mileage from Olympia = 98 miles

From Bellingham: drive south on I-5 to Exit 230 for Highway 20 West, Whidbey Island and Anacortes. Exit from I-5, and follow signs to Deception Pass, Whidbey Island, Oak Harbor and Coupeville. Turn right in Oak Harbor and drive toward Coupeville for 9.7 miles, then turn right, immediately past a foot bridge, to Fort Casey and the Keystone Ferry. Ride the ferry across Puget Sound to Port Townsend. Turn left from the Port Townsend Ferry Dock onto Water Street (becomes Sims Way). Drive 0.5 mile, turn right onto Kearney Street, and follow the directions below.

From Seattle: drive north on I-5 to the Edmonds-Kingston Ferry Exit 177. Turn west onto 244th Street SW and follow Highway 104 West to the Kingston Ferry in Edmonds. Cross Puget Sound to Kingston, and drive 9.0 miles west on Highway 104 to the Hood Canal Bridge. Turn right onto the bridge (still Highway 104), and follow signs to Port Townsend. After entering Port Townsend on Sims Road, turn left onto Kearney Street. In 0.3 mile, Kearney Street ends where it forms a tee with Blaine Street. At the tee, turn left onto Blaine Street. Then, in two blocks, turn right onto San Juan Avenue and drive 1.5 miles to where the roadway makes a sharp left turn onto 49th Street. Take the next right turn onto Kuhn Street and drive the remaining 0.5 mile to North Beach.

From Olympia: drive north on Highway 101 along the Olympic Peninsula to the south end of Discovery Bay. Turn east onto Highway 20, and drive 12.0 miles to Kearney Street in Port Townsend. Turn left onto Kearney Street and follow the above directions.

Current Table: Admiralty Inlet.
Look up the daily current predictions for Admiralty Inlet. Apply the following time corrections to calculate slack current times:

Time corrections for subordinate station 945:
Minimum current before flood: −113 minutes
Minimum current before ebb: −08 minutes

Telephone Location: None at the immediate site. Drive 1.6 miles back to the intersection of San Juan Avenue and "F" Street.

Non-Diver Activities: Visit Fort Worden (see pages 143-144) or stroll through historic Port Townsend to see its old homes and interesting shops. Catch some sunshine on a sandy beach, go for a beach walk, toss a frisbee, build a sand castle or share a picnic lunch with friends.

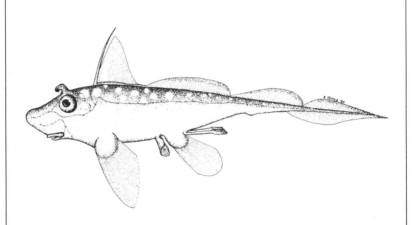

Ratfish

The ratfish, *Hydrolagus colliei*, is a beautiful reddish-brown animal with vivid silver-white spots and large blue-green eyes. It seems curious about its surroundings, often following divers during a dive, but turning to drift out of visibility range when divers stop to look at it. Contrary to its latin name *Hydrolagus*, meaning "water hare," ratfish glide gracefully through the water on immense pectoral fins. They use their swimming ability as a primary means of defense. A long spine, forming the leading edge of the dorsal fin, can also be used for defense when necessary.

The ratfish feeds on shellfish, crab, shrimp and fish. It uses a tooth-like bony ridge on the front edge of its upper jaw to crush shells. Ratfish grow to a length of 3 feet (91 cm). Their eggs are laid during spring and summer, enclosed in long protective ridged brown cases.

Figure 39

FRESHWATER BAY COUNTY PARK

Habitat and Depth: The swim across Freshwater Bay to Bachelor Rock is perhaps the longest swim in this book. On a sunny day, when the bottom is well lit, both divers and snorkelers can see a variety of small and interesting animals. Watching small animals is a great way to rest during this swim.

When swimming between the boat ramp and Bachelor Rock, divers will pass over a sandy bottom and eelgrass bed. They will see many animals actively competing for survival. Moon snails, sunflower sea stars and flounder can often be seen hunting for their next meals. With a little patience and a sharp eye, divers can watch flatfish lunge out of the sand to gulp down small bottom animals. Hairy helmet crabs (a favorite of mine), hermit crabs, jellyfish, an occasional skate and various small fish are other common inhabitants of this area. The comical interactions frequently occurring between hermit crabs are also fun to watch, but are serious business for the hermits as they compete for food and larger shells.

The types and number of animals change dramatically at the basalt reef near Bachelor Rock. The lee side of the reef is covered with a colorful carpet of small anemones. Submerged rocks provide attachment points for a forest of bull kelp. White plumose sea anemones and both red and purple sea urchins cling to the outside wall of Bachelor Rock. Gumboot chitons, orange cucumbers, kelp crabs, sun stars, blood stars, rat fish, sand lances and perch are a few of the other animals living on this reef.

Bottom depth between the boat ramp and Bachelor Rock is shallow, reaching a depth of 19 feet about half way out. The bottom continues to gradually deepen to a depth of 32 feet just inside the basalt reef that stretches between Bachelor Rock and the shoreline. Bottom depth at the base of the wall on the outside of Bachelor Rock deepens to 53 feet (10 foot tidal height).

Site Description: Be prepared for a long swim of 30 to 40 minutes from the boat ramp to Bachelor Rock. The shoreline on the west side of Freshwater Bay is private land and is marked "No Trespassing." Please respect the owner's privacy by not trespassing.

Freshwater Bay and Bachelor Rock

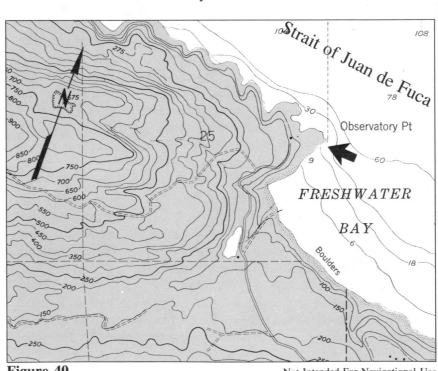

Figure 40   Not Intended For Navigational Use

Swim out from the public boat launch ramp toward Bachelor Rock. Just before reaching the outside of the bay, divers will come to a basalt reef that stretches between Observatory Point and Bachelor Rock. Instead of climbing over the reef, damaging animals and tearing your exposure suit, follow the lee side of the rock formation through the kelp to the east side of Bachelor Rock. Beyond this narrow band of rocks and kelp, bottom depth will increase sharply.

Skill Level: Advanced.

Hazards: A long swim, current, kelp, and small boats.

Due to the long swim, this dive can easily become more work than pleasure. If you do not feel up to a 30 minute swim (one way), it would be better to choose a different dive site with a shorter swim. Take your time swimming out so that you will not be too tired to enjoy your dive once you reach Bachelor Rock.

When swimming in the bay, stay to the side of the main boat lane between the boat ramp and Bachelor rock. In shallow water, stay on the surface where you are visible to boat operators. Once the bottom has deepened enough to allow a descent below 10 feet, submerge and stay below 10 feet throughout your dive. Always listen for engine noise and check the surface before making an ascent. Carry a dive knife and display a dive flag.

Facilities: Rest rooms in the upper parking area, outhouses in the lower parking lot by the boat ramp, and a Day Use Picnic Area with picnic tables, wood burners and concrete trails winding through the woods. Air fills are available in Port Angeles, Joyce, Sekiu and Neah Bay.

Travel Distance and Directions: Freshwater Bay is located on the Strait of Juan de Fuca, 13 miles west of Port Angeles.

> Mileage from Bellingham = 125 miles
> Mileage from Seattle = 82 miles
> Mileage from Olympia = 130 miles

As you drive into Port Angeles, you will be on East Front Street. Look for a sign marking a left hand turn to the Olympic National Park and Hurricane Ridge. At this sign, turn left onto Race Street and drive past the high school stadium. Turn right onto Lauridsen Boulevard and drive across a small bridge. Lauridsen Boulevard will soon become East Boulevard. Turn left at the next stop sign onto West Boulevard to Highway 101 West. Continue west for 4.2 miles to the Highway 101/112 junction. Turn right onto Highway 112 West and head toward Sekiu and Neah Bay. In 7.4 miles, turn right onto Freshwater Bay Road and drive the remaining 2.5 miles to Freshwater Bay.

Current Table: Race Rocks.

Look up the daily current predictions for Race Rocks. Apply the following time corrections to calculate slack current times:

> Time corrections for subordinate station 825:
>
> | | |
> |---|---|
> | Minimum current before flood: | +82 minutes |
> | Minimum current before ebb: | −32 minutes |

Telephone Location: None at the immediate site. The closest public phone is at Salt Creek Inn, 6.2 miles west on Highway 112 at the intersection of Camp Hayden Road and Highway 112 (the road to Salt Creek Recreational Area and Tongue Point).

Non-Diver Activities: Freshwater Bay is a good place to launch a canoe or rubber raft and paddle to Observation Point to see the rock formations. On a clear day, this is also a great way to catch some sun while floating in a beautiful bay. This shallow sandy bay is great for snorkeling and watching small marine animals as they scurry about on the bottom.

Another venture for non-divers is to drive from the bay to the Striped Peak Scenic Area, located on the top of Striped Peak. When the fog has cleared, there is a wonderful view over the tops of trees, across the Strait of Juan de Fuca and Freshwater Bay, to Vancouver Island.

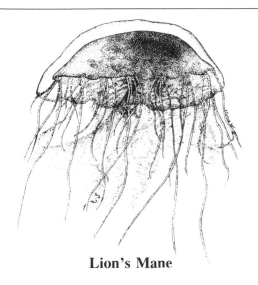

Lion's Mane

The lion's mane, *Cyanea capillata*, is the largest species of jellyfish in the Pacific Northwest. This richly colored orange-brown animal is also known as the sea nettle or sea blubber jellyfish (Plate 2). Its semi-translucent mantle typically grows to a diameter of 10 inches (25 cm), yet individuals reaching twice this size may be seen by late summer. The tentacles of jellyfish are retractile. When fully extended, (for a jellyfish with a 10 inch diameter mantle) the tentacles from *Cyanea* will reach 20 feet in length (6 meters). Tentacles are attached to the edge of the mantle in eight separate bundles containing more than seventy tentacles apiece. Each thread-like tentacle is armed with stinging cells, called nematocysts, that discharge poisonous barbs on contact. These are used to capture small animals, which are paralyzed by the nematocysts and then pulled to the mouth at the underside of the mantle.

Nematocysts also discharge when contact is made with a diver's uncovered face or hands. The resulting sting is uncomfortable and may persist for several hours. When approaching this animal, avoid swimming into the tentacles.

Figure 41

SALT CREEK COUNTY PARK

Habitat and Depth: The Tongue Point Marine Life Sanctuary is one of the most beautiful dive areas in the State of Washington. The prominently rocky shoreline is composed of fused chunks of dark basalt that slope down to the water. Beneath the surface, divers will find a fantastically beautiful realm with submerged rocks, sand channels, thick kelp and thousands of attached and free-swimming animals. There is so much life along this shoreline that divers must carefully choose areas that they come in contact with to avoid squashing animals.

The marine sanctuary status of this park and its rugged shoreline protect marine life from collection. Without this protection, the cumulative effect from the large number of people using this park each year would significantly impact animal life and the natural beauty of the area. Please respect the area, leaving it intact so that others may enjoy its natural beauty.

A few of the animals divers often see while diving at this site include sea urchins, sea cucumbers, sea anemones, octopuses, nudibranchs, sunflower sea stars, brittle stars, kelp greenling, wolf eels, ratfish, schools of small fish and dense schools of amphipods and small shrimp-like mysids.

The cobblestone bottom reaches a depth of approximately 60 feet (10 foot tide) outside the kelp canopy.

Site Description: There are four different dives that can be made from the end of beach access trails. One of these trails leads past Campsite 5, on the east side of the park; another one passes between campsites 55 and 57; a third passes between campsites 60 and 62; and the fourth trail cuts through a day use area west of Campsite 66, on the west side of the park. The western trail is the steepest and longest of the four.

The first three trails lead out onto rock formations along the shoreline east of Tongue Point. At each of these entry sites, divers should enter the water at points that are at least partially protected from tidal surge. Avoid placing yourself between a rock and breaking waves.

Basalt formations slope down to the water

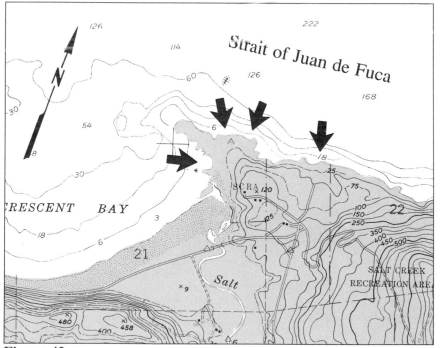

Figure 42   Not Intended For Navigational Use

Once in the water, either swim out over the kelp or drop down under its canopy and slowly begin to work your way through the mass of vegetation. The fourth entry point is on Tongue Point at the west side of the park. Divers can enter on either side of the point. East of Tongue Point the bottom and shoreline is rocky, while west of the point divers will find a sandy bottom extending into Crescent Bay.

Skill Level: Advanced.

Hazards: Waves breaking on the rocky shore, surge, strong currents and thick kelp during summer and fall months.

Waves breaking against a rocky shoreline can be dangerous to divers when entering or exiting the water. Before making a dive at this site, watch the height and frequency of incoming waves to decide if a safe entry and exit are possible. Do not enter the water if waves are continually breaking against the shoreline. Enter during a quiet period and move quickly offshore.

When returning to shore after your dive, choose an exit point where you will not have to climb out over a rock structure while the surge pushes and pulls at you. Swim for a narrow cobblestone beach, a channel between rocks, or a low rock that is in the lee of another rock. These formations will provide at least some shelter from the surge, allowing an easier and safer exit. Do not attempt to exit over rocks where waves are breaking.

Exit points are easy to see from the vantage point of the shoreline, but are often very difficult to see when looking inshore at water level. Before entering the water, note a landmark or leave a brightly colored object on shore that will mark your exit point. When returning, locate your exit point before swimming inshore.

Be sure to carry a knife when diving in kelp. Use the buddy system and help each other with kelp tangles. Enjoy your dive.

Facilities: Facilities at this site include 80 campsites, picnic areas with barbecue pits, a kitchen shelter, rest rooms and hot showers. There is also a large grass field with a playground, a baseball field and horseshoe pits. Hiking trails are nearby, and firewood is available for a fee. If you get tired of your own cooking, a grocery/restaurant is located at the junction of Camp Hayden Road and Highway 112. Air fills are available in Port Angeles, Joyce, Sekiu and Neah Bay.

Travel Distance and Directions: Salt Creek County Park is on the Strait of Juan de Fuca, 11 miles west of Port Angeles.

Mileage from Bellingham = 129 miles
Mileage from Seattle = 86 miles
Mileage from Olympia = 134 miles

As you drive into Port Angeles you will be on East Front Street. Look for a sign marking a left hand turn to the Olympic National Park and Hurricane Ridge. At the sign, turn left onto Race Street and drive past the high school stadium. Turn right onto Lauridsen Boulevard and drive across a small bridge. Lauridsen Boulevard will soon become East Boulevard. Turn left at the next stop sign onto West Boulevard to Highway 101 West. Continue west for 4.2 miles to the Highway 101/112 junction. Turn right onto Highway 112 West toward Sekiu and Neah Bay. In 11.0 miles, begin to watch for the Salt Creek Recreational Area and Tongue Point sign. Turn right onto Camp Hayden Road and drive the remaining distance to Salt Creek County Park.

Current Table: Race Rocks.
Look up the daily current predictions for Race Rocks. Apply the following time corrections to calculate slack current times:

Time corrections for subordinate station 825:
Minimum current before flood: +82 minutes
Minimum current before ebb: −32 minutes

Telephone Location: On the outside of the park office.

Non-Diver Activities: Originally a WWII harbor defense site, Salt Creek County Park covers 196 acres, and has a spectacular view of the Strait of Juan de Fuca. Two big guns were once mounted on the hillside above Crescent Bay to guard the entrance into the Strait of Juan de Fuca. The guns have been sold for scrap metal, but a long concrete gunnery bunker and a small spotting bunker remain. The area is now a beautiful park that the whole family can enjoy. Local activities include hiking, beach combing, tide pool discovery, snorkeling in Crescent Bay, camping, fishing, picnicking, baseball and exploring the harbor defense bunkers. Bring your tennis shoes, rubber boots, a good book and a camera.

Purple Sea Star

The aggressive purple sea star, *Pisaster ochraceus*, is frequently found along the exposed shores of the San Juan Islands, the Strait of Juan de Fuca and the open coast. There, the purple sea star lives primarily in rocky intertidal areas, feeding on mussels, clams and barnacles. Coloration within the species varies from light and dark purple to yellow and orange (Plate 15).

Divers often find this sea star perched on top of a bed of mussels or barnacles. *Pisaster* opens shells by attaching tube feet to each side and applying traction. The sea star everts its stomach through its mouth, and when a small gap occurs between the shell halves, slips the stomach inside and proceeds to digest the shellfish. Dissolved nutrients are absorbed across the stomach membrane. Once the meal is completed, the sea star retracts its stomach and leaves behind a clean shell.

Figure 43

LAKE CRESCENT

Habitat and Depth: Looking down into Lake Crescent from the shallows, one can easily see across the gently sloping and narrow shale bottom. The bottom seems to end a few feet from shore where a deep blue band of crystal clear water floats above the edge of a steep slope. Beyond this edge, a sterile looking silty bottom slopes rapidly downward into a hidden canyon, well past the limits of sport diving and compressed air.

I looked at my depth gauge at 80 feet and rolled onto my back to watch the exhaust bubbles shimmering toward the surface, expanding as they rose. The next time I looked at my depth gauge we were at 120 feet. Again I rolled onto my back and saw that we could still see the surface ripples in the sun spot. Below us the bottom continued to plunge downward, but it was time to come up.

Site Description: Diving in water that is clearer than most home drinking water can be a real treat. Excellent visibility and a noticeable lack of salt taste in your mouth are only two advantages of diving in a freshwater lake. There is also no current or surge to contend with, and no kelp to get tangled in. All of these contribute to an intriguing dive. Diving in fresh water is a great way to wash equipment, too! Your exposure suit zippers will be squeaky clean.

One of several entry points is in the La Poel day use area. Here the park road curves down past the shoreline, providing an easy access to the water. Enter the water, put your mask and fins on and move a few feet out from shore to submerge onto a steep slope. During your descent, you may see a few dead trees with smooth gray trunks pointing downward, with bare limbs curled and twisted. There is also a limited supply of tires, bottles, license plates and cast iron frying pans resting on the slope. Occasional small sculpins may be the only fish you will see during this dive.

Skill Level: All divers.

Hazards: The main hazard at this site is excellent visibility. Divers used to associating the dim light in Puget Sound with depth, may

The entry site at the La Poel day use area

unknowingly exceed their planned maximum depth limit. This mistake can easily be prevented by frequently monitoring your depth gauge during the dive. Use a dive table when planning your dive and be careful to stay within the no-decompression limits.

Facilities: Parking and picnic tables.   Air fills are available in Joyce, Sekiu and Port Angeles.

Travel Distance and Directions: The La Poel day use area is part of the Olympic National Park. It is 24 miles west of Port Angeles, on the south shore of Lake Crescent.

> Mileage from Bellingham = 137 miles
> Mileage from Seattle = 94 miles
> Mileage from Olympia = 142 miles

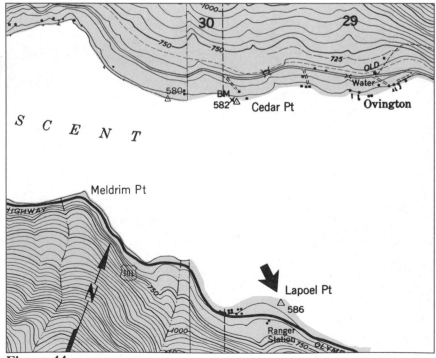

Figure 44   Not Intended For Navigational Use

As you drive into Port Angeles, you will be on East Front Street. Look for a sign marking a left hand turn to the Olympic National Park and Hurricane Ridge. At the sign, turn left onto Race Street and drive past the high school stadium. Turn right onto Lauridsen Boulevard and drive across a small bridge. Lauridsen Boulevard will soon becomes East Boulevard. Turn left at the next stop sign onto West Boulevard to Highway 101 South. Continue west for 4.2 miles to the Highway 101/112 junction. Stay to the left, following Highway 101 South for 19.1 miles toward Lake Crescent and Fairholm. Before reaching Fairholm, turn right into the La Poel day use area. Follow the park road to the edge of Lake Crescent.

Current Table: Predicted times for the occurrence of slack current in this lake are easily and accurately calculated. Check your watch when you arrive at the lake and add 30 minutes to allow time for suiting up!

Telephone Location: None at site. Turn right onto Highway 101 and drive 2.6 miles to the Fairholm General Store.

Non-Diver Activities: Lake Crescent is a clear deep mountain lake surrounded by the Olympic National Park. Visitors will find camping facilities, with places to hike, fish, swim and go boating.

The Storm King Ranger Station and Visitor Center are located between East Beach and La Poel. Visitors will find an interpretive display and a 1.5 mile (round trip) trail leading to Marymere Falls. Crescent Lodge is also nearby.

In the opposite direction, 2 miles west of Fairholm, is the turn off for Soleduck Valley Hot Springs Resort.

SEKIU JETTY

Habitat and Depth: Just beneath the surface, we stopped to watch the water break and recede over the rocks. Barnacles and purple sea stars clung to the rocks in a churning swirl of bubbles. There are so many small animals living along this shoreline that it is difficult to put a hand down without crushing an animal or colony of animals. This is a great dive for those who like to look at or photograph small animals.

Many of the rocks scattered over this sandy bottom are wrapped in kelp and hidden from view. Some larger rock formations stand alone, while others lean toward each other to form narrow spaces between them. We were delighted at the large number and variety of colorful animals that were concealed beneath the kelp.

Large purple and red sea urchins cling to the rock formations, sometimes all but filling the spaces between adjacent rocks. In one of these spaces, after gently pulling the kelp aside and moving carefully past the urchins, we discovered an orange finger sponge. We stopped to watch its orange, swollen fingers quietly waving in the surge. Chitons, limpets, red sea squirts and stalked sea squirts clung to almost every rock. Tens of thousands of amphipods and mysids (small shrimp-like swimming animals) formed dense clouds in the water. Countless comb jellies floated past our masks. Yellow bread crumb sponges covered patches of rock while yet another sponge covered broken kelp stipes. Colorful sea stars were actively feeding on other invertebrates, and large sea anemones displayed their thick tentacles as they patiently waited for their next meal.

Bottom depth along the outside of the rocky area ranges between 34 and 40 feet (10 foot tide). The bottom remains sandy and is covered with empty shells down to a depth of 68 feet (10 foot tide). Bands of eelgrass also grow in the shallows.

Site Description: A shore entry can be made over a rock embankment at either end of the parking area northwest of the marina office. This area provides access to either the jetty or to the rocky area northwest of the jetty, where there are many sculptured rocks and heavy kelp. The number of rocks that can be seen from the

Rock formations and kelp lie northwest of the jetty

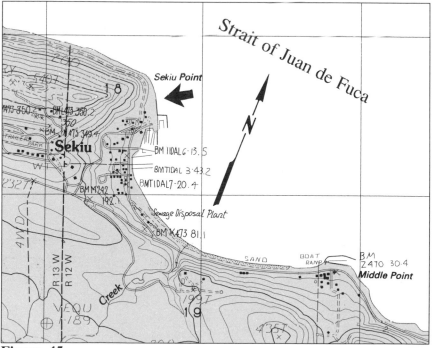

Figure 45

Not Intended For Navigational Use

surface constantly changes as the tide rises and falls. Sometimes there are twenty-one rocks protruding above the water and surge, while at other times there are twelve or less. This rocky area has more intriguing shapes to explore than the jetty or sandy beach area next to the jetty.

Skill Level: Advanced.

Hazards: Current, surge, fishing line, and heavy kelp.

Facilities: The marina offers a boat launch, boat rentals, rest rooms and parking for vehicles. Food and lodging are available in both Sekiu and Clallam Bay. Air fills are available in Sekiu.

Travel Distance and Directions: The Sekiu Recreational Area is on the northern end of the Olympic Peninsula, 35 nautical miles west of Port Angeles.

> Mileage from Bellingham = 165 Miles
> Mileage from Seattle = 121 Miles
> Mileage from Olympia = 169 Miles

Drive west from Port Angeles on Highway 101 to the Highway 101/112 Junction, then turn right onto Highway 112 West toward Sekiu and Neah Bay. Follow Highway 112 West for 46.5 miles to the Sekiu Recreational Area. Turn right into the Sekiu Recreational Area, and drive 0.5 mile before turning right at the Olson's Marina sign. Continue past the sign for 0.2 mile and park along the shoreline at the far end of the marina parking lot.

Current Table: Strait of Juan de Fuca.

Look up the daily current predictions for the Strait of Juan de Fuca. Apply the following time corrections to calculate slack current times:

> Time corrections for subordinate station 820:
> Minimum current before flood: −35 minutes
> Minimum current before ebb: +52 minutes

Telephone Location: In front of Olson's Marina in Sekiu

Non-Diver Activities: Rental boats are available in Sekiu for fishing, diving or playing. You can also walk out onto the jetty, fish from the jetty, and feed the sea gulls.

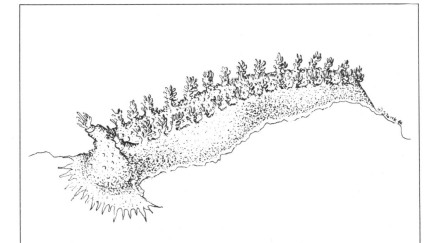

Festive Triton

The festive triton, *Tritonia festiva*, lives subtidally, reaching a length of 5 inches (12 cm). This colorful nudibranch has a soft pink color with a row of white branchial plumes along the sides of its back. A front pair of larger appendages resemble branchial plumes, but are actually retractable sensory organs called rhinophores. A prominent white veil extends in front of the festive triton. It is an additional sensory organ that is used by the nudibranch to feel its way across the bottom and to locate food. The primary foods consumed by *Tritonia festiva* are sea pens, other soft corals, and hydroids.

Figure 46

SEKIU
ONE-MILE BEACH

Habitat and Depth: The impressive number of logs often found on this sandy beach allude to the pounding this shoreline receives during winter storms. Offshore, during quieter times, divers will find a series of tunnels winding through thick kelp and around submerged rocks. These are especially beautiful on a clear day with sunlight filtering through the water and around the kelp stipes.

Animals often seen by divers in this area include sea urchins, sea cucumbers, kelp greenling, wolf-eels, octopuses, sun stars, sunflower stars, blood stars, lemon nudibranchs, schools of small fish and large, dense schools of mysids and amphipods (small shrimp-like animals).

Bottom depths average between 45 and 55 feet along the inshore area (10 foot tide). Bottom depth gradually increases as you move offshore until, at the 70 foot depth, it begins to drop rapidly.

Site Description: To reach the water, follow a steep trail downhill from the roadway to the beach, then through tall grass and over logs scattered across the shoreline.

There are many rocks and channels to explore at this site. You may even discover a wolf-eel or octopus living in one of the holes beneath the rocks. Octopuses and wolf-eels are beautiful animals which, if not frightened, are usually willing to take food out of a diver's hand. Try carrying some fish or crab with you on your dive to feed one of these animals. With a little patience, your feeding attempts could develop into an exciting and rewarding experience that you will not soon forget.

Skill Level: Advanced.

Hazards: Strong current, surge and thick kelp during the growing season. Due to the strong surge in this area, dive only on calm days, preferably during slack current periods. Both flood and ebb currents move parallel to shore, with flood currents moving to the east and ebb currents moving to the west.

An isolated beach of basalt, clay and sand

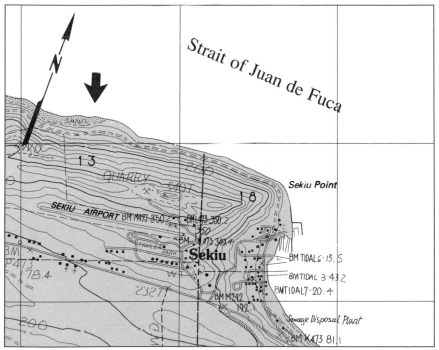

Figure 47   Not Intended For Navigational Use

If you choose to dive during an exchange period, plan and execute your dive as a drift dive. Be sure to use a current table to find the direction of main water flow so that you can plan your entry and exit points accordingly.

Facilities: None at the immediate dive site. Air fills are available in Neah Bay, Sekiu and Port Angeles.

Travel Distance and Directions: One-Mile beach is on the Strait of Juan de Fuca, 0.7 mile west of the Sekiu Recreational Area marina parking lot.

Mileage from Bellingham = 166 miles
Mileage from Seattle = 122 miles
Mileage from Olympia = 171 miles

Drive to Port Angeles, located on the northern end of the Olympic Peninsula. As you drive into Port Angeles, Highway 101 becomes East Front Street. Look for a sign that marks a left hand turn to the Olympic National Park and Hurricane Ridge. At this sign, turn left onto Race Street and drive past the high school stadium, then turn right onto Lauridsen Boulevard and drive across a small bridge. Lauridsen Boulevard soon becomes West Boulevard, which then joins Highway 101. Continue west on Highway 101 to the Highway 112 junction. Turn right onto Highway 112 West, drive 49 miles toward Sekiu and Neah Bay, then turn right into the Sekiu Recreational Area. Drive into Sekiu and turn right at the Olson's Marina sign, just past Washington Street. Make an immediate left-hand turn uphill onto a dirt road (it becomes very muddy during the rainy season). Drive the remaining 0.9 mile to a trail that leads down to the beach.

Current Table: Strait of Juan de Fuca.
Look up the daily current predictions for the Strait of Juan de Fuca. Apply the following time corrections to calculate slack current times:

Time corrections for subordinate station 820:
Minimum current before flood: −35 minutes
Minimum current before ebb: +87 minutes

Telephone Location: None at the immediate dive site. Drive back to Sekiu.

Non-Diver Activities: Enjoy the thrill of walking down a wooded trail to discover a log-strewn isolated beach. Soak up some sunshine while you watch ship traffic on the Strait of Juan de Fuca. Take time to watch the birds, take pictures, dig for shellfish, feed sea gulls or walk along the beach. There are rock formations to explore, tide pools to look into, and shells to collect.

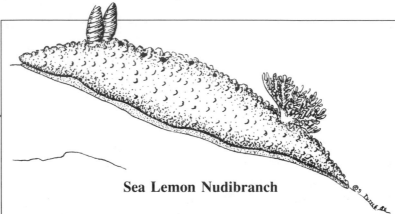

Sea Lemon Nudibranch

As is characteristic of dorid nudibranchs, the sea lemon, *Archidoris montereyensis*, has a branchial plume encircling its anus; which is on its back at the opposite end from its rhinophores. This nudibranch is often confused with two other dorid nudibranchs: Cooper's dorid, *Aldisa cooperi*, and the speckled sea lemon, *Anisodoris nobilis*. The dorsums (backs) of all three nudibranchs are covered with small bumps called tubercles. The positioning of black spots on their dorsums and tubercles, along with the color of their branchial plumes, distinguish the three species.

The sea lemon has a lemon-yellow to brownish-yellow body with a variable number of black spots that are positioned both between and on its tubercles. Its branchial plume is the same color as its body, often lemon-yellow.

In contrast, the speckled sea lemon has a yellow to orange-yellow body with a variable number of black spots on its dorsum. The spots are positioned only between the tubercles, and its branchial plume is white.

Cooper's dorid is recognized by a single distinctive row of 6 to 10 black spots running along the crest of its lemon-yellow to orange-yellow dorsum. Its branchial plume is the same color as its body.

The sea lemon, *Archidoris montereyensis*, lives in both intertidal and subtidal zones where it feeds on yellow sponges. It typically grows to 3 inches (5 cm) in length, but may occasionally reach 6 inches (15 cm).

Figure 48

PINNACLE ROCK

Habitat and Depth: This is another beautiful and rich dive site that is well worth the drive to see. The beach is separated from the roadway by a row of trees. After stepping past the trees, visitors have a sweeping view of the Strait of Juan de Fuca. A large rock formation rises out of the water a short distance offshore. Beneath the surface, rocks and long kelp stalks form tunnels that are fun to swim through and exciting to explore. The bottom is rocky with areas of a sandy-cobblestone bottom showing between the rocks and beneath patches of eelgrass. A few large rocks are exposed above water, but most are submerged.

Animals divers may see during this dive include kelp greenling, sea urchins, large dense schools of mysids and amphipods (small shrimp-like animals), moon snails, sunflower sea stars and ochre sea stars.

Bottom depths range from 20 to 45 feet in the kelp bed.

Site Description: Follow a path through a narrow band of trees to the rocky beach and enter the water. Divers can explore the rocky bottom in either direction from their point of entry.

Skill Level: Advanced.

Hazards: Strong current, surge and thick kelp. When waves are breaking along the shoreline, entry can be difficult and dangerous.

Due to the current and waves common to this area, dive only on calm days, and preferably during slack current periods. The main water flow is parallel to shore, but localized changes in directional flow occur around inshore rock formations. If you choose to dive during an exchange period, plan on a drift dive. During the dive, be willing to change your direction of movement to move either with the water flow or perpendicular to it.

Always make a visual check of surface conditions before entering. Be willing to abort a dive if either you or your buddy are not comfortable with the area or surface conditions. Be careful and enjoy your dive.

Submerged rocks and sand channels are fun to explore

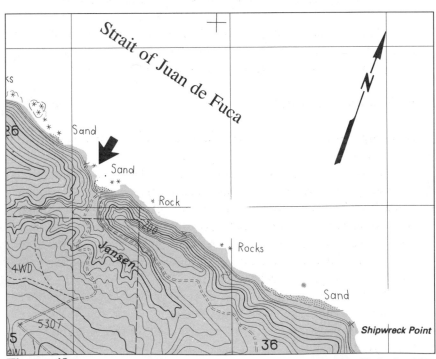

Figure 49

Facilities: None at the immediate site. Drive west to Neah Bay or east to Sekiu. Air fills are available in Neah Bay, Sekiu, Joyce and Port Angeles.

Travel Distance and Directions: This dive site is between Sekiu and Neah Bay, 11 miles west of the Sekiu Recreational Area.

Mileage from Bellingham = 176 miles
Mileage from Seattle = 132 miles
Mileage from Olympia = 180 miles

Drive to Port Angeles on Highway 101 North. Turn onto Highway 112 West and continue to Sekiu. Continue past the Sekiu Recreational Area turn-off for 11 miles to where the roadway drops down to the water, just past mile marker four. Look for a tall, slender rock pinnacle standing in the intertidal area. Trees grow on top of this unusual rock formation. Park on the north side of the roadway in a dirt turn-out.

Current Table: Strait of Juan de Fuca.

Use the daily current predictions for the Strait of Juan de Fuca reference station. Time corrections are not needed.

Telephone Location: None at the immediate site. Drive 7 miles west to the Thunderbird Resort in Neah Bay, or 11 miles east to the Sekiu Recreational Area.

Non-Diver Activities: Between Sekiu and Neah Bay, Highway 101 passes through a naturally beautiful and wild area of Washington. This sometimes narrow roadway winds through trees and along the edge of the Strait of Juan de Fuca. Visitors interested in the shoreline and marine life will not only enjoy the drive, but will enjoy walking along the beach while exploring the rock formations and tide pools. Seals are commonly sighted offshore, their heads just showing above the surface as they pause to look around. Whales are sighted less often.

To visit the Makah Museum, drive 6.5 miles west of Pinnacle Rock to the outskirts of Neah Bay. Turn left to the Makah Museum.

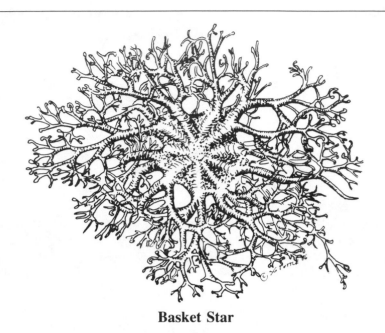

Basket Star

The white basket star, *Gorgonocephalus eucnemis*, is the largest species of brittle star in the Pacific Northwest. It has ten main arms, each branching several times to form a delicate basket-like shape (Plate 25). The basket star is usually found in high current areas north of Puget Sound. It feeds on plankton and small animals, captured with its tentacles from the surrounding water.

Brittle stars are different from sea stars in that they do not have pedicellariae, their tube feet are small, and the tube feet are not used for locomotion. While the white basket star remains relatively fixed in one location, smaller brittle stars are more active. The small brittle stars move about by lifting their central disc off the bottom with two or three arms, then push themselves in the direction that they wish to go with the remaining non-supportive arms. Their movements are jerky, but effective. The white basket star can move also, but not as fast.

Figure 50

PART 8. **NORTH PUGET SOUND**

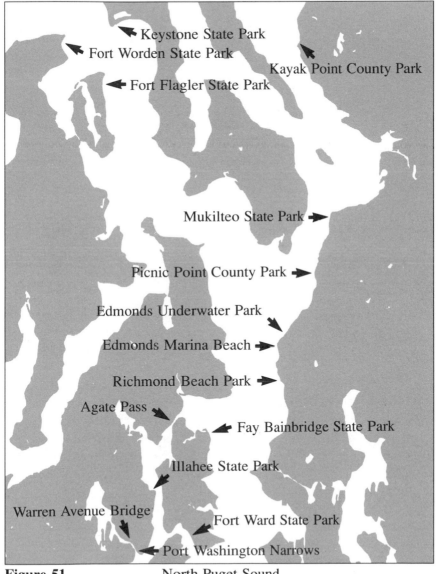

Figure 51   North Puget Sound

FORT WORDEN STATE PARK
PIER AND REEF

Habitat and Depth: A few feet from shore, divers will find an artificial reef and adjacent pier. The south end of the reef contains small mounds of old tires, while the northern half is made of scattered logs and hollow concrete piles. Both areas contain a variety of intriguing underwater structures for divers to explore. Spear fishing is not permitted in the park.

Although there are more animals living on the reef than under the pier, both structures provide protection and support for many interesting animals. A few of these include schools of perch and tube-snouts, flounder, rockfish, sculpins, blackeye gobies, painted greenling, sea anemones, sponges, tube worms, octopuses, red sea squirts, sea cucumbers, large gumboot chitons, shrimp, large barnacles, and sea stars.

The area has a sandy bottom that changes to mud beyond the 26 foot depth (10 foot tide). During the sunnier months of the year, species of flat brown kelp (*Laminaria* sp.) cover much of the bottom around the reef, while bull kelp and feather-boa kelp rise to the surface. Depth at the end of the pier is 31 feet (10 foot tide).

Site Description: The center of the artificial reef is marked by a single buoy (white with red stripes), located north of the pier. Swim out from the parking area to a point 100 feet south of the buoy, over the south end of the tire reef. Descend and swim northward over the reef, away from the boat harbor entrance. The boat launch area on the north side of the pier is closed to swimming.

Long, hollow concrete piles are scattered over the bottom. They are open at each end, providing convenient access points for animals using them for shelter. What more could an octopus or rockfish ask for? A light will be useful when peering into these dark openings.

Divers also may want to use a light when diving beneath the pier. Vertical wood planks line the south side of the pier from the beach outward, but turn to wrap in underneath the deck before reaching the end of the pier. Swim out along the south side of the

A Marine Science Center is located on the Fort Worden pier.

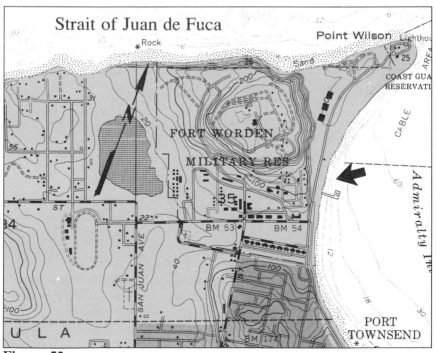

Figure 52   Not Intended For Navigational Use

pier to where the planks wrap in underneath the deck. Take a look at the surface to confirm that it is clear and unobstructed, then submerge and swim under the deck. The piles are covered with white plumose anemones and large purple tube worms. Notice the differences in numbers and types of animals living in this dark environment, as compared to the animals living in the sunnier habitats on either side of the pier.

Skill Level: All divers.

Hazards: Current, fishing line and small boats.

Currents move parallel to shore in a counterclockwise direction, from Point Wilson toward the pier, during both flood and ebb cycles.

Facilities: Facilities available between the wharf and the northern camping area include camping, picnic tables, barbecue stands, rest rooms, hot showers, a cold shower for washing equipment (located halfway between the pier and lighthouse), a boat launch on the north side of the wharf, a sink with running water on the end of the wharf, a kitchen shelter and a snack bar/grocery store (located across the road from the wharf). Air fills are available in Port Townsend, Hadlock and Port Angeles.

Travel Distance and Directions: Fort Worden State Park is located on the northeast tip of the Olympic Peninsula, 3 miles from the Port Townsend ferry pier.

> Mileage from Bellingham = 69 miles
> Mileage from Seattle = 48 miles
> Mileage from Olympia = 97 miles

From Bellingham: drive south on I-5 to Exit 230 for Highway 20 West, Whidbey Island and Anacortes. Exit from I-5, and follow signs to Deception Pass, Whidbey Island, Oak Harbor and Coupeville. Turn right in Oak Harbor toward Coupeville. Drive 9.7 miles, then turn right immediately past a foot bridge to Fort Casey and the Keystone Ferry. Ride the ferry across Puget Sound to Port

Townsend. After leaving the Port Townsend Ferry Dock, turn left onto Water Street (becomes Sims Way), drive 0.5 mile and turn right onto Kearney Street. Follow the directions below.

From Seattle: drive north on I-5 to the Edmonds/Kingston Ferry Exit 177. Exit from I-5, then turn west onto 244th Street SW at the bottom of the exit ramp. Follow Highway 104 West to the Kingston Ferry in Edmonds, then ride the ferry across Puget Sound to Kingston. From Kingston, drive 9.0 miles west on Highway 104 to the Hood Canal Bridge. Turn right onto the bridge (still Highway 104) and follow signs to Port Townsend. After entering Port Townsend on Sims Way, turn left onto Kearney Street. Follow the signs to Fort Worden State Park. After entering Fort Worden, take the third right hand turn onto Ft. Worden Way. Drive past the park office and turn left onto Harbor Defense Way. Drive downhill to the pier and parking lots.

From Olympia: follow Highway 101 North for 83 miles, through the town of Quilcene, to the southern tip of Discovery Bay. Turn right onto Highway 20 East, drive 12 miles to Port Townsend, turn left onto Kearney Street and follow the above directions.

Current Table: Admiralty Inlet.

Look up the daily current predictions for Admiralty Inlet. Apply the following time corrections to calculate slack current times:

> Time corrections for subordinate station 950:
> Minimum current before flood: −68 minutes
> Minimum current before ebb: −47 minutes

Telephone Location: The closest phone is located across the road from the wharf. A second phone can be found at the park office.

Non-diver Activities: Fort Worden was originally one of three artillery fortifications that guarded the entrance into Puget Sound. Although operational during both World War I and II, the guns were never fired at an enemy. Visitors can walk up to Artillery Hill to see the concrete bunkers and gunnery emplacements. Beneath the two gunnery pads are cavernous magazines where explosives were once stored. Now empty and abandoned, a flashlight is needed when walking through these dark magazines and connecting tunnels. The observation post at the top of bunker Battery D. Kinzie has a dramatic view of the Strait of Juan de Fuca. Seeing this magnificent view is well worth the climb to the top of the bunker.

There are also hiking trails, a play structure, a Marine Science Center (located on the Fort Warden pier) and lots of open area to run and play in. Visitors can walk the beach to the Point Wilson Lighthouse, fly a kite or play baseball on the grassy parade ground.

Nearby Port Townsend is fun to visit, too. Historical attractions in this old sea port include the Rothschild House and the Jefferson County Historical Museum. The Rothschild House built in 1868, was the home of a merchant. It is open daily for tours during the summer, and on weekends during the winter.

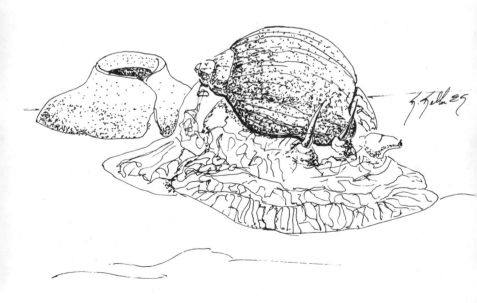

Figure 53

Moon Snail

Moon snails, *Polinices lewisii*, live on soft bottoms where they are often seen plowing through the substrate in search of food (Plates 16-18). They feed on clams and other moon snails after drilling a small hole through the shells of their prey. To accomplish this feat, the moon snail comes equipped with an array of specialized structures. It first uses suction to attach the end of a long tongue-like organ, called a proboscis, to its prey's shell. It then secretes an acid from the end of the proboscis to soften a small area of shell. The end of the proboscis (the snail's mouth) contains a rasp-like structure, called a radula, that is covered with rows of replaceable teeth. The snail uses its radula to rasp out the newly softened layer of shell. Softening and rasping actions continue over several hours until a small hole is completed. The moon snail's proboscis is then extended through the hole to begin feeding. The radula goes to work again, tearing out soft chunks of tissue. At the same time, the loosened pieces of tissue are sucked through the hollow proboscis and deposited in the moon snail's stomach.

Moon snails lay a gelatinous layer of eggs that become embedded with sand as they emerge from the parent and wrap around the snail's foot and shell. The eggs are held together with a sticky mucus, which soon hardens the egg mass into a curious and flexible collar-like shape. The gray egg cases left behind look like round pieces of old rubber. They eventually disintegrate, releasing about a half million free-swimming larvae.

FORT FLAGLER STATE PARK FISHING PIER

Habitat and Depth: Sunshine, bull kelp and wharf pilings each contribute to the enchantment of diving beneath this picturesque fishing pier. Swimming out over the sandy bottom, divers can glide between the pilings or explore large, abandoned concrete cylinders on either side of the pier. The concrete structures now form small reefs that support and protect many small animals.

A few of the animals living in this area include rockfish, flounder, kelp greenling, hermit crabs, sponges, gunnels, sea anemones and giant acorn barnacles.

Depth at the end of the pier is approximately 31 feet (10 foot tide). Beyond the outer pilings of the pier, the bottom slope drops rapidly to 40 feet, then changes to a more gradual slope.

Site Description: A trail leads down to the beach on the north side of the pier. Enter the water from the beach on either side of the pier and swim out along the pilings and over the eelgrass. During the sunnier months, bull kelp grows around the end of the pier and beneath an opening in the pier decking. This dive site is a state park game sanctuary. Spear fishing is not allowed.

Skill Level: Intermediate.

Hazards: Current, kelp and fishing line.

Strong currents are common at this site because Admiralty Inlet is the main channel for water flowing into and out of Puget Sound. Due to a reverse current along the shoreline south of Marrowstone Point, both flood and ebb currents flow north-northwest, past the fishing pier toward Marrowstone Point.

Dive during periods of minimal current, and always make a visual check of water movement before entering. Carry a knife so you can cut fishing line if necessary.

The Fort Flagler Fishing Pier during a low tide

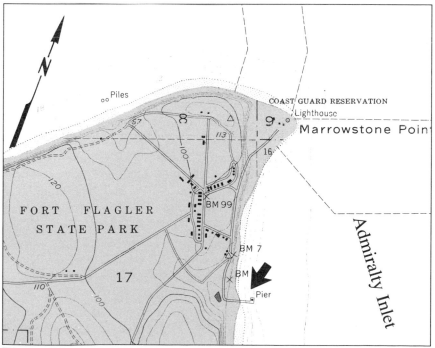

Figure 54   Not Intended For Navigational Use

Facilities: None at the fishing pier. Facilities available in other areas of the park include camping, barbecue stands, picnic tables, rest rooms, hot showers, a small grocery store that also serves hot food, a dock and boat launch. Air fills are available in Hadlock and Port Townsend.

Travel Distance and Directions: Fort Flagler State Park is located on Marrowstone Island, 21 miles from Port Townsend.

> Mileage from Bellingham = 86 miles
> Mileage from Seattle = 46 miles
> Mileage from Olympia = 97 miles

From Bellingham: drive south on I-5 to the Anacortes Exit 230 for Highway 20 West, Whidbey Island and Anacortes. Exit from I-5, then follow signs to Deception Pass, Whidbey Island, Oak Harbor and Coupeville. Turn right in Oak Harbor toward Coupeville. Drive 9.7 miles before turning right, immediately past a foot bridge, to Fort Casey and the Keystone Ferry. Ride the ferry across Puget Sound to Port Townsend.

From the Port Townsend Ferry Dock, turn left onto Water Street (becomes Sims Way). Drive out of Port Townsend to a "Y" in the roadway. Bear to the left toward Fort Flagler, then drive 3.5 miles before turning left onto Charles Street. Continue into the Town of Hadlock. In Hadlock, turn left onto Oak Bay Road and follow the directions below.

From Seattle: drive north on I-5 to the Edmonds-Kingston Ferry Exit 177. At the bottom of the exit ramp, turn west onto 244th Street SW and follow signs for Highway 104 West to the Edmonds-Kingston Ferry Dock. Board the ferry and cross Puget Sound to Kingston. From Kingston, drive 9.0 miles west on Highway 104 to the Hood Canal Bridge. Turn right onto the bridge (still Highway 104), cross the canal and continue 5.0 miles to the Port Ludlow Recreational Area turn-off. Turn right onto Beaverton Valley Road, then continue 9.1 miles to the town of Chimacum. Turn right onto Chimacum Road and drive 1.6 miles into the Town of Hadlock. In Hadlock, turn right onto Oak Bay Road, and then left onto Flagler Road. Follow Flagler Road onto Indian Island and then onto

Marrowstone Island. Watch for signs leading the way to Fort Flagler State Park. Maps of the park are available at the gate.

From Olympia: drive north on Highway 101 to the junction for Highway 101/Highway 8. Exit to the right onto Highway 101. Drive 65 miles, past Shelton and Hoodsport, to Quilcene. In Quilcene, turn right onto the Quilcene-Chimacum Road. Drive 16.8 miles, through Center, to the town of Hadlock. Turn right onto Oak Bay Road and follow the above directions.

Current Table: Admiralty Inlet.

Look up the daily current predictions for Admiralty Inlet. Apply the following time corrections to calculate slack current times:

> Time corrections for subordinate station 995:
>   Minimum current before flood: −53 minutes
>   Minimum current before ebb: −73 minutes

Telephone Location: On the outside of the ranger residence, across the road from the park office.

Non-Diver Activities: Visit the gun emplacements, play on the grass, camp, hike, fish from the dock or go for a walk along the beach.

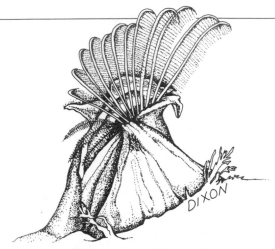

Giant Acorn Barnacle

Originally described by Darwin in the mid 1800's, the giant acorn barnacle, *Balanus nubilus*, is the largest barnacle in the Pacific Northwest. Living subtidally, its shell may reach a diameter of 3 inches (8 cm) and a height of 2 1/2 inches (6 cm).

A barnacle begins life as a tiny, crab-like, free-swimming larva. After undergoing a series of molts, it attaches its head to a supporting structure with glue produced in the base of the first antenna. The barnacle then rotates its legs (now called cirri) up and over the attachment point. It also begins to build its protective outer shell. For the remainder of a barnacle's life, cirri are no longer used for locomotion, but instead are used to sweep in and out of its shell, bringing plankton (food) and water (oxygen) to the animal.

Barnacles belong to the only group of sessile crustaceans. Just as crabs do, they must periodically molt by shedding their carapaces to allow room for growth. With each molt, they also must enlarge their outer shell. To accommodate this need, the hard outer shell is secreted in a series of cxpandable, interlocking plates that can be enlarged as needed.

Figure 55

KEYSTONE STATE PARK

Habitat and Depth: The current-swept Keystone Jetty is a magical world where cabezon and lingcod disappear into walls of white plumose anemones with the flick of their tails. It is also a world where clouds of sand lances shimmer in the sunlight as they sweep past overhead, swimming in unison as one entity. Large boulders piled on top of each other form the jetty, providing hundreds of hiding places into which animals can easily retreat. The rocks provide an immense structural support for bull kelp, as well as many invertebrates, such as heart crabs, giant acorn barnacles and a variety of sea stars and anemones.

East of the jetty is a group of old pilings where divers will find still more plumose anemones. Bushes of purple and green feather duster worms, Puget Sound's largest species of tube worm, are also found here.

Other animals common to this beautiful wildlife preserve include schools of rockfish and herring, kelp greenling, whitespotted greenling, painted greenling, tube-snouts, sea urchins, sea cucumbers, shrimp, crab, nudibranchs, chitons, limpets and an occasional wolf-eel or octopus.

A sandy bottom stretches between wharf pilings and a rock jetty. Bottom depths on the outside of the pilings and at the end of the jetty reach 28 feet and 62 feet respectively (10 foot tide).

Site Description: Enter the water on the east side of the jetty, submerge and begin to explore the large boulders. Divers will quickly discover that the jetty is built like a pyramid, with more rocks extending beneath the surface than above. It is a good location for both wide-angle and macro photography. If the current allows, the end of the jetty and opposite side are fun to explore, too.

An alternate dive can be made around a group of old wharf pilings during either flood or ebb exchanges. The pilings are covered with small colorful animals that are fun to watch or photograph. After exploring the pilings, divers can often ride the current toward the jetty (see the Hazards section and map on pages 152-154 for a description of current patterns). As they near the

A pier once connected the Keystone wharf with the shore.

jetty, they should start swimming for shore before the current flow changes direction and begins to flow out along the jetty. During the early part of a flood exchange, the water is moving in the opposite direction. At this time, divers can drift from the jetty to the pilings. When swimming in current, remember to swim with the flow or perpendicular to it, but not against it.

Visibility is usually best during the last part of a flood exchange and during slack before ebb.

Skill Level: Intermediate divers.

Hazards: Strong current, fishing line and kelp.

Ferry traffic and small boats are additional hazards when diving on the side of the jetty closest to the ferry pier and boat launch. When diving on this side of the jetty, be sure to stay out of the ferry traffic and small boat lanes by staying close to the jetty.

During the initial phase of a flood exchange, water flows in along the jetty, then turns in the shallows and flows parallel to shore toward the old wharf. A second slack occurs during a flood cycle when the flow reverses and begins to flow toward the jetty.

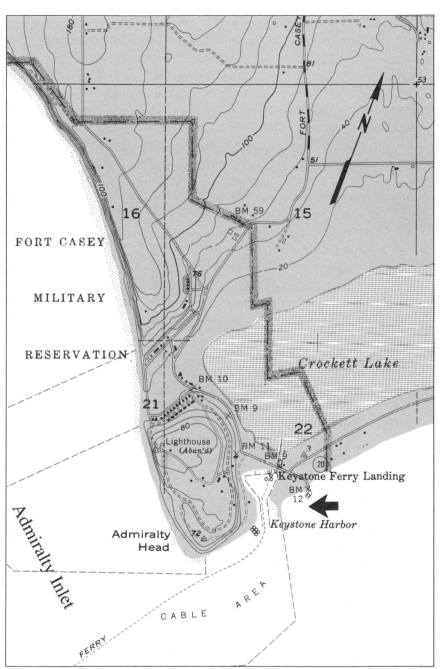

Figure 56

A true slack before ebb does not occur at Keystone. Instead, the current only slows before picking up speed again and continuing to flow southwest, past the wharf toward the jetty. Currents flow out along the jetty during both ebb exchanges and the last half of flood exchanges. During large exchanges, current striking the jetty will divide into two segments; one flowing out along the jetty, and one flowing inshore.

Use a current table (not a tide table) to plan your dive at Keystone. Enter the water approximately 30 minutes before the predicted time for slack current. If you should find yourself in current, remember that the flow is slower on the bottom. Also, rocks can be used for hand holds to pull yourself along the jetty. Use the big boulders for shelter from current if a rest is needed.

Facilities: Rest rooms with hot showers, an outside cold shower for cleaning equipment, picnic tables, a boat launch and parking. There is a restaurant across the street from the park. Air fills are available in Oak Harbor, Port Townsend and Anacortes.

Travel Distance and Directions: Keystone State Park is located in Admiralty Bay on the west side of Whidbey Island, 5 miles south of Coupeville.

> Mileage from Bellingham = 66 miles
> Mileage from Seattle = 47 miles
> Mileage from Olympia = 96 miles

From Bellingham: drive south to I-5 Exit 230 for Anacortes and Whidbey Island. Exit from I-5, then follow Highway 20 West for 11.9 miles before turning left to Deception Pass. Continue on Highway 20 West for 16.2 miles, across Deception Pass and into Oak Harbor. Turn right to Coupeville, then drive 9.7 miles and, just past a foot bridge, turn right onto Engle Road. Drive the remaining 4.2 miles, through Fort Casey State Park and past the Keystone Ferry Dock, to Keystone State Park.

From Seattle: drive to Mukilteo, then ride the ferry to Clinton on Whidbey Island. Drive north from Clinton on Highway 525 for 22 miles, through Freeland and Greenbank, before turning left to the Port Townsend Ferry and Fort Casey State Park. Drive the remaining 3.4 miles to Keystone State Park.

From Olympia: drive north on Highway 101 to Port Townsend, then ride the ferry to Keystone. Turn right as you leave the ferry dock, then make the next right turn into Keystone State Park.

Current Table: Admiralty Inlet.

Look up the daily current predictions for Admiralty Inlet. Apply the following time corrections to calculate slack current times:

> Time corrections for subordinate station 965:
> Minimum current before flood: −31 minutes
> Minimum current before ebb: +01 minutes

Telephone Location: Across the street at the restaurant.

Non-Diver Activities: Visit the concrete gun emplacements at Fort Casey, ride the ferry to Port Townsend (there are many interesting shops and restaurants in this historical seaport), go for a walk along the beach, fish from the jetty, catch some sunshine on the sandy beach, camp, picnic or barbecue a meal at Fort Casey State Park.

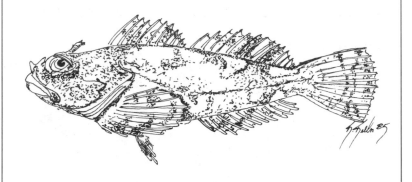

Cabezon

The cabezon, *Scorpaenichthys marmoratus*, is one of the largest sculpins in the northwest, growing to 36 inches (91 cm) in length. It lives in intertidal and subtidal areas around rocky reefs and kelp beds where it feeds on crustaceans, fish and shellfish. Cabezon have a distinctive marbled coloration of black splotches on a variable greenish to yellow background. Typical of sculpins, their head is large in comparison with the rest of the body. Large bulbous eyes protrude from the top of the head, along with a large cirrus that decorates the area above each eye.

Spawning occurs in January through March when large masses of eggs are attached to rocks. The male positions himself on top of the fertilized egg mass, guarding it until the eggs hatch. During this period, the fish is reluctant to leave the egg mass and is especially vulnerable to spear fishing. The uneducated diver spearing such a fish not only kills the adult, but cssentially kills up to 100,000 eggs by exposing them to predation from other fish (Plate 19).

Figure 57

Kayak Point County Park has a number of sheltered picnic areas

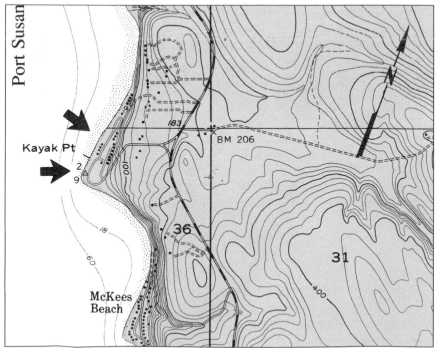

Figure 58

KAYAK POINT COUNTY PARK

Habitat and Depth: Although there are a limited number of animals living on the bottom at this site, it is a good dive for beginning divers who are becoming familiar with their equipment. The site has an easy entry with weak current and infrequent surge. Some of the animals that you will find are flounder, C-O sole, hermit crab, moon snails, orange plumose sea anemones and mottled sea stars (*Evasterias troschelii*).

North of the fishing pier, the bottom is a silty sandy-gravel that slopes to a mud flat. The slope is gradual at first, then steepens somewhat at the 21 foot and 71 foot depths (10 foot tide). By 50 feet, the bottom has changed to silty sand, but changes again at about 60 feet to mud. By 89 feet the mud bottom levels out.

Kayak Point is located south of the fishing pier. Offshore from Kayak Point, a steep sandy slope quickly exceeds 110 feet in depth.

Site Description: The fishing pier and boat ramp are located in the middle of the park shoreline, dividing the beach into north and south segments. Enter the water and dive from any point along the beach, remembering to stay clear of the boat launching area and any people fishing from the pier.

Skill Level: All divers.

Hazards: Fishing line and small boats.

The boat ramp is located immediately north of the fishing pier. It is a good idea to stay clear of both the boat ramp and pier to avoid boat traffic and fish hooks. Listen for motor noise before ascending. Minimal current flows to the northwest during flood exchanges and to the southeast during ebb exchanges.

Facilities: The park has a long grass field that stretches the length of the lower parking area. It also has rest rooms with dry changing areas, a fishing pier, covered picnic tables, barbecue pits, camping, a boat ramp and parking. Air fills are available in Everett, Lynnwood and Edmonds.

Travel Distance and Directions: Kayak Point County Park is located on the east shore of Port Susan, 12 miles northwest of Marysville.

> Mileage from Bellingham = 67 miles
> Mileage from Seattle = 37 miles
> Mileage from Olympia = 106 miles

Follow I-5 to Marysville (north of Everett) and Exit 199. Exit from the freeway and turn west onto the Marine Drive-Tulalip Road. Drive 12 miles, turn left onto Kayak Point Park Road, and follow the signs downhill to the beach. Park on the north side of the boat ramp.

Current Table: Admiralty Inlet.
Look up the daily current predictions for Admiralty Inlet. Apply the following time corrections to calculate slack current times:

> Time corrections for subordinate station 1400:
> Minimum current before flood: +44 minutes
> Minimum current before ebb: +13 minutes

Telephone Location: In the upper parking lot, next to the park office.

Non-Diver Activities: This is a beautiful county park with a long stretch of lawn to run and play on. There is also room for a softball game and frisbee and kite flying. Visitors can enjoy a nature trail and a great view of Camano Island while they fish from the pier, barbecue their lunch, photograph sea gulls, or just enjoy being outside.

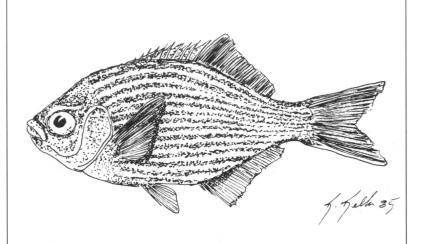

Striped Seaperch

The striped seaperch, *Embiotoca lateralis*, is easily recognized by its distinctive horizontal blue stripes below the lateral line. It is often seen in schools around kelp, eelgrass and wharf pilings in both intertidal and high subtidal areas.

Another easily recognized seaperch is the pile perch, *Rhacochilus vacca*. This fish is recognized by dark blotches or vertical bars on its back and sides. It also is seen near pilings where it feeds on mussels and barnacles after using its mouth as a battering ram to break their protective shells. Generous coverings of broken shells, along with clumps of mussels and barnacles, occur on bottoms around pilings primarily because of perch feeding activity.

Once fertilized, perch eggs develop inside the female until fully developed young fish are released in June, July and August. Seaperch eat many small animals including mussels, barnacles, worms, small crustaceans and the eggs of other fish.

Figure 59

Plate 1   A magical world lies hidden beneath the surface.

Plate 2 The Lion's Mane, the Northwest's largest jellyfish, feeds on small animals that it captures with its tentacles.

Plate 3 Hermit crabs actively compete for empty shells.

Plate 4 In the spring, male hermit crabs can be seen dragging females across the bottom prior to mating.

Plate 5 Sea pens are colonial animals that feed on plankton captured from the surrounding water.

Plate 6 A spiny sea star slowly digests a sea pen.

Plate 7 In hopes of obtaining a meal, a leather star moves toward a sea anemone.

Plate 8 Following contact with the sea star's tube feet, the anemone responds by stinging this potential predator.

Plate 9 Then, if stinging does not discourage the predator, the swimming anemone detaches from its rocky perch...

Plate 10 ...and swims out of the sea star's reach.

Plate 11 The aggressive Sunflower sea star...

Plate 12 ...actively hunts for its meals.

Plate 13 The basket cockle often escapes...

Plate 14 ...from this aggressive predator by extending its large foot and pushing itself out of the sea star's path.

Plate 15 The foraging of purple sea stars limits the populations of mussels and barnacles in the lower intertidal zone.

Plate 16 Moon snails hunt for clams and snails.

Plate 17 Basket cockles will attempt to jump...

Plate 18 ...from a moon snail's path.

Plate 19 A male cabezon guards its purple egg mass.

Plate 20 A quillback rockfish will often display a territorial behavior by raising its dorsal fin and swimming toward a diver.

Plate 21 Feeding a wolf eel or octopus is an exciting experience
that is not easily forgotten. If not frightened by a diver's
approach, a wolf eel will often take a split sea urchin from
a diver's hand.

Plate 22 A diver slowly offers a Dungeness crab to an octopus.

Plate 23 If hungry, and not frightened by the diver, an octopus often responds by reaching out with its tentacles.

Plate 24 The octopus will grip a crab with a few suction cups, then pull it from the diver's hand.

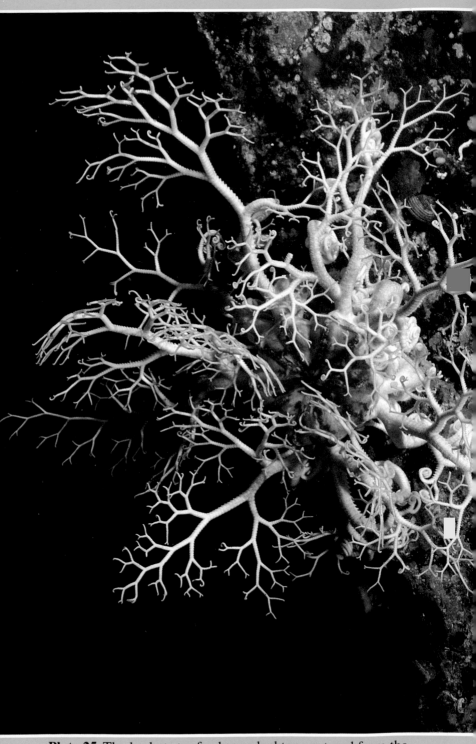

Plate 25 The basket star feeds on plankton captured from the surrounding water with its tentacles.

MUKILTEO STATE PARK

Habitat and Depth: As I surfaced and the water cleared from my face plate, I realized that a sea monster was swimming past me with occasional snorts and puffs of steam. Upon taking a second look, the monster disappeared, leaving behind four sea lions, swimming in line as they headed south. One sea lion turned its whiskered nose toward me long enough to snort before continuing on its way.

Below the surface, flounder and speckled sanddabs glide over the sandy bottom while looking for their next meal. Green and purple shore crabs inhabit the inshore sandy-cobblestone bottom, along with gunnels that can be found hiding under rocks. Other animals living here include moon snails, sea anemones, frosted nudibranchs, sea stars, piddock clams, sea squirts, hermit crabs, heart crabs, kelp crabs and an occasional passing sea monster.

The inshore sandy-cobblestone bottom changes abruptly to sand at the 13 foot depth (10 foot tide).

Site Description: At the 23 foot depth, the bottom angles sharply downward to 86 feet, then levels out to a gentler slope. Low vertical clay banks, 3 to 5 feet in height, cut across the slope at the 41, 56 and 73 foot depths. To find these, swim out from the lone tree that stands near the rest rooms south of Elliot Point, submerge and follow the slope down to the clay banks. This barren slope is steep enough so that vegetation does not remain attached, but slides downward to form a deep pile at the base of the slope.

Skill Level: All divers.

Hazards: Current and small boats.

A boat ramp, located at the north end of Mukilteo State Park, receives frequent use. Dive to the south of the launching area, display a dive flag, and listen for motor noise before ascending.

Facilities: Include rest rooms with changing areas, picnic tables, barbecue stands, a large grass field and a boat launch. Air fills are available in Everett, Lynnwood and Edmonds.

A lone tree stands on the shoreline south of Elliot Point.

Travel Distance and Directions: Mukilteo State Park is located in Mukilteo, 0.1 mile south of Taylor's Landing.

Mileage from Bellingham = 73 miles
Mileage from Seattle = 22 miles
Mileage from Olympia = 91 miles

Follow I-5 to Exit 189 in South Everett, then exit to Highway 526 West. Continue on Highway 526 West for 5.4 miles, past Boeing, to the Highway 525 North junction. Turn right onto Highway 525 North (Mukilteo Speedway). Drive 2.0 miles to the bottom of the hill in Mukilteo, turn left onto Front Street (in front of Taylor's Landing), then left into the park.

Current Table: Admiralty Inlet.
Look up the daily current predictions for Admiralty Inlet. Apply the following time corrections to calculate slack current times:

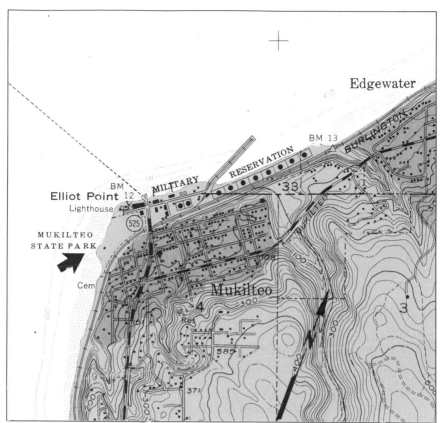

Figure 60   Not Intended For Navigational Use

Time corrections for subordinate station 1090:
  Minimal current before flood: +44 minutes
  Minimal current before ebb: +13 minutes

Telephone Location: In front of the store on Taylor's Landing.

Non-Diver Activities: Mukilteo is a small town with interesting shops to visit, excellent restaurants, and a great view across Possession Sound to Whidbey Island. A public fishing pier is located at Taylor's Landing, next to the ferry pier. With fishing poles and a picnic lunch, non-divers can spend a morning or afternoon fishing while watching ferry traffic, people and birds.

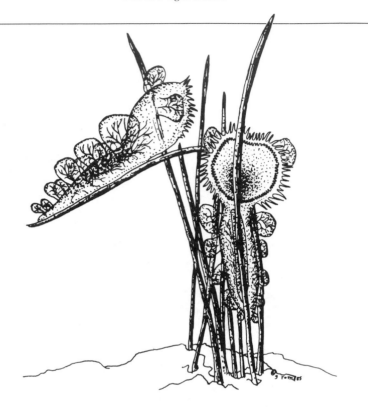

Hooded Nudibranch

The hooded nudibranch, *Melibe leonina*, is usually found attached to eelgrass or kelp in areas that are at least partially sheltered from current. This unusual nudibranch uses a scoop-like oral hood, ringed with short tentacles, to capture small animals from the surrounding water. In a single year, the translucent *Melibe* grows to a length of 4 to 6 inches (10 cm), reproduces and then apparently dies. Its life span is not known, but large populations have been observed to disappear within a single month (Nybakken, 1984).

The hooded nudibranch belongs to the suborder, *Dendronotacea*, along with the giant nudibranch, *Dendronotus sp.*, and the festive triton, *Tritonia festiva*.

Figure 61

PICNIC POINT COUNTY PARK

Habitat and Depth: The main attractions at this site are its public access and its accessibility to the North Seattle area. Be prepared for a long walk (290 yards) from the parking lot to the beach. Given the limited number of animals living in this area, there are a surprising variety of species. Animals divers may see include sea pens, flounder, striped nudibranchs, tube-snouts, pipe fish, moon snails, several species of sea stars and an occasional skate.

Picnic Point has a cobblestone beach that quickly changes to a gradually sloping sandy bottom with an eelgrass bed. The bottom slopes downward past 70 feet, but the eelgrass and most of the animals will be found above 40 feet.

Site Description: From the parking lot, walk across the foot bridge to the beach and enter the water.

While exploring the sandy bottom, notice which animals are limited to one type of habitat. Sea pens, striped nudibranchs and sunflower sea stars usually live only in subtidal habitats, below the eelgrass line. Other animals, like perch and hermit crabs, frequent both intertidal and subtidal habitats. In what ways have these and other animals adapted to their respective habitat ranges?

Skill Level: All divers.

Hazards: Occasional small boats.

Minimal current moves parallel to shore, generally moving northward during a flood cycle and southward during an ebb cycle.

Facilities: A foot bridge leads over the railroad tracks, from a large parking area at the end of Picnic Road, to a grass lawn and beach. A few picnic tables and barbecue stands are located on the grass, while outhouses are in the parking lot. There are no other facilities. Park hours are from 6:00 A.M. to dusk. Air fills are available in Everett, Lynnwood and Edmonds.

A foot bridge crosses the RR tracks from the parking lot

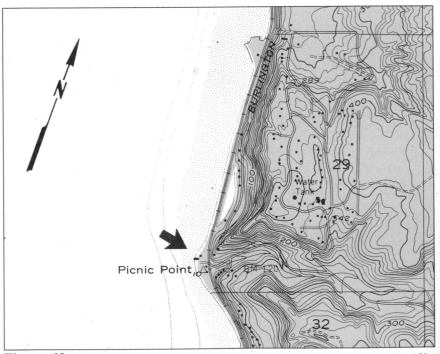

Figure 62   Not Intended For Navigational Use

Travel Distance and Directions: Picnic Point is located on the east shore of Possession Sound, between Mukilteo and Edmonds.

> Mileage from Bellingham = 75 miles
> Mileage from Seattle = 15 miles
> Mileage from Olympia = 84 miles

Follow I-5 to Exit 183, located between Everett and North Seattle, exit and drive west on 164th Street SW. Turn right onto 36th Avenue West, left onto 148th Street SW, right onto Highway 99, and then left onto Shelby Road. In 1.4 miles the road (now Picnic Point Road) will fork to the right, then in 0.9 mile it will fork to the left. Follow Picnic Point Road the remaining 0.5 mile to Picnic Point County Park.

Current Table: Admiralty Inlet.

Look up the daily current predictions for Admiralty Inlet. Apply the following time corrections to calculate slack current times:

> Time corrections for subordinate station 1090:
> Minimum current before flood: +44 minutes
> Minimal current before ebb: +13 minutes

Telephone Location: Drive 2.8 miles back to the intersection of Shelby Road and Highway 99.

Non-Diver Activities: Explore the beach and the animals that live on it. Sea gulls, small crabs and gunnels are just a few of the more prominent animals that are fun to watch.

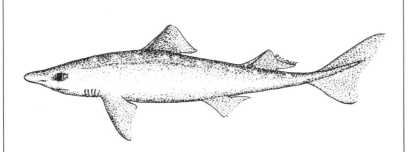

Pacific Spiny Dogfish

The spiny dogfish, *Squalus acanthias*, is the smallest species of shark. It is slate gray in color and, like other sharks, has tough sandpaper-like skin, gill slits and multiple rows of sharp teeth. It grows to a length of 4 to 5 feet (1.2-1.5 meters), reaching a weight of 20 pounds (9 kg). On the front of each dorsal fin is a poisonous spine that is used for defense. The stab wounds that a dogfish is capable of inflicting with these spines are not only painful, but are often followed by significant swelling. Some fishermen cut their lines after hooking a dogfish to avoid handling the animal.

Dogfish may live longer than 40 years. Males become sexually mature at 13 years and females mature at about 23 years. Each egg is fertilized inside the female and then enclosed in a membrane. A developing dogfish reaches a length of about one inch before breaking their surrounding membrane and swimming free into the uterus. Development continues in the uterus until the fully formed sharks are released following a total development period of 22-24 months. Litter size is between 4 to 20 sharks.

This small shark is usually considered to be a scrap fish by people in the Northwest, although if broiled in butter, it makes an excellent meal.

Figure 63

EDMONDS UNDERWATER PARK

Habitat and Depth: The "wrecks" that form the artificial reef in the Edmonds Underwater Park are not actually wrecks, but instead are the side walls of the sunken DeLion dry dock. They rise 34 feet above the inner deck, are 80 feet apart and 325 feet in length. Halfway between the two walls is a low concrete ledge, which once served as a keel support for ships while being worked on. The ledge now acts as a half-way mark for divers swimming between the walls. During extreme low tides, the top of the dry dock is visible from the surface.

Protected by wildlife sanctuary status, the hundreds of invertebrates and fish that live on and around the walls of the dry dock make this a special dive, either by day or night. The dry dock is covered with white sea anemones and colorful tube worms. Lingcod, cabezon, rockfish, flounder, scallops, sea stars, nudibranchs, hydromedusae, crab, ratfish, painted greenling, dogfish, pipefish, tube-snouts, shrimp and hermit crabs all live in this area and are commonly seen by divers.

This area has a sandy bottom with eelgrass, kelp and an artificial reef. Maximum depth in the park reaches 43 feet (10 foot tide).

Site Description: Oriented in a parallel direction to the ferry slip, the dry dock rests on the bottom between the slip and park surface rafts. During the summer, the dry dock is also marked by attached kelp floating on the surface over each wall. A map of the underwater park is posted near the west end of the rest room.

The easiest way to find the dry dock is to swim to the southern pile, located between the shore and surface rafts. Submerge and follow a guide rope from the base of this pile to the northern wall of the dry dock. After reaching the dry dock and swimming the length of the wall, remember that 80 feet to the south is the second parallel wall structure. During your return swim, take time to float on the surface while watching the ferry traffic and clouds or stars. This can be a wonderful way to end a dive!

Skill Level: Intermediate.

Edmonds Underwater Park during a low tide

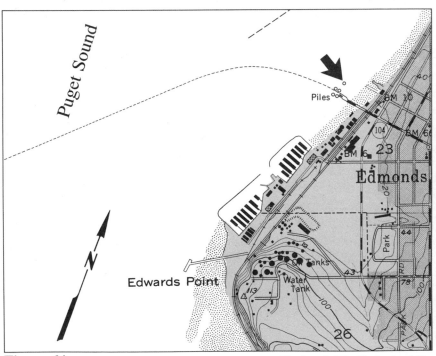

Figure 64   Not Intended For Navigational Use

Hazards: Current, kelp and ferry traffic.

The park boundary is marked on the bottom by a row of tires. Stay inside the tires and do not venture into the ferry lane. Both you and your buddy should carry knives.

Facilities: Parking, rest rooms, dry changing areas, a cold shower in front of the rest room, and a map of structure locations in the underwater park.

Travel Distance and Directions: Edmonds Underwater Park is located in Edmonds, immediately north of the ferry pier.

> Mileage from Bellingham = 81 miles
> Mileage from Seattle = 8 miles
> Mileage from Olympia = 78 miles

From Bellingham: drive south on I-5 to the Edmonds-Kingston Ferry Exit 177. Exit and follow the directions below.

From Seattle and Olympia: drive north on I-5 to Exit 177 for the Edmonds-Kingston Ferry. Exit and turn right onto 244th Street SW, then follow Highway 104 West (becomes Edmonds Way) for 3.4 miles before exiting to the right toward the Kingston Ferry. Continue on Highway 104 West to the bottom of the hill and a stoplight. Turn left onto Dayton Street, cross the railroad tracks, and make an immediate sharp right turn onto Railroad Avenue. Follow Railroad Avenue to the park entrance, just past the ferry pier.

Current Table: Admiralty Inlet.

Look up the daily current predictions for Admiralty Inlet. Apply the following time corrections to calculate slack current times:

> Time corrections for subordinate station 1090:
> Minimum current before flood: +44 minutes
> Minimum current before ebb: +13 minutes

Telephone Location: At the end of the ferry pier.

Non-Diver Activities: A paved path leads out onto the end of a short jetty at the north end of the park where there is a wonderful view of the water surface, the nearby ferry dock, and boat traffic. Large rocks provide seating for those who wish to sit and enjoy the view. Outside of the park visitors can discover the captivating charm of downtown Edmonds while exploring its unique small shops and cozy cafes. Walk along Main Street to the Cultural Arts Center and Public Library or visit the interesting stores in Old Milltown. The nearby Edmonds Museum (north of Main Street on Fifth Street) has historical displays of logging, sawmills and maritime shipping. The fishing pier is also within easy walking distance, just a few blocks south of the ferry pier, where Dayton Street intersects Admiral Way. Walk through the marina, watch the sun set over the Olympic Mountains, relax on the beach or ride the Edmonds-Kingston Ferry.

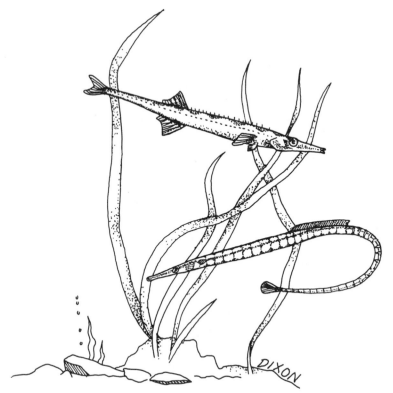

Figure 65   The tube-snout and bay pipefish

Tube-snout

The tube-snout, *Aulorhynchus flavidus*, is usually seen around kelp and in eelgrass beds. This fish grows to a length of 7 inches (18 cm). It is recognized by a long, straight, green body, a well developed caudal fin, and its swimming motion of sudden short sprints. The tube-snout swims primarily with its caudal fin. It has a dorsal fin located immediately opposite the anal fin, a long pointed snout, and small mouth.

During the spawning season the male tube-snout builds a nest in the kelp or eelgrass and defends it from other males. Females are accepted into the nest to lay eggs. The fertilized eggs are then guarded by the male until they hatch.

Bay Pipefish

Related to the sea horse, the bay pipefish, *Syngnathus griseolineatus*, has a slender green body, long tapering tail, and small caudal fin. It is easily distinguished from a tube-snout by its flexible, often curved body. It swims with a gliding motion, has bony plates covering its body, and does not have pelvic fins.

Unlike the tube-snout, which swims with its caudal fin, the pipefish swims primarily with its pectoral and dorsal fins. Pipefish live in eelgrass, where their green coloration and long body shape provide excellent camouflage.

Courtship and mating occur in late June, after which the female wraps herself around the male and deposits the eggs into the male's brood pouch. The male caries the developing eggs until the young fish grow to lengths of about 3/4 inch, when they are released fully developed.

EDMONDS MARINA BEACH
EDMONDS OIL DOCK

Habitat and Depth: This marine sanctuary offers both wharf pilings and a sandy bottom to explore. It also has a small topside park that is convenient to North Seattle. Look for the outline of flounder that have buried themselves in the sand, small sea pens, colorful nudibranchs and hermit crabs. Beneath the pier are clusters of large green and purple tube worms (*Eudistylia vancouveri*), perch feeding on mussels and barnacles, scallops covered with yellow sponge, and clusters of white plumose anemones. Other animals divers may see include cabezon, lingcod, small sculpins, rockfish, swimming anemones (*Stomphia*), sea cucumbers, sunflower sea stars, sun stars, moon snails, and an occasional wolf-eel or octopus.

While swimming between the shoreline and the end of the pier, divers will pass over a shallow, sandy bottom approximately halfway out. Here, the bottom becomes shallower before abruptly angling downward near the end of the pier. Bottom depth at the northeast pile is 48 feet (10 foot tide), while the bottom at the northwest pile is 56 feet (10 foot tide). Outside the pier, the bottom slopes downward rapidly over an area covered with shale.

Site Description: There is a bit of a swim to the end of the pier, so take time to explore the pilings as you snorkel out. Once you have submerged and moved among the pilings at the end of the pier, roll onto your back to check out the streaks of light slanting through the water between the pilings and sea anemones. This is especially beautiful on a bright, sunny day.

Underneath the dock the light dims, but it is here that you will find the largest number of animals. An artificial light is useful in the darkness to brighten colors that otherwise appear drab and uninteresting.

Skill Level: All divers.

Hundreds of small animals live in this protected marine sanctuary.

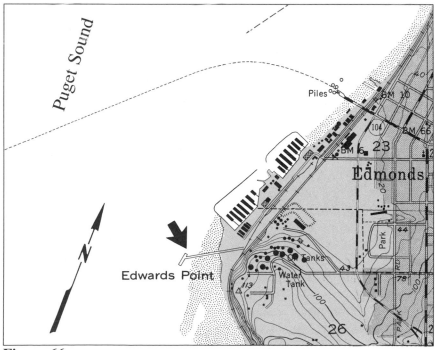

Figure 66

Not Intended For Navigational Use

Hazards: Current and a long swim. This is a working pier. Stay clear of any docked oil tankers, barges or tugboats. Flood currents are usually weaker than ebb currents at this site. By timing your entry prior to an ebbing current, you can easily avoid a hard swim. When diving here during slack before flood, enter the water only about 10 minutes before slack, so that most of your dive will occur during the early flood exchange. When diving here during slack before ebb, enter the water at least 30 minutes before slack, so that slack occurs about halfway through your dive.

Facilities: A parking area, outhouses, picnic tables, a play structure, a grass lawn and beachside fire pit. Changing rooms, a cold shower and rest rooms are located a few blocks away at the Edmonds Underwater Park. There are also two cold showers for divers on the back wall of Skipper's Seafood and Chowder House. Rinsing the salt off in a fresh water shower, followed by a hot meal of fish & chips with chowder, is a great way to end a dive. Air fills are available in Edmonds.

Travel Distance and Directions: Edmonds Marina Beach is located in Edmonds, 1 mile south of the ferry pier.

      Mileage from Bellingham = 82 miles
      Mileage from Seattle = 8 miles
      Mileage from Olympia = 78 miles

    From Bellingham: drive south on I-5 to the Edmonds-Kingston Ferry Exit 177. Exit and follow the directions below.
    From Seattle and Olympia: drive north on I-5 to Exit 177 for the Edmonds-Kingston Ferry. Exit from I-5, turn right at the bottom of the exit ramp onto 244th Street SW, then follow Highway 104 West (becomes Edmonds Way) for 3.4 miles before exiting to the right toward the Kingston Ferry. Continue on Highway 104 West to the bottom of the hill, where there is a stoplight and ferry ticket booth. Turn left onto Dayton Street, cross the railroad tracks, and follow Dayton Street around a curve to the left where it becomes Admiral Way. Follow Admiral Way past the Edmonds Marina to the Edmonds Marina Beach Park.

Current Table: Admiralty Inlet.
Look up the daily current predictions for Admiralty Inlet. Apply the following time corrections to calculate slack current times:

Time corrections for Edmonds Marina Beach:
Minimum inshore current before flood: −10 minutes
Minimum inshore current before ebb: −92 minutes

Telephone Location: At the end of the parking lot near the play structures.

Non-Diver Activities: The Edmonds Marina Beach is a city park with an inviting grass lawn. The lawn is often used for sunning, kite flying, volleyball and frisbee. There is a log play structure for kids, a sandy beach, fire pits and a great view of the Olympic Peninsula.

Visitors also can walk back through the marina toward Edmonds. There are restaurants along the waterfront and a public fishing pier at the corner of Dayton and Admiral Way. You can watch the ferries from the fishing pier, fish for dinner or watch other people fish. Bring a picnic lunch and enjoy the view from the lawn, fishing pier or sandy beach. Don't forget to visit the shops in Old Milltown, located on the corner of Dayton and Fifth Street in Edmonds.

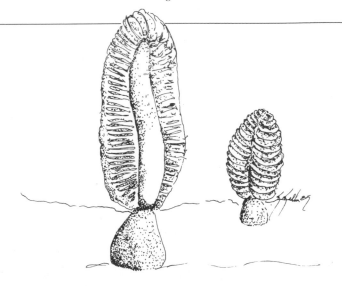

Sea Pen

The orange sea pen, *Ptilosarcus gurneyi*, lives subtidally in soft sand or mud bottoms, with approximately one-third of its long body extending down into the bottom like a carrot. Looking more like plant than animal, a sea pen is actually a colonial animal composed of many small polyps that are supported by a single large structural polyp. Each polyp has a specialized function for filter feeding, water circulation, reproduction or structural support.

Sea pens are a soft coral and, like other types of coral, feed primarily during the night by extending their tentacles to capture plankton. During this time, divers can see the tiny tentacles of feeding polyps extended along the upper feather-like structure of a sea pen.

Sea pens are preyed upon by several types of nudibranchs and sea stars, such as the striped nudibranch, orange peel nudibranch and spiny sea star. When divers encounter large populations of these beautiful orange colonial animals, they frequently will find predators in the same area, often busily eating (Plates 5 and 6).

Figure 67

RICHMOND BEACH PARK

Habitat: This is a dive to enjoy with friends for the pleasure of getting wet, visiting the varied and continually changing animal populations, and playing on a long sandy beach. The site is best during the late summer and fall months, when the bull kelp has grown and there are more animals to be seen. During the rest of the year, especially the winter months, expect to see a limited number of animals.

While the density of animal life at this site is lower than that found farther north in the San Juan Islands or the Strait of Juan de Fuca, there is an interesting variety of species living in this sandy habitat. These include hermit crabs, white plumose anemones, stubby rose anemones (*Urticina coriacea*), yellow sponges, solitary glassy sea squirts, stalked sea squirts, nudibranchs, schools of tubesnouts, ratfish, colorful sea stars, sea pens, sea cucumbers, flounder, speckled sanddabs and an occasional skate.

The beach above the high water line is sandy, while the intertidal area is a sandy-cobblestone with scattered chunks of rusted iron from a ship that burned offshore. By 12 feet in depth (10 foot tide), the bottom changes to sand without cobbles. It remains shallow to the 18 foot depth (10 foot tide), then drops steeply to 37 feet (10 foot tide), where it levels out to a gentle slope.

Site Description: Enter the water in front of the rest rooms, submerge and swim out from shore. The cobble bottom will soon change to sand, followed by an apparent horizon marking the top of the slope. Swim down the slope while exploring bottom and looking for the small animals that live here. Turning west, parallel to shore, divers will find rusty pieces of metal scattered over the bottom, remnants from the burned ship.

Skill Level: All divers.

Hazards: Moderate current and bull kelp.

Current moves parallel to the beach with the main channel flow, often becoming more noticeable below the 30 foot level.

Richmond Beach Park has a long sandy beach.

Facilities: Parking, rest rooms, changing areas, picnic tables, barbecue stands and metal fire rings. Air fills are available in Edmonds, Lynnwood, Kenmore, Bothell, Kirkland and Seattle.

Travel Distance and Directions: Richmond Beach Park is located in North Seattle, approximately 1 mile south of Point Wells.

> Mileage from Bellingham = 82 miles
> Mileage from Seattle = 5 miles
> Mileage from Olympia = 75 miles

Drive to North Seattle via either I-5 or Highway 99. Exit from I-5 at the NE 175th Street/Aurora Avenue North Exit 176, then turn west at the bottom of the exit ramp and drive to Aurora Avenue North. Turn right onto Aurora Avenue North, and drive north to North 185th Street. Turn left onto North 185th Street (becomes Richmond Beach Road), follow it down the hill, and turn left onto 20th Avenue NW. Follow 20th Avenue to the Richmond Beach Park entrance, drive down a steep hill to a large parking area, park and walk over a foot bridge to the beach.

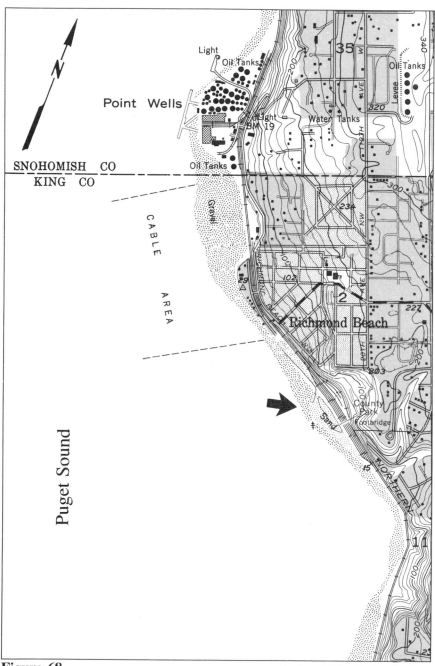

Figure 68

Not Intended For Navigational Use

Current Table: Admiralty Inlet.
Look up the daily current predictions for Admiralty Inlet. Apply the following time corrections to calculate slack current times:

Time corrections for subordinate station 1090:
Minimum current before flood: +44 minutes
Minimum current before ebb: +13 minutes

Telephone Location: None at the immediate site. Drive back up the hill to the intersection of 20th Avenue NW and Richmond Beach Road.

Non-Diver Activities: Walk along the sandy shoreline or sun yourself on the beach. This is a good place to enjoy a picnic lunch with friends or family, go for a run on a long beach, play with a frisbee or fly a kite.

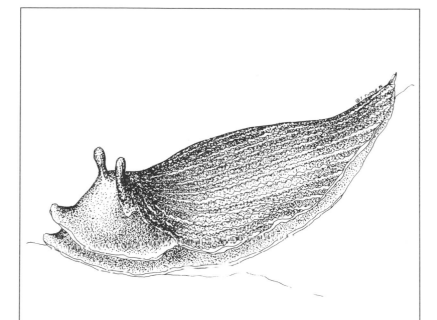

Striped Nudibranch

The striped nudibranch, *Armina californica*, is often seen partially buried in sandy bottoms beside the base of sea pens, its primary food. It grows to 3 inches (8 cm) in length and is easily distinguished by its lengthwise brown and white stripes and lack of visible cerata (respiratory structures) on its dorsum (back). Unlike most other nudibranchs, *Armina* has its cerata tucked underneath a fold of skin along each side of the dorsum, just above the foot. The only visible projections from the dorsum are two club shaped sensory organs (rhinophores) extending forward from a central spot at the anterior end of the animal. *Armina* lays soft, pale yellow coils of eggs on the surface of sandy bottoms.

Figure 69

AGATE PASSAGE

Habitat and Depth: Thousands of animals, both large and small, make this current swept environment an impressive dive site.

Giant acorn barnacles and small white sea anemones carpet many of the larger rocks. Bushes of tube worms perch on structures above the bottom, their red and green feather-like plumes extending outward to catch food. Chunks of yellow sponge are attached to many of the smaller rocks, and colorful sea stars are scattered across the bottom. Grunt sculpins, chitons, limpets and red Irish lords are also frequently seen by divers in Agate Passage.

The bottom is primarily sandy cobblestone, with intermittent patches of clay, shoals of shell fragments, sandy areas and a few large rocks. Eelgrass grows in the shallows at both ends of the channel. Maximum depth in the center of the channel is 43 feet (10 foot tide).

Site Description: Agate Passage can be dived either during slack current periods or as a drift dive in current. When diving during the short periods of slack, divers can stop to look at the small animals living on and around the concrete bridge pylons and on the bottom between the pylons. The rest of the time, divers will be in strong current that will sweep them over the bottom. Diving in current is fun, but makes stopping to explore difficult. It also requires active communication between buddies to prevent separation.

Drift diving produces a flying sensation that will leave you excited and grinning. Swept over the bottom on an invisible magic carpet, you can stretch your arms out and fly like an airplane, banking left or right within your imagination. As you fly over the cobblestone bottom, try turning a somersault by placing your hands on the bottom, ducking your head and beginning to roll. Suddenly your feet are pushed over your head and you will find yourself lying on your back, heading downstream feet first. To complete your roll, kick into the current while sitting upright (be ready to adjust buoyancy if necessary). Your upper body will be pushed gently forward, your legs will fall behind, and you will again be moving headfirst.

Agate Passage is at the north end of Bainbridge Island

When doing a drift dive from the Agate Passage Bridge to the Suquamish Dock, a pick-up car can be left in the parking area above the Suquamish Dock, on the west side of the channel. If a non-diver in the group is willing to drive a car across the bridge, and pick divers up at the Suquamish Dock, only one car will be needed. Otherwise, two cars are needed; one for each side of the channel.

By drifting northward on an ebb current, from the bridge to the Suquamish Dock, divers will have an easier exit because the channel is wider and the current slower. Begin the dive by submerging and actively swimming toward the middle of the channel. Relax and drift for approximately 15 minutes, then turn perpendicular to the current and complete your swim to the opposite shore. During the middle of a ten foot exchange, plan on about a 30 minute drift between the bridge and Suquamish Dock (1.1 nautical miles), but surface after 20 minutes to check your position.

Skill Level: Intermediate/Advanced. This dive requires intermediate skills when diving beneath the bridge during slack, or when diving in current along the eastern shoreline of the Bainbridge side.

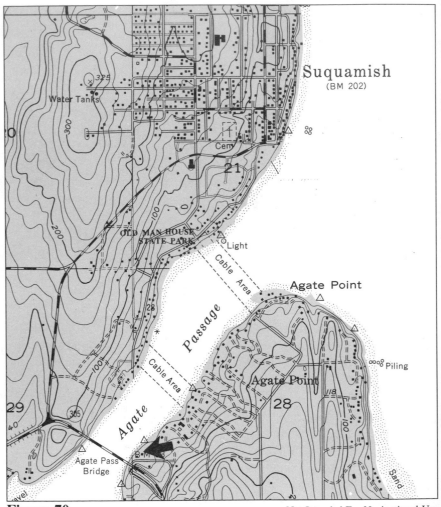

Figure 70   Not Intended For Navigational Use

The dive requires advanced diving skills when crossing the channel in current and exiting at the Suquamish Dock. If divers miss the dock they may be swept into Port Madison.

Hazards: Strong current and frequent overhead boat traffic.
     The narrowest section of the channel is beneath the bridge. It is here that water movement is swiftest, slowing as the water moves

toward the northern end of Agate Passage and the Suquamish Dock. At the north end of Agate Passage, maximum ebb current is predicted to be 1.8 knots (182 feet per minute), but at the south end of Agate Passage the maximum ebb current is predicted at 3.6 knots (365 feet per minute). Current flow is parallel to the shore.

Due to overhead boat traffic, do not dive at this site if you are weighted lightly or unsure of how much weight to use. Adjust your weights before diving this site.

When drift diving, move with the current (or perpendicular to it) and be careful not to snag your exposure suit on barnacles as you are swept past the rocks.

Facilities: None. Air fills are available in Bremerton and Seattle.

Travel Distance and Directions: Agate Passage is located between the northwest end of Bainbridge Island and the Kitsap Peninsula, 7 miles north of the Winslow Ferry Dock.

> Mileage from Bellingham = 97 miles
> Mileage from downtown Seattle = 9 miles
> Mileage from Olympia = 81 miles

From Bellingham: drive south on I-5 for 77 miles to Exit 177 for the Edmonds-Kingston Ferry. Exit from I-5, and turn right at the bottom of the exit ramp onto 244th Street SW. Follow Highway 104 West (becomes Edmonds Way) to the Edmonds-Kingston Ferry Dock on the Edmonds waterfront. Ride the ferry across Puget Sound to Kingston.

From Kingston, drive 3.9 miles from the ferry dock to the junction of Bond Road and Highway 104. Angle to the left onto Bond Road toward Highway 305 and Poulsbo. Follow Bond Road for 5.3 miles, then turn left at a stoplight onto Highway 305 South, and drive toward Winslow and the Agate Passage Bridge. After crossing the Agate Passage Bridge, drive 0.1 mile, and turn left onto Reitan Road (first left-hand turn after bridge). Drive the remaining 0.3 mile to a limited parking area below the bridge.

From the Seattle waterfront: ride the Seattle-Winslow Ferry to Bainbridge Island. After leaving the ferry, follow Highway 305 North for 6.7 miles, then make a right turn onto Reitan Road (last right-hand turn before reaching Agate Passage Bridge). Drive 0.3 mile to the parking area beneath the bridge.

From Olympia: drive north on I-5 to Exit 132 for Bremerton and Highway 16 West. Exit from I-5, and then follow Highway 16 West across the Tacoma Narrows Bridge. After crossing the bridge, continue north for 22.8 miles, through the town of Gorst and around the tip of Sinclair Inlet. Turn left at the Highway 3 North/Highway 304 East junction. Follow Highway 3 North for 16.0 miles, until it curves to the right and becomes Highway 305 South at a four-way intersection and stoplight. Continue straight through the intersection toward Winslow, following Highway 305 South for 6.2 miles to the Agate Passage Bridge and Bainbridge Island. After crossing Agate Passage Bridge, drive 0.1 mile, turn left onto Reitan Road (first left-hand turn after bridge), and drive 0.3 mile to the parking area below the bridge.

Current Table: Admiralty Inlet
Look up the daily current predictions for Admiralty Inlet. Apply the following time corrections to calculate slack current times:

Time corrections for subordinate station 1110:
Minimum current before flood: −88 minutes
Minimum current before ebb: −18 minutes

Telephone Location: None at the immediate site. Drive back to Highway 305, turn right and drive 0.9 mile, across the bridge to a gas station and deli located on the right-hand side of the road.

Non-Diver Activities: There are several dry activities near Agate Passage. The closest attraction, other than enjoying Agate Passage Beach, is a totem pole display near the north end of the Agate Pass Bridge. Another attraction is the Suquamish Museum and Tribal Center. Located less than 2 miles north of the dive site, the Suquamish Museum provides a rich glimpse into the history and culture of the Suquamish Tribe. Large photos are used throughout the museum to tell visitors about daily Indian life before the intrusion of the white man, how daily life changed as a result of "civilization", and how Indian culture was impacted. The exhibits are presented in an organized, interesting and factual manner. One display even includes a "Please Touch" sign. Moving outside, visitors can walk along a nature trail where plants and trees are numbered to correspond to an interpretive list available from the museum.

Near the town of Suquamish, Chief Seattle Park marks the site of "Old Man House," the longhouse Chief Sealth built during the 1800's. It was razed by order of the U.S. Army in 1870, about four years after the death of Chief Sealth. To visit the site of "Old Man House", drive 1.2 miles toward Suquamish from Highway 305, turn left onto Division Street and drive to Chief Seattle Park. Chief Sealth's grave is nearby, in the town of Suquamish.

Other dry activities include visiting the Bainbridge Island Winery on Highway 305 near Winslow, visiting shops or a restaurant in Winslow, and visiting historic Poulsbo and its Waterfront Park. Also located on Bainbridge Island are Fort Ward State Park, Fay Bainbridge State Park and Battle Point Park.

Figure 71 Giant tube worms

Giant Tube Worm

The largest tube worm in the Pacific Northwest, *Eudistylia vancouveri*, is a segmented worm (Phylum *Annelida*) that builds leather-like tubes for protection (Family *Sabellidae*). Related to the common earthworm, tube-worms have a complete digestive tract with both a mouth and anus. They also have a closed circulatory system and the ability to elongate or contract each segment of their body wall. Tube worms are known for the ability to snap back into their protective tubes when a sudden movement or change in light pattern is sensed. This protective reflex is an effective defense mechanism from potential predators such as hungry fish who might otherwise feed on the extended plumes.

Eudistylia vancouveri may be seen growing singularly or in bush-like clumps, reaching heights of 12 to 14 inches with plume diameters of 1.5 inches. Each worm has a dark red plume with green stripes. This feather-like plume is usually seen extended from the top of the worm's tube, where it is used for both gas exchange and feeding. Floating plankton and organic debris that contact the plume become entrapped on a mucous layer and are then conveyed to the mouth by cilia.

Another common group of segmented worms (Family *Serpulidae*) secretes smaller and harder tubes, often in white serpent-like coils.

      "*Annelida*" = animals with little rings
      "*Sabellidae*" = sand family
      "*Serpulidae*" = little snake family

FAY BAINBRIDGE STATE PARK

Habitat and Depth: Diving over a sandy bottom to observe the interactions between animals can result in intriguing dives with many surprises. Animal interactions divers may see in a sandy habitat include a male hermit crab dragging a female across the bottom, a beaded anemone (*Urticina coriacea*) disgorging the remains of a small crab, a group of striped nudibranchs feeding on a sea pen, a skate lying quietly on the bottom, or a flounder lunging out of its hiding place in the sandy bottom to gulp down a passing beast. Divers willing to slow down to watch for animal behavior are likely to enjoy this dive, but those looking for larger animals will probably find this site uninteresting.

Additional animals you may see while diving at this site include perch, moon snails, frosted nudibranchs, sea stars, geoducks, sea anemones, comb jellies and jellyfish.

This site has a long sandy-cobblestone beach, an eelgrass bed and a sandy bottom that slopes downward past 100 feet in depth.

Site Description: Swim out from shore toward the two yellow buoys, which are anchored on the slope. Descend and follow the bottom contour downward. There are no outstanding structures, only a gently sloping sandy terrain.

Skill Level: All divers.

Hazards: Occasional small boats.

Current movement is parallel to shore, with flood currents moving toward the southeast. Ebb currents move to the northwest in front of the dive site, but change direction to the west as the water rounds Point Monroe and flows into Port Madison.

Display a dive flag when diving at this site, and listen for engine noise before ascending.

Facilities: Camping, picnic tables, a covered eating area with a large rock fireplace, barbecue stands, fire pits along the beach, a

Looking southeast toward Mount Rainier

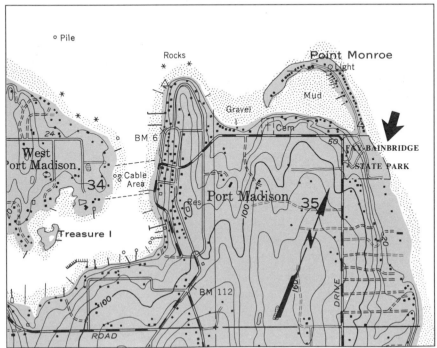

Figure 72   Not Intended For Navigational Use

volleyball sand court with net stands, a play structure for the kids, rest rooms, hot showers and a boat launch. Air fills are available in Bremerton, Tacoma and Seattle.

Travel Distance and Directions: Fay Bainbridge State Park is located on the northeast end of Bainbridge Island, 8 miles north of the Winslow ferry landing.

> Mileage from Bellingham = 98 miles
> Mileage from North Seattle = 17 miles
> Mileage from Olympia = 72 miles

From Bellingham: drive south on I-5 for 77 miles to Exit 177 for the Edmonds-Kingston Ferry. Exit from I-5, and turn right at the bottom of the exit ramp onto 244th Street SW. Follow Highway 104 West (becomes Edmonds Way) to the Edmonds-Kingston Ferry Dock on the Edmonds waterfront. Ride the ferry to Kingston. From the Kingston Ferry Dock, drive 3.9 miles to the Bond Road Junction. Angle to the left onto Bond Road toward Highway 305 and Poulsbo. Follow Bond Road for 5.3 miles, turn left at a stoplight onto Highway 305 South, then drive toward Winslow and the Agate Passage Bridge. After crossing over Agate Passage onto Bainbridge Island, continue for 2.7 miles before turning left onto NE Day Road East. Follow the directions below.

From the Seattle waterfront: ride the Seattle-Winslow Ferry to Bainbridge Island. After leaving the ferry, follow Highway 305 North for 4.4 miles before turning right onto NE Day Road East. Turn left onto Sunrise Drive NE, and follow to Fay Bainbridge State Park. Turn right onto NE Lafayette Avenue and drive down into the park.

From Olympia: drive north on I-5 to Exit 132 for Bremerton and Highway 16 West. Exit from I-5, then follow Highway 16 West across the Tacoma Narrows Bridge. After crossing the bridge, continue north for 22.8 miles, through the town of Gorst and around the tip of Sinclair Inlet. Turn left at the Highway 3 North/Highway 304 East junction. Follow Highway 3 North for 16.0 miles, until it curves to the right and becomes Highway 305 South at a four-way intersection and stoplight. Continue straight through the intersection toward Winslow, following Highway 305 South for 6.2 miles to the Agate Pass Bridge and Bainbridge Island. Cross over Agate Passage onto Bainbridge Island, continue for 2.7 miles, turn left onto NE Day Road East and follow the above directions.

Current Table: Admiralty Inlet.
Look up the daily current predictions for Admiralty Inlet. Apply the following time corrections to calculate slack current times:

Time corrections for subordinate station 1110:
Minimal current before flood: −88 minutes
Minimal current before ebb: −18 minutes

Telephone Location: Located in front of the rest room at the north end of the lower park.

Non-Diver Activities: Walk along the beach and enjoy the view of Seattle while watching the different types of ships that seem to pass within touching distance. Camp for a weekend, play volleyball or horseshoes, sit around a beach-side fire built in one of the provided fire rings, or drive into Winslow or Poulsbo to visit the shops and restaurants.

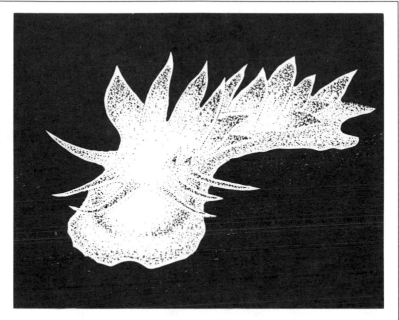

Frosted Nudibranch

The frosted nudibranch, *Dirona albolineata*, also known as the alabaster nudibranch or white-lined dirona, has a striking appearance setting it apart from other nudibranchs. Projecting from the dorsum of this animal's grayish-white translucent body are many long, triangular distinctive respiratory structures (called cerata), each edged with a brilliant white line. When this nudibranch is handled by a diver, the fragile looking cerata soon begin to separate from its body. The cerata are detached deliberately as a means of detracting a predator from the main part of the animal's body. The lost cerata are later regenerated. Nudibranchs also apparently taste bad (personally unconfirmed), as they are spit out by most fish.

The frosted nudibranch lives in the subtidal zone, feeding on small snails, sea squirts, hydroids, anemones and bryozoans. It grows to a length of 3 inches (8 cm).

Figure 73

FORT WARD STATE PARK

Habitat and Depth: While submerged in Rich Passage, divers may hear the thunderous prop noise of the Bremerton ferry as it passes overhead. Beneath the surface, rocks are scattered over the sandy bottom, providing attachment points for sea anemones, sea squirts, sea lettuce, brown algae and bull kelp.

An interesting animal that lives on this sandy bottom is the tube-dwelling anemone. This tall, slender anemone is selective in what it eats. Try feeding it a small animal, such as a shrimp, hermit crab or nudibranch. The anemone will either reject the offering or, after passing it to an inner ring of smaller tentacles, will accept it by stuffing it into its mouth.

A few of the other animals often seen while diving here include sea pens, flounder, hermit crabs, kelp crabs, moon snails, yellow sponges, sea cucumbers, gumboot chitons, nudibranchs, sea squirts, pink sea stars, perch, ratfish and shrimp.

Beyond the cobblestone beach, the sandy bottom slopes gently to 41 feet (10 foot tide) before beginning to level out.

Site Description: Walk down the beach a short distance in order to move away from the immediate boat launching area. Then enter the water, snorkel out and descend.

When swimming straight out from shore, divers will reach a depth of 61 feet (10 foot tide) approximately 300 feet from shore. Most animal life will be found above this depth.

Skill Level: All divers.

Hazards: Minimal current and small boats.

Current movement is parallel to shore, with ebb currents flowing southeast and flood currents flowing northwest. Listen for small boat noise before ascending.

Facilities: Picnic tables, outhouses and a boat launch. Air fills are available in Bremerton, Tacoma and Seattle.

Enter the water southeast of the boat launching area.

Travel Distance and Directions: Fort Ward State Park is located on the south end of Bainbridge Island, 7 miles south of the Winslow ferry landing.

> Mileage from Bellingham = 96 miles
> Mileage from North Seattle = 16 miles
> Mileage from Olympia = 70 miles

From Bellingham: drive south on I-5 for 77 miles to Exit 177 (exit for the Edmonds-Kingston Ferry). Exit from I-5, turn right at the bottom of the exit ramp onto 244th Street SW, and follow Highway 104 West (becomes Edmonds Way) to the Edmonds-Kingston Ferry Dock. Ride the ferry to Kingston. From the Kingston Ferry Dock, drive 3.9 miles to the Bond Road Junction, then angle to the left onto Bond Road toward Highway 305 and Poulsbo. Follow Bond Road for 5.3 miles, turn left at a stoplight onto Highway 305 South, and drive toward Winslow and the Agate Pass Bridge. After crossing over Agate Pass, continue for 6.0 miles, then turn right onto NE Highschool Road. Follow the directions below.

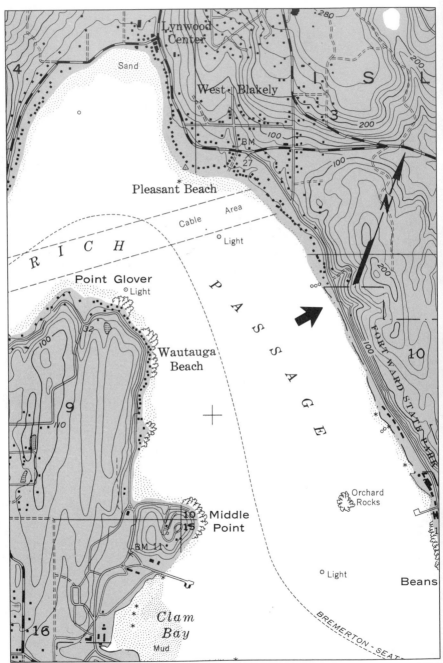

Figure 74

From the Seattle waterfront: ride the Winslow ferry to Bainbridge Island. After leaving the ferry, drive north on Highway 305 for 0.9 mile, then turn left onto NE Highschool Road. Follow NE Highschool Road to a tee, turn left onto Fletcher Bay Road NE, then drive to a second tee. Turn right onto Lynwood Center Road NE (Lynwood Center Road NE will become Pleasant Beach Drive NE). Stay to the right when the road forks and follow Pleasant Beach Drive NE into Fort Ward State Park.

From Olympia: drive north on I-5 to Exit 132 for Bremerton and Highway 16 West. Exit from I-5, then follow Highway 16 West across the Tacoma Narrows Bridge. After crossing the bridge, continue north for 22.8 miles, through the town of Gorst and around the southwest tip of Sinclair Inlet (becomes Highway 3 North). Turn left at the Highway 3 North/Highway 304 East junction. Follow Highway 3 North for 16.0 miles, until it curves to the right and becomes Highway 305 South at a four-way intersection and stoplight. Continue straight through the intersection toward Winslow, following Highway 305 South for 6.2 miles to the Agate Pass Bridge and Bainbridge Island. Cross over Agate Pass onto Bainbridge Island, then continue for 6.0 miles before turning right onto NE Highschool Road. Follow the above directions.

Current Table: Admiralty Inlet.

Look up the daily current predictions for Admiralty Inlet. Apply the following time corrections to calculate slack current times:

Time corrections for subordinate station 1175:
Minimum current before flood: −14 minutes
Minimum current before ebb: +36 minutes

Telephone Location: None at the immediate site. Drive 1.2 miles back along Pleasant Beach Drive NE to Lynwood Center. A public phone is located in front of the Lynwood Theater.

Non-Diver Activities: Hike through the wooded 480 acres of Fort Ward State Park, enjoy the view of Rich Passage, photograph birds, picnic or drive into Winslow to visit the shops and restaurants.

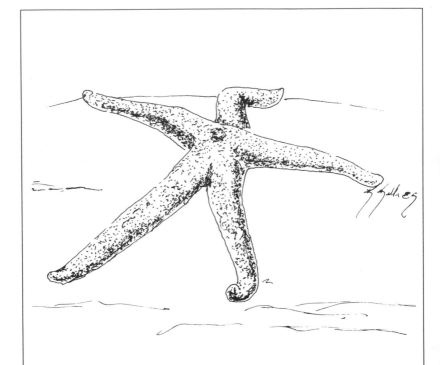

Blood Star

The blood star, *Henricia leviuscula*, is distinguished from other sea stars by its five narrow, rounded arms and small central disc. It has a bright red-orange color, which is either solid red-orange or a red-orange mottled with white splotches. The blood star is commonly seen both intertidally and subtidally where it grows to a diameter of 5 inches (13 cm). This colorful sea star moves slowly; its diet of sessile sponges and bryozoans precluding the need for rapid movement to compete successfully for food.

Early in the year, females produce a cluster of eggs. They stop feeding and disappear into hiding to brood their eggs, which are retained around the mouth area. After hatching occurs, the females emerge from hiding and resume feeding.

Figure 75

ILLAHEE STATE PARK

Habitat and Depth: The Illahee State Park fishing pier and boat dock is just a short swim from shore. Here divers can see many animals frequently found on the underside of floating docks. These animals form a community as they interact with each other while competing for food, living space and mates. Many animals live on the body surfaces of other animals.

Animals living in this type of environment include colorful sea anemones, giant tube worms, pile perch, striped sea perch, hermit crabs, flounder, sea squirts, blood stars, leather stars, sun stars, sunflower stars, sea cucumbers and jellyfish.

This site has wharf pilings, and a floating dock for both fishing and boating. Beneath the floating dock the depth is 33 feet (10 foot tide). Outside the dock, the smooth sandy bottom slopes gradually outward to more than 85 feet in depth (10 foot tide).

Site Description: Walk down a short flight of stairs (located beside the pier next to the bulkhead), enter the water beside the pier and swim out along the pilings. Be careful to stay clear of both boats and fishing line.

After exploring the pier and the animals attached to the underside of the float, swim down the slope to see which animals are living on this sandy bottom (most will be above the 50 foot depth). Some of these animals will overlap between sandy and wharf habitats, but many will not. Animals have structural adaptations that help them in their competition for survival in specific habitats. As a result, animals are found most frequently in the respective habitats that they are equipped to survive in.

Skill Level: All divers.

Hazards: Small boats and fishing line.

Stay clear of the underside of boats that may be docked at the floating pier. Also, remember to listen for engine noise before beginning your ascent. When there is an active boat on the surface, either remain submerged or move to the pilings before ascending.

This public pier is used for both fishing and boating.

Facilities: Camping sites, a fishing pier, moorage for small boats, a boat launch, rest rooms with changing areas, hot showers, picnic tables, a covered eating area, barbecue stands, hiking trails and parking next to the beach. Air fills are available in Bremerton.

Travel Distance and Directions: Illahee State Park is located on the Kitsap Peninsula, 5 miles north of the Bremerton ferry landing.

> Mileage from Bellingham = 95 miles
> Mileage from North Seattle = 15 miles
> Mileage from Olympia = 64 miles

From Bellingham: drive south on I-5 for 77 miles to Exit 177 (exit for the Edmonds-Kingston Ferry). Exit from I-5, turn right at the bottom of the exit ramp onto 244th Street SW, then follow Highway 104 West (becomes Edmonds Way) to the ferry dock in Edmonds. Ride the ferry to Kingston. From the Kingston Ferry Dock, drive 3.9 miles to the Bond Road Junction. Angle to the left onto Bond Road toward Highway 305 and Poulsbo, then follow Bond Road for 5.4 miles. Turn right at a four-way intersection and

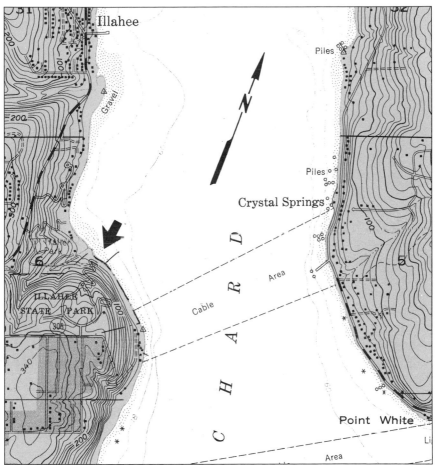

Figure 76

stoplight onto Highway 305 North. Continue straight through the next stoplight onto Highway 3 South. Follow Highway 3 South for 7.1 miles, then exit to Silverdale and East Bremerton. While still on this exit ramp, exit to the right toward East Bremerton and Waaga Way. In 3.6 miles, Waaga Way curves to the right and becomes Highway 303 South (also Wheaton Way). Follow Wheaton Way, which becomes Warren Avenue, past NE Riddell Road for 0.8 mile, to Sylvan Way. Turn left onto Sylvan Way and drive the remaining 1.4 miles to Illahee State Park.

From the Seattle waterfront: ride the Seattle/Bremerton Ferry to Bremerton. After leaving the ferry, turn left onto Burwell Street and then right onto Highway 303 North (Warren Avenue). Follow Highway 303 North over the Warren Avenue Bridge. After crossing the bridge, drive 1.4 miles to the next stoplight and turn right onto Sylvan Way (also Highway 306 East). Follow Highway 306 East to Illahee State Park.

From Olympia: drive north on I-5 to Exit 132 for Bremerton and Highway 16 West. Exit from I-5, then follow Highway 16 West across the Tacoma Narrows Bridge. After crossing the bridge, continue north for 24.0 miles, through the town of Gorst and around the tip of Sinclair Inlet (becomes Highway 3 North and then Highway 304 East). After rounding the southwest end of Sinclair Inlet, follow the highway along the water (becomes Highway 304 East), past the Naval Shipyard and into Bremerton. Turn right onto Farragut Street toward the City Center, Seattle Ferry and Highway 304 East. Drive two blocks and turn left onto Callow Avenue. Follow Callow avenue for four blocks (0.5 mile), turn right onto Burwell Street, then left onto Highway 303 North (Warren Avenue). After crossing the Warren Avenue Bridge continue for 1.4 miles. Turn right at the next stoplight onto Sylvan Way (Highway 306 East) and drive the remaining 1.4 miles to Illahee State Park.

Current Table: Admiralty Inlet.

Look up the daily current predictions for Admiralty Inlet. Apply the following time corrections to calculate slack current times:

> Time corrections for subordinate station 1180:
> Minimal current before flood: –44 minutes
> Minimal current before ebb: +46 minutes

Telephone Location: Just inside the park entrance, beside a cannon display.

Non-Diver Activities: Camp for the weekend, go hiking, fish or crab from the pier, walk along the beach and enjoy the view of Bainbridge Island, bring along a book to read or visit the shops and restaurants in Bremerton.

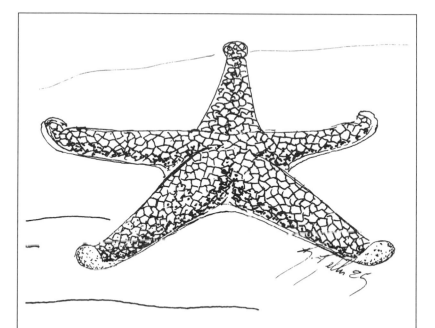

Vermilion Star

The vermilion star, *Mediaster aequalis,* lives primarily subtidally, but is occasionally seen in low intertidal areas. Also known as the equal sea star, it is bright red in color and has five triangular shaped arms that widen into a broad central disc. The upper surface of the central disc, arms and the sides of each arm are covered with a distinctive pattern of calcareous plates. Additionally, the tip of each arm is turned upwards.

Vermilion and blood stars have similar coloring, but are easily distinguished by the shape of their arms and size of their central disc (the blood star has narrow, rounded arms and a small central disc).

Vermilion stars grow to reach a diameter of 6 inches (15 cm) on a diet of sea pens, sea squirts, sponges and algae. Because this sea star preys on sessile bottom dwelling animals, it has not developed a rapid means of locomotion.

Figure 77

WARREN AVENUE BRIDGE

Habitat and Depth: As is typical in high current areas, there is little silt beneath the Warren Avenue Bridge. Looking freshly scrubbed, small particles of sand, rocks and pieces of broken shells are routinely washed free of silt as current sweeps over the bottom.

Some areas of bottom at this site are clay, shaped into small steps by current. Piddock clams use their shells to cut burrows into this hard clay bottom, leaving it riddled with a maze of holes. Many holes are occupied by these remarkable clams, whose necks can often be seen extending a few inches above the top of their rigid burrows. The clam is easily recognized by its red-brown neck that is covered with many small raised white projections. Each neck has two siphons, with the larger of the two having fringes on the inside. Small sculpins and gunnels also use the holes for shelter.

Other animals that divers may see include red Irish lords, perch, flounder, sailfin sculpins, sun stars, sunflower sea stars, tube worms, pink sea stars, blood stars, plumose anemones, acorn barnacles, snails and nudibranchs. In shallower water, small colorful pink tipped anemones (*Anthopleura elegantissima*) grow along the cobblestone bottom.

The bottom along the shoreline is sandy-cobblestone, changing to a mixture of large and small cobbles as you move offshore toward the concrete bridge pylons. Depth at the base of the first pylon is 20 feet (10 foot tide); depth at the base of the second pylon is 32-35 feet (10 foot tide); and depth at the base of the rocks surrounding the third pylon is 48 feet deep (10 foot tide).

Site Description: A short trail leads down to the water from the end of Elizabeth Avenue. Follow the trail to the beach and enter the water beneath the bridge.

During slack current periods, divers can swim out to the first bridge pylon, submerge, explore this structure, then move on to the second and third pylons. On a sunny day when the water visibility is good, divers can use the shimmering image of the overhead bridge to guide them between the pylons. During periods of lower visibility, a compass is useful when swimming between the pylons.

The Warren Avenue Bridge crosses Port Washington Narrows.

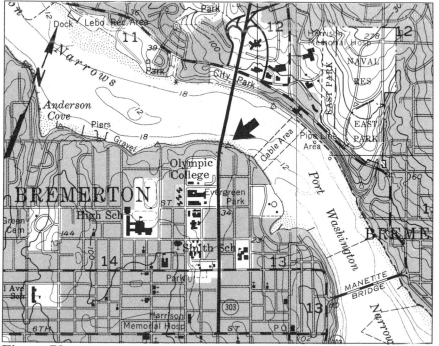

Figure 78

Not Intended For Navigational Use

At the first pylon, divers will find a concrete ledge that appears to skirt the outside of this support, but is actually part of the buried pylon. Each of the deeper pylons have a similar ledge fully exposed above the bottom. Boulders piled around the bases of the second and third pylons provide an environment where fish and invertebrates congregate. Schools of small sea perch often cloud the water around these structures, creating a panorama that is delightful to swim through. A mixture of white plumose anemones and giant acorn barnacles blanket the hard surfaces, while red-brown sea squirts and chunks of yellow sponges are attached to smaller rocks scattered about.

Skill Level: Intermediate divers.

Hazards: Strong current and small boats. Current direction changes very rapidly, becoming noticeable within 5 to 10 minutes after slack water. Begin your dive 30 to 40 minutes prior to the predicted time for slack current. Start your return swim to shore as soon as the current changes direction.

Facilities: None. This is a residential neighborhood. Please be considerate of the people that live on Elizabeth Street. Do not block their driveways, and be sure to carry out all your garbage. Air fills are available in Bremerton.

Travel Distance and Directions: The Warren Avenue Bridge crosses the Port Washington Narrows in Bremerton, approximately 1 mile west-northwest of Point Herron.

Mileage from Bellingham = 107 miles
Mileage from Seattle = 3 miles
Mileage from Olympia = 61 miles

From Bellingham: drive south on I-5 for 77 miles to Exit 177 (exit for the Edmonds-Kingston Ferry). Exit from I-5, then turn right at the bottom of the exit ramp onto 244th Street SW. Follow Highway 104 West (becomes Edmonds Way) to the Edmonds-Kingston Ferry Dock in Edmonds. Ride the ferry across Puget

Sound to Kingston. From the Kingston Ferry Dock, drive 4.0 miles to the Bond Road Junction, angle to the left onto Bond Road toward Highway 305 and Poulsbo, then follow Bond Road for 5.4 miles. Turn right at a four-way intersection and stoplight onto Highway 305 North, and continue straight through the next stoplight onto Highway 3 South. Follow Highway 3 South for 7.1 miles before exiting to Silverdale and East Bremerton. While still on the exit ramp, exit to the right toward East Bremerton and Waaga Way. In 3.6 miles, Waaga Way curves to the right and becomes Highway 303 South (also Wheaton Way). Follow Wheaton Way (becomes Warren Avenue) to the Warren Avenue Bridge, cross the bridge and take the first left turn onto 17th Street. Drive one block, turn left onto Elizabeth Avenue, drive to the end of Elizabeth Avenue and park beside the road.

From the Seattle Waterfront: ride the Seattle-Bremerton Ferry to Bremerton (allow for a 60 minute ferry ride, plus waiting time on the dock). Within 0.1 mile after leaving the Bremerton Ferry, turn right onto Washington Avenue. Follow Washington Avenue (curves to the left and becomes 11th Street) for 0.9 mile and turn right onto Warren Avenue. Follow Warren Avenue for 0.4 mile, then turn right onto 17th Street (last right turn before reaching the Warren Avenue Bridge). Drive one block, turn left onto Elizabeth Avenue, drive to the end of Elizabeth Avenue and park beside the road.

From Olympia: drive north on I-5 to Exit 132 for Bremerton and Highway 16 West. Exit from I-5, then follow Highway 16 West across the Tacoma Narrows Bridge. After crossing the bridge, continue north for 24.0 miles, through the town of Gorst and around the tip of Sinclair Inlet (becomes Highway 3 North and then Highway 304 East). After rounding the end of Sinclair Inlet, follow the highway along the water, past the Naval Shipyard and into Bremerton. Turn right onto Farragut Street toward the City Center, Seattle Ferry and Highway 304 East. Drive two blocks and turn left onto Callow Avenue. Follow Callow avenue for four blocks (0.5 mile), then turn right onto Burwell Street. Drive 0.9 mile, turn left onto Warren Avenue, drive 0.8 mile along Warren Avenue and turn right onto 17th Street (last right turn before reaching the Warren Avenue Bridge). Drive one block, turn left onto Elizabeth Avenue and drive to the end of the road.

Figure 79   Piddock clams in a hard clay bottom

Piddock Clam

Colonies of piddock clams, *Penitella penita*, are often found living in clay or soft rock where they use their shells to cut burrows into the hard bottom. As a section of bottom becomes riddled with holes, it may be weakened to the point that chunks are stripped out by current or wave action. When diving in areas inhabited by these clams, divers will see the distinctive clam necks extending two to three inches above the bottom. At first glance the color of the necks may appear to be a textured off-white, but a closer look will reveal a reddish neck studded with many small white projections. The larger of the clam's two siphons (incurrent) has a ring of short flap-like projections on the inside of its bore, while the smaller syphon (excurrent) is smooth on the inside.

Many other animals, such as small fish and crabs, use the holes cut by piddock clams for shelter. These secondary dwellers seem to prefer empty burrows, but can sometimes be found sharing them with clams.

Current Table: Admiralty Inlet
   Look up the daily current predictions for Admiralty Inlet. Apply
the following time corrections to calculate slack current times:

   Time corrections beneath the Warren Avenue Bridge:
      Minimum inshore current before flood: –23 minutes
      Minimum inshore current before ebb: +55 minutes

Telephone Location: On the northwest corner of Wheaton Way
and Sheridan Road, 1.1 miles from the dive site. Follow Warren
Avenue across the Warren Avenue Bridge to the intersection of
Wheaton Way and Sheridan Road (Warren Avenue becomes
Wheaton Way).

Non-Diver Activities: Evergreen Park, located along the shoreline
of Port Washington Narrows, is within easy walking distance from
the end of Elizabeth Avenue (0.4 mile from the dive site). The park
has rest rooms, picnic tables, barbecue stands, a covered eating area
with a large cooking grill, a horse swing with two seats, regular
swings, horseshoe pits and a boat launch. There is room to play on
the grass or go for a walk along a dirt road that winds through the
park. To reach the park, walk to 17th Street and turn left. In one
block, turn right onto Park Avenue and follow to Evergreen Park.
   The Bremerton Municipal Pool and Kitsap Family YMCA are
located 2 miles from the dive site. They are open year-round, but
you may want to call ahead to check on hours. To drive to the
pool/YMCA, cross to the north side of the Warren Avenue Bridge,
turn right onto Sheridan Road, then take an immediate right onto
Wheaton Way. Follow Wheaton Way for 0.8 mile before turning
left to the Bremerton Municipal Pool.
   Other activities in Bremerton include touring the Bremerton
Naval Shipyard, riding a bike to the Lebo Recreational Area or
visiting the Kitsap Regional Library which is located on the corner
of Sylvan Way and Spruce Avenue (see additional Non-Diver
Activities listed on page 233).

PORT WASHINGTON NARROWS

Habitat and Depth: Occasional large rocks loomed up in front of us as we were swept over the bottom of Port Washington Narrows. At one such spot, my slate lodged between two rocks, stopping me like a sea anchor on the end of a line. Grabbing a large barnacle, I pulled myself into the current to take the strain off the line and release the slate from the rocks. After letting go of the barnacle, I was once again flying over the bottom. Drift diving in current can be an exhilarating way to glimpse a large area of bottom with little effort.

As we flew over the cobblestone bottom, we saw fewer animals than we had seen in Agate Pass. Even so, the variety of animals that we saw, along with the excitement of a drift dive, made this a swim worth repeating. On the bottom, common five-rayed pink stars and multi-rayed sunflower stars were busy digging holes in pursuit of their next meal of clam. Besides these large active sea stars, smaller, slow-moving sea stars were scattered about. Some were red and white mottled stars, while others were reddish-brown leather stars and orange-red blood stars.

Still other animals that we saw included octopuses, piddock clams, kelp crabs, hermit crabs, flounder, C-O sole, whelks, giant acorn barnacles, white plumose anemones, orange sea cucumbers and beaded sea anemones (*Urticina coriacea*).

Maximum bottom depth between the two bridges in Port Washington Narrows reaches 44 feet (10 foot tide).

Site Description: The Bremerton Park Department maintains a small parking lot at street level above the Boat House Restaurant. Because parking space is limited in the lower lot next to the restaurant, please park in the upper lot and walk down the wooden stairs to the beach.

Enter the water beneath the bridge, swim out to the fourth pylon (current permitting) and descend to begin your drift dive. It will take about 48 minutes to drift to the Warren Avenue Bridge in a one knot current. Use a current table to determine how fast the current will be moving during your dive, then adjust the estimated

The fishing pier and exit point at the Lebo Recreation Area

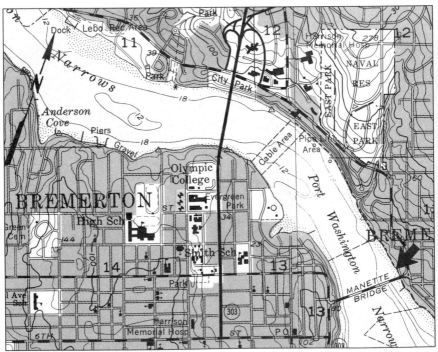

Figure 80   Not Intended For Navigational Use

drift time accordingly. Begin to swim toward shore no later than 10 minutes (for a 1 knot current) after passing beneath the Warren Avenue Bridge. Your exit point is a fishing pier on the north side of the channel, just past a long row of trees at the west end of the Lebo Recreational Area. The total drift distance from the Manette Bridge to the fishing pier is 1.4 nautical miles.

Divers can either leave a second car in the parking lot at the west end of the Lebo Recreational Area, or have a non-diver move a car from the Manette Bridge to the exit point in the park. Enjoy your dive.

Skill Level: Advanced

Hazards: Current and small boats.

Current movement is parallel to shore. Flooding currents move into Port Washington Narrows from Sinclair Inlet, passing first beneath the Manette Street Bridge and then flowing northwest toward the Warren Avenue Bridge. Ebbing currents flow out of Dyes Inlet, through Port Washington Narrows and into Sinclair Inlet.

Dive this site only on a flooding current. Diving this site during an ebbing current is not recommended because it is too easy to miss your exit at the Manette Bridge and be swept into Sinclair Inlet. Also, to avoid being struck by an overhead boat, be sure to maintain a depth of at least 10 feet or more throughout your dive.

Facilities: None at the entry point beneath the Manette Street Bridge. Rest rooms are located near the exit point in the Lebo Recreational Area. Air fills are available in Bremerton.

Travel Distance and Directions: Port Washington Narrows stretches through Bremerton, between Dyes Inlet and Sinclair Inlet. The Manette Street Bridge spans the south end of Port Washington Narrows, where the passage opens into Sinclair Inlet.

> Mileage from Bellingham = 107 miles
> Mileage from Seattle = 3 miles
> Mileage from Olympia = 62 miles

From Bellingham: drive south on I-5 for 77 miles to Exit 177 (exit for the Edmonds-Kingston Ferry). Exit from I-5, then turn right at the bottom of the exit ramp onto 244th Street SW. Follow Highway 104 West (becomes Edmonds Way) to the Edmonds-Kingston Ferry Dock in Edmonds. Ride the ferry to Kingston. From the Kingston Ferry Dock, drive 3.9 miles to the Bond Road Junction. Angle to the left onto Bond Road, toward Highway 305 and Poulsbo. Follow Bond Road for 5.4 miles, then turn right at a four-way intersection and stoplight onto Highway 305 North. Continue straight through the next stoplight onto Highway 3 South. Follow Highway 3 South for 7.1 miles, then exit to Silverdale and East Bremerton. While still on the exit ramp, exit to the right toward East Bremerton and Waaga Way. In 3.6 miles, Waaga Way curves to the right and becomes Highway 303 South (also Wheaton Way). Follow Wheaton Way (becomes Warren Avenue) 1.3 miles beyond NE Riddell Road, and turn left onto Sheridan Street. Make an immediate right turn onto Wheaton Way and drive 1.5 miles to a stop sign at the Manette Bridge. Continue past the bridge, then take the next right turn into a small parking area next to the bridge.

From the Seattle Waterfront: ride the ferry to Bremerton (allow for a 60 minute ferry ride, plus your waiting time on the dock). Within 0.1 mile after leaving the Bremerton Ferry, turn right onto Washington Avenue and follow Washington Avenue to the Manette Bridge. Turn right onto the Manette Bridge, cross Port Washington Narrows and take the first right turn after crossing the bridge. Turn right again into a small parking lot beside the bridge.

From Olympia: drive north on I-5 to Exit 132 for Bremerton and Highway 16 West. Exit from I-5 and follow Highway 16 West across the Tacoma Narrows Bridge. After crossing the bridge, continue north for 24.0 miles, through the town of Gorst and around the tip of Sinclair Inlet (becomes Highway 3 North and then Highway 304 East). After rounding the end of Sinclair Inlet, follow the highway along the water, past the Naval Shipyard and into Bremerton. Turn right onto Farragut Street toward the City Center, Seattle Ferry and Highway 304 East. Drive two blocks and turn left onto Callow Avenue. Follow Callow avenue for four blocks (0.5 mile), then turn right onto Burwell Street. Drive 1.3 miles and turn left onto Washington Avenue. In 0.5 mile, turn right onto the

Manette Bridge. Cross the bridge, take the first right turn, then turn right again into a small parking lot beside the bridge.

Current Table: Admiralty Inlet.

Look up the daily current predictions for Admiralty Inlet. Apply the following time corrections to calculate slack current and maximum current times. Use the current speed ratios for calculating the speed of maximum current.

Time corrections for subordinate station 1195:
Minimum current before flood: −09 minutes
Minimum current before ebb: +55 minutes

Maximum flood current: +13 minutes
Maximum ebb current: +68 minutes

Maximum current speed ratios: 0.6 flood / 0.7 ebb

Telephone Location: A public phone is located near the Manette Bridge, on Harkins Street, one block east of Wheaton Way. Near the Lebo Recreation Area, phones are located in front of the Bay View Apartments, 0.1 mile from the parking lot at the west end of the park. To reach them, turn left from the parking lot onto Lebo Boulevard, make the first right turn onto Sheridan Road and drive to the top of the hill. Two phone booths are located on the left side of the road, just inside the apartment entrance.

Non-Diver Activities: The Lions Community Playfield is located in the Lebo Recreational Area. This large park has three baseball fields, a paved running track, and two play structures for the kids (the larger of the two is fenced). There is also lots of room for kite flying, even with baseball games in progress. A food concession stand is often open during baseball games.

To drive to the playfield from the Manette Bridge, drive west on Wheaton Way (1.0 mile) to the intersection of Lebo Boulevard and Wheaton Way. Turn left onto Lebo Boulevard and drive 0.9 mile before turning left into a parking lot next to the pier and boat launch (see page 228 for additional Non-Diver Activities).

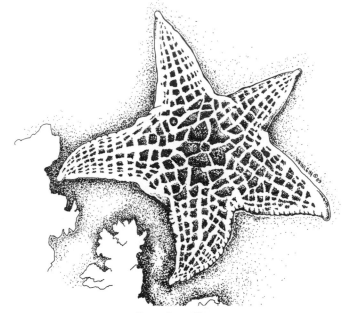

Leather Star

The soft skin of the leather star, *Dermasterias imbricata*, feels like wet leather. This blotchy, reddish-brown animal has five wide, triangular-shaped arms and a broad central disc. The leather star grows to 10 inches in diameter (25 cm). It feeds on sea anemones, sea urchins and sea cucumbers. When rubbed gently, the leather star smells like gunpowder or rotten garlic.

The swimming anemone, *Stomphia*, when touched by the leather star's sensory tube feet, will begin to thrash its oral disc and tentacles from side to side. The anemone will usually push its tentacles down onto the sea star, presumably stinging it with nematocysts (Plates 7-8). Then, if contact from this predatory sea star continues, the small orange anemone will detach itself from its rocky perch and swim off a short distance (Plates 9-10). The anemone then settles down and reattaches to another rock.

Figure 81

PART 9. SOUTH PUGET SOUND

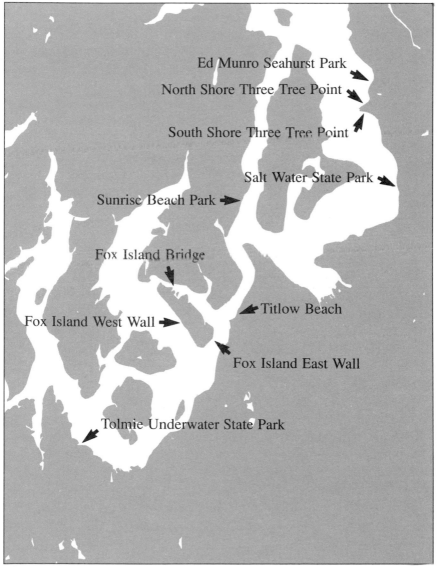

Ed Munro Seahurst Park

North Shore Three Tree Point

South Shore Three Tree Point

Salt Water State Park

Sunrise Beach Park

Fox Island Bridge

Titlow Beach

Fox Island West Wall

Fox Island East Wall

Tolmie Underwater State Park

Figure 82

ED MUNRO SEAHURST PARK

Habitat and Depth: The long sandy-cobblestone beach at Ed Munro Seahurst Park provides an easy entry into the water. Once in the water, divers will find only minimal currents, along with a sunken barge and an interesting community of colorful animals. North of the barge there is a beautiful field of large orange sea pens, which are a form of soft coral. Often scattered throughout a field of sea pens are brown and white striped nudibranchs. When present, they can be seen moving about in the top layer of sand and sometimes feeding on the sea pens. Delicate pale-yellow egg coils from this nudibranch may lie partially buried in the sand.

Other animals you may see while diving here include flounder, C-O sole, moon snails, hermit crabs, burrowing sea cucumbers, perch, sea anemones and sea stars.

Directly out from the parking lot, where a stream crosses the beach, divers will find a sandy bottom with a small eelgrass bed. North of the eelgrass bed the sandy bottom slopes slowly downward past 90 feet in depth (10 foot tide).

Site Description: Swimming directly out from the parking area, divers will descend along a gradually sloping bottom to find occasional sea pens and flounder.

To locate the barge, descend to a depth of 45 feet (10 foot tide), turn in a northward direction, and follow the bottom contour at 45 feet. The shallow end of the barge is located north of the stream at 39 feet. The deeper end is located at 49 feet (10 foot tide).

An alternate way of finding the barge is to swim a compass heading of 270 degrees from the "donut" sculpture, located on shore near the bath house. If you reach the 50 foot depth (10 foot tide) without sighting the barge, surface and take compass readings back toward shore. When directly over the barge, a sighting to the "donut" sculpture will be 90 degrees. A second sighting, to the first picnic shelter south of the stream, will be 150 degrees.

Skill Level: All divers.

The long beach at Seahurst is great for a walk or picnic

Hazards: Moderate current during exchange periods and occasional small boats. Both flood and ebb currents move southward
along the shoreline in front of the entry point.

Facilities: Rest rooms, dry changing areas, covered picnic areas
with barbecue stands, and an outside cold shower for washing
equipment. Air fills are available in Renton, Kent, Federal Way,
Puyallup, Seattle and the Tacoma area.

Travel Distance and Directions: Seahurst Park is located south
of Seattle in Burien, 1.4 nautical miles north of Three Tree Point.

> Mileage from Bellingham = 106 miles
> Mileage from South Seattle = 10 miles
> Mileage from Olympia = 56 miles

From the South Seattle area: follow I-5 to the Burien/Sea-Tac
Airport Exit 154B and exit onto Highway 518 West. Continue on
Highway 518 West into Burien, where the highway then becomes
SW 148th Street. Follow SW 148th Street across 1st Avenue South,

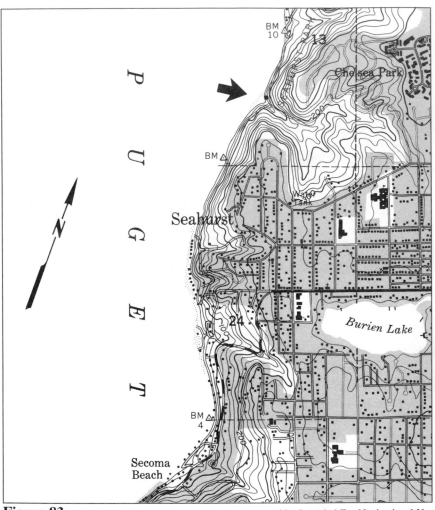

Figure 83   Not Intended For Navigational Use

and 9th Avenue South. Turn right at the next street onto Ambaum Boulevard, then left onto SW 144th Street. In three blocks turn right onto 13th Avenue SW, and drive downhill to the park.

Current Table: Admiralty Inlet.

Look up the daily current predictions for Admiralty Inlet. Apply the following time corrections to calculate slack current times:

Time corrections for subordinate station 1155:
   Minimum current before flood: −36 minutes
   Minimum current before ebb: −13 minutes

Telephone Location: None in the park. Drive up the hill 1.0 mile to the intersection of Ambaum Boulevard and SW 144th Street.

Non-Diver Activities: Go for a walk along a path that leads across a small bridge toward the beach. After crossing the bridge, the path turns and leads southward between the trees and a long, beautiful beach. Visitors can also explore a rock sea-wall north of the bridge, dig for clams (be sure to check game regulations and red-tide warnings before digging), fly a kite or share some quiet moments with friends. Bring a picnic lunch and enjoy the view of Vashon and Blake Islands.

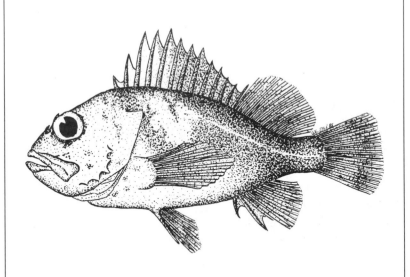

Quillback Rockfish

The quillback rockfish, *Sebastes maliger*, has a brownish coloration with an undefined pattern of yellow blotches behind the head, on its side, and extending up onto the dorsal fin. Additional orange-brown spots are often seen on the head. It lives primarily in rocky areas from 35 feet on down to 900 feet (10 to 274 meters). The quillback rockfish reaches 24 inches (61 cm) in length, although most specimens seen by divers will be less than 14 inches (36 cm).

When approached by an intruder, such as a diver, this solitary rockfish may display an aggressive territorial behavior by raising its long, deeply notched dorsal fin and swimming toward the diver (Plate 20).

Figure 84

NORTH SHORE
THREE TREE POINT

Habitat and Depth: Marine animals have incredibly diverse physical structures and behavior characteristics. Because of this diversity, every dive in the Northwest holds surprises for the divers who are willing to take time to look at small animals. Divers who are uninterested in small animals may find the bottom at Three Tree Point disappointing. This dive is for those who are willing to look. The site is close to Seattle and easily accessible.

Although this sandy habitat does not have large numbers of animals, there are many different species living here. Moon snails plow through the sandy bottom looking for their next shellfish meal. Tube dwelling anemones live farther down the sandy slope, quietly waiting for a meal to bump into their long, white, deadly tentacles. Occasional flounder and sole erupt from their hiding places in the sand to scurry off to a safer spot. Hermit crabs scurry across the bottom while looking for food and the often elusive bigger shell. Filter feeding sessile animals, such as sponges, orange colonial sea pens and reddish sea squirts protrude from the bottom. In turn, they are fed upon by bright-red blood and vermilion sea stars.

Other animals divers may see during a dive at this site include painted greenling, pile perch, sunflower sea stars, pink sea stars, rose stars, sun stars, white plumose anemones, geoduck clams, sharp-nosed crabs, rockfish, burrowing anemones, chitons, shrimp and nudibranchs.

The inshore bottom is sandy-cobblestone. It changes to silty-sand along the top of a steep slope, where eel grass grows between the 17 and 27 foot depths (10 foot tide). Part way down this slope, the bottom changes back to sandy-cobblestone. Two clusters of tires, at the 44 and 60 foot depths, provide support for groups of colorful tube worms and sea squirts. A small boat sits on the bottom with its bow at the 46 depth level. The entire structure of the boat is encased with barnacles and small white anemones. The slope continues downward beyond 130 feet in depth.

The public access trail on the north shore of Three Tree Point

Site Description: Follow the trail from the parking area, at the end of SW Three Tree Point Lane, to the beach. Enter the water over the public access, directly in front of where the trail ends. Private beaches are located on each side of the public access. Please respect this private property by not walking along the beach.

To find the tires or boat, swim out from shore and down the slope in the general direction of west-by-northwest. Turn south-by-southwest and follow the bottom contour along either the 44 or 60 foot depths to find the tires, or along the 48 foot depth to find the boat (10 foot tide).

After ascending to the top of the slope, divers can make a safety stop while watching the animals that live in this sandy habitat. Enjoy your dive.

Skill Level: All divers.

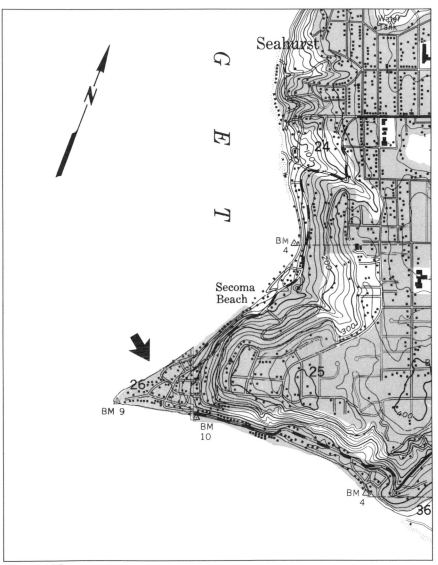

Figure 85

Not Intended For Navigational Use

Hazards: Current and occasional small boats. Both flood and ebb currents move in a clockwise pattern along the north side of Three Tree Point, toward the point and parallel to shore. During comparable tidal exchanges, flood currents are stronger than ebb currents.

Facilities: None. This is a residential neighborhood with limited parking. Access is closed between sunset and sunrise, thus there is no night diving. Air fills are available in Kent and Federal Way.

Travel Distance and Directions: Three Tree Point is located in Burien, 7.7 nautical miles south-southeast by southeast of Seattle's Alki Point.

> Mileage from Bellingham = 105
> Mileage from South Seattle = 11
> Mileage from Olympia = 56

From the South Seattle area: follow I-5 South to the Burien/Sea-Tac Airport Exit 154B and exit onto Highway 518 West toward Burien. Continue on Highway 518 West past the airport exit and into Burien, then across 1st Avenue South onto SW 148th Street. Drive one block past 9th Avenue South, turn left onto Ambaum Boulevard, drive to SW 152nd Street and turn right. Follow SW 152nd Street to 23rd Avenue SW, where SW 152nd Street curves to the left onto Maplewild Avenue SW. Continue along Maplewild Avenue SW for 1.6 miles, down a hill, back up and then down again before turning right onto SW 170th Street. Park at the end of SW 170th Place.

Current Table: Admiralty Inlet
Look up the daily current predictions for Admiralty Inlet. Apply the following time corrections to calculate slack current times:

> Time corrections for subordinate station 1155:
> Minimum current before flood: −36 minutes
> Minimum current before ebb: −13 minutes

Telephone Location: None at the immediate site. Turn left onto Maplewild Avenue SW and drive 1.7 miles back up the hill to the intersection of SW 152nd Street and 21st Avenue SW. A phone is located in a parking lot on the right.

Non-Diver Activities: Go for a walk along an Indian trail from the parking area or walk back to Maplewild Avenue and then downhill along the roadway to the south side of Three Tree Point where there is a sandy stretch of public beach.

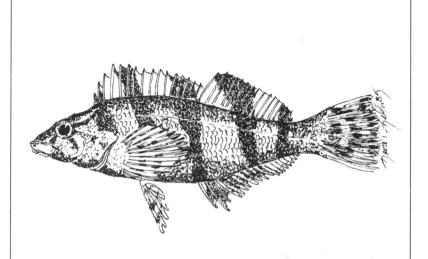

Painted Greenling

Painted greenlings, *Oxylebius pictus*, are commonly seen in rock, kelp and piling habitats. They are recognized by seven dark maroon, vertical bars along each side of the fish (two of these bars may be lost in the color pattern of the tail). Additional distinguishing characteristics include a pointed head with three dark lines radiating from each eye; one extends forward onto the snout, while the other two diverge backward. Painted greenlings feed on small crustacea, and grow to 10 inches (25 cm) in length.

Figure 86

SOUTH SHORE
THREE TREE POINT

Habitat and Depth: Here is your chance (with a little imagination) to drive not one, but three cars over a sandy bottom in your scuba gear! The cars, plus a small boat, rest on the bottom a short distance from the boat launch. This site is also open for night diving, but bring a good light because the headlights on the cars don't work.

Animals living in this area include orange sea pens, white sea anemones, vermilion sea stars, spiny sea stars, leather stars, brown and white striped nudibranchs, brilliant white alabaster nudibranchs (*Dirona albolineata*), sea cucumbers, tube worms attached to tires, sunflower sea stars, flounder, speckled sanddabs, cockles, hermit crabs, ratfish and schools of perch.

The sandy-cobblestone beach slopes gradually downward to 14 feet (10 foot tide), where a sandy slope steepens and drops beyond 96 feet. The cars are at the 35, 60 and 87 foot depths (10 foot tide). The small boat sits on the bottom in a north-south line, with its bow at the 82 foot depth and its stern at the 87 foot depth (10 foot tide).

Site Description: Swim out from the public access (next to the guard rail at the sharp bend in the road) to the southeast on a compass heading of 135 degrees. The deepest of the three cars is on this heading at depth of 87 feet (10 foot tide). From the car, turn east-northeast on a heading of 70 degrees and swim 106 feet to the remains of a small boat. To find the second car from the boat, turn northwest to a heading of 320 degrees and swim 63 feet to the 60 foot depth. To find the shallow car from the car at the 60 foot depth, swim uphill to a depth of 21 feet (almost at the crest of the hill), turn right and swim down into a valley to a depth of 35 feet.

When beginning this dive, you may wish to conserve air by swimming to the buoys on the surface. After reaching the buoys, locate the position of the deep car with the above surface headings, then drop to the bottom.

Skill Level: Intermediate.

The residential area at Three Tree Point has limited parking.

Hazards: Current and occasional small boats.

Both flood and ebb currents move in a counterclockwise pattern on the south side of Three Tree Point, flowing westward along the shoreline toward the point. Ebb currents, during comparable tidal exchanges, are noticeably stronger at this location than flood currents. As a result, divers will encounter less current when diving this site during slack before flood or during a flood exchange. The reverse is true for North Three Tree Point.

Do not allow yourself to be swept past the tip of Three Tree Point into the shipping lane. Also, be sure to monitor your depth and bottom time to stay within the no-decompression limits.

Facilities: There are no facilities at this site other than a public access across the beach, which is open between sunrise and sunset only. This is a residential neighborhood. Air fills are available in Kent and Federal Way.

Travel Distance and Directions: Three Tree Point is located in Burien, 7.7 miles south-southeast by southeast of Seattle's Alki Point.

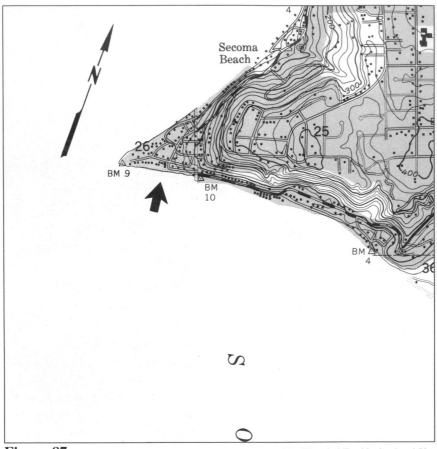

Figure 87   Not Intended For Navigational Use

Mileage from Bellingham = 105 miles
Mileage from South Seattle = 11 miles
Mileage from Olympia = 56 miles

From the South Seattle area: follow I-5 South to the Burien/Sea-
Tac Airport Exit 154B and exit onto Highway 518 West toward
Burien. Continue on Highway 518 West past the airport exit and
into Burien, then across 1st Avenue South onto SW 148th Street.
Drive one block past 9th Avenue South, turn left onto Ambaum
Boulevard, drive to SW 152nd Street and turn right. Follow SW

152nd Street to 23rd Avenue SW, where SW 152nd Street curves to the left onto Maplewild Avenue SW. Continue along Maplewild Avenue SW for 1.7 miles, up and down hills, and eventually down to the water. The public access is to the right of a sharp curve in the roadway, just as you reach the shoreline. Drive onto the public access, unload your gear and then move your car to the side of the roadway to park.

Current Table: Admiralty Inlet.

Look up the daily current predictions for Admiralty Inlet. Apply the following time corrections to calculate slack current times:

> Time corrections for subordinate station 1155:
> Minimum current before flood: −36 minutes
> Minimum current before ebb: −13 minutes

Telephone Location: None at the immediate site. Drive 1.8 miles back up the hill to the intersection of SW 152nd Street and 21st Avenue SW. A phone is in the parking lot on the right.

Non-Diver Activities: Bring a pair of binoculars so that you can watch the ships that pass between Vashon Island and Three Tree Point. Go for a walk along the sandy beach or relax in the sun and read a book.

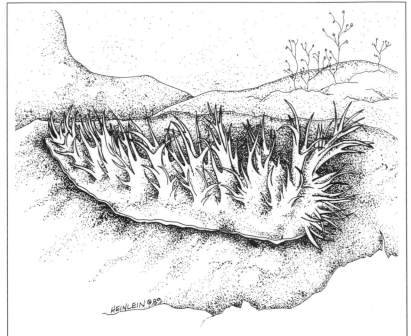

Giant Nudibranch

The giant nudibranch, *Dendronotus rufus*, is an impressive animal, growing to 10 inches (25 cm) in length. This animal belongs to a group of nudibranchs that have been named for their naked gills (order *Nudibranchia*) and for the tree-like appendages that extend from each side of their dorsum (suborder *Dendronotacea*). The giant nudibranch's large and highly branched cerata resemble two colorful rows of 6 to 9 small bushy trees, each with white trunks and deep red branches. Its body is white, with a contrasting thin red line marking the outer edge of the foot. *Dendronotus rufus* feeds on small polyps, including sessile forms of jellyfish.

Figure 88

SALT WATER STATE PARK

Habitat and Depth: Two tire reefs and a sunken barge (still loaded with gravel) provide support for hundreds of colorful tube worms and sea anemones. The wood borers have been busy, as the barge hull is now a sculptured hulk riddled with a maze of holes.

Look for an octopus under the bow of the barge, but please leave this beautiful animal uninjured, so that it may live out its natural life. It continues to thrill the many divers who visit this barge each year, especially the ones who feed it. Try feeding the octopus a crab or some fresh herring (herring is inexpensive and available from many fish markets).

Other animals common to this area include perch, flounder, speckled sanddabs, moon snails, sea pens, nudibranchs, sea cucumbers, hairy and stalked sea squirts, hermit crabs, great sculpins, a variety of colorful sea stars, geoducks, white and orange plumose anemones, gunnels, painted greenling and kelp greenling.

A band of eelgrass grows at the 15 foot depth (10 foot tide), where the inshore sandy-cobblestone bottom changes to sand.

Site Description: Walk down the entry stairs and out along the rock retaining wall. The barge is located in 40 feet of water (10 foot tide), approximately 50 feet north of the southern white and red buoy. The barge also can be located by swimming out from the southwest edge of the rock retaining wall on a compass course of 270 degrees west.

Tire reefs are located on both ends of the barge. The southern reef lies approximately 70 yards south of the barge on a compass course of 170 degrees. The northern reef is located only 20 yards north of the barge on a compass course of 350 degrees.

Skill Level: All divers.

Hazards: Current is light to moderate, with flooding currents flowing parallel to the beach in a south-southeast direction. Conversely, ebbing currents also flow parallel to shore, but in a north-northwest direction. Plan your dive around slack current.

Salt Water State Park on a winter morning

Facilities: Parking, camping, hot showers, a food concession stand, picnic tables, barbecue stands, beach fire rings, rest rooms, a covered eating area for groups (reserve ahead of time), a grass lawn, play structure and nature trail. The beach closes at dusk, thus no night diving. Air fills are available in Kent and Federal Way.

Travel Distance and Directions: Salt Water State Park is located 5.4 nautical miles southeast of Three Tree Point.

> Mileage from Bellingham = 108 miles
> Mileage from South Seattle = 12 miles
> Mileage from Olympia = 49 miles

From the South Seattle area: follow I-5 to the Kent-Des Moines Exit 149. Exit from the freeway, turn west onto the Kent-Des Moines Road (Highway 516 West) and follow it across Highway 99 and down a hill for 1.9 miles. At the bottom of the hill turn left onto Highway 509 South (also Marine View Drive), continue for 1.4 miles, then turn right to Salt Water State Park. Follow the road down a short hill to the beach parking lot.

Figure 89

Not Intended For Navigational Use

Current Table: The Narrows.

Use the daily predictions for The Narrows reference station. Time corrections are not needed.

Telephone Location: Located beside the snack bar in the lower parking lot.

Non-Diver Activities: Located across the road from the upper parking lot is a trail that leads to a secluded hill overlooking the beach. Here you will find a sheltered picnic area with a fantastic view of Maury Island.

After dark, enjoy a fire on the beach around a large stone fire pit. The sound of waves lapping on the beach, the smell of salt water, and the flickering firelight help create a romantic setting and great place to spend some quiet time with a special friend.

A play structure for the kids, constructed from peeled logs, is in the lower parking lot. The log structure supports a tire swing, two regular swings, a slide and climbing bars.

Visitors can spend time wading through the tide pools or walking along a nature trail. They also can camp overnight or for the weekend.

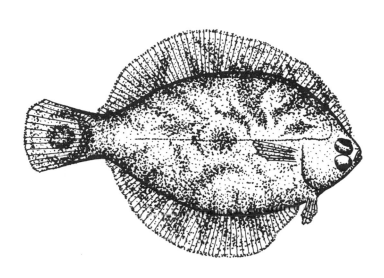

C-O Sole

The C-O sole, *Pleuronichthys coenosus*, is one of at least twenty-five species of flatfish found in the northwest. This fish is easily recognized by a distinctive C-O marking on the upper side of the fish. The C-O pattern is formed by a curved dark bar at the base of the tail and a dark spot on the tail. There is an additional dark spot about midway between the head and tail, also on its upper side.

When a flatfish first hatches, it has an eye on each side of its head. One eye soon begins to migrate, moving across the top of the head to the other side of the fish. This characteristic may look a little strange, but it makes sense for flatfish. With both eyes located on the same side of the head, flounder and sole are able to camouflage themselves by laying flat on the bottom and flipping sand onto their backs. Both eyes are left exposed, slightly raised above the sediment, where they can watch for the next unsuspecting meal to come within striking distance.

Figure 90

SUNRISE BEACH PARK

Habitat and Depth: Octopuses and wolf-eels live in the crevices that are part of the rock ledges at Sunrise Beach. Feeding these beautiful animals is a thrilling experience that is being shared by an increasing number of divers. These divers are choosing to leave their spear guns at home so that they can pursue less damaging activities (it is illegal to spear an octopus). Some of these activities include observing and feeding marine life, and underwater photography. Both wolf-eels and octopuses will accept food from divers (Plates 21-24). To feed these animals, all a diver needs are a few herring, smelt or crab (crab is the octopus' favorite food), along with patience and a hungry animal that has not been frightened. Both animals are usually non-aggressive, but are unpredictable when threatened. Wolf-eels also may not recognize the difference between fingers and food, so be cautious when feeding them.

Many animal species live on the bottom below the intertidal zone. These animals include moon snails, gumboot chitons, leather sea stars, blood stars, sun stars, sunflower stars, mottled stars, slime stars, tube worms, sea squirts, blackeye gobies, piddock clams, nudibranchs, flounder, C-O soles, sailfin sculpins, painted greenling, red Irish lords, mosshead warbonnets, sharp-nosed crabs, hermit crabs, sponge, California sea cucumbers, white sea cucumbers, orange sea cucumbers and small colorful anemones.

Depths for the rock ledge during a 10 foot tide are listed below. The beach and bottom are sandy cobblestone.

Site Description: From the upper parking lot, walk down the dirt road to the lower parking area, then down a trail to a log retaining wall and the beach.

Except for an area of beach between the entry point and the southern park boundary (prior to reaching the first cabin), the beach is private. Please do not trespass. Be considerate of the owner's privacy by staying in the water when south of the park boundary.

Enter the water from the beach in front of the trail and swim southward, past a cabin and two houses, to a deformed evergreen tree. To find the rock ledge from the deformed tree, set a compass

The beach trail ends beside a boat shelter and log retaining wall

Sunrise Beach Rock Ledge Depth in feet during a 10 foot tide			
Ledge Section	North End	Center	South End
Top	41	37	38
Bottom	50	60	49

course of 115 degrees, submerge and swim out to the ledge. This course will place you at the approximate top center of the ledge and a depth of 37 feet (10 foot tide).

Skill Level: Intermediate.

Hazards: Strong and variable currents, with a moderately long swim that seems longer when swimming against current.

Current moves northward past Sunrise Beach during both flood and ebb tidal cycles, except during two periods; during the first 94

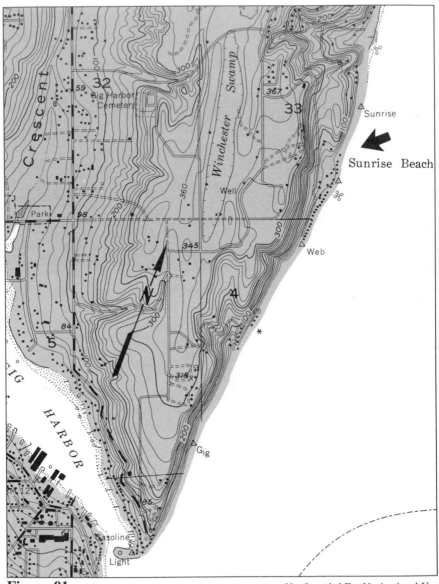

Figure 91

Not Intended For Navigational Use

minutes of a flood cycle when water flows southward, and during a period preceding slack before flood when ebb flow weakens and fluctuates widely, having both south and north vectors.

Slack before flood at Sunrise Beach occurs about 90 minutes before slack occurs at The Narrows. Approximately four minutes after flood begins at The Narrows, flooding current along Sunrise Beach will go slack again, then begin to flow northwards past the rock ledge and back toward the entry point.

Divers can take advantage of this reverse flood current by entering the water 30 minutes before the occurrence of slack before flood at The Narrows. At this time, water will be moving southward past the entry point and rock ledge. Divers can swim southward with the current, past the cabin and two houses, to the rock ledge. Shortly after The Narrows current begins to flood, current direction along Sunrise Beach will reverse and begin to flow northward. Divers making a return swim following this flood reversal, will again be swimming with the current.

A slack period before an ebb current cycle does not occur at Sunrise Beach. The already northern bound flooding current only slows, before picking up speed again and continuing to flow northward as an ebbing current.

Facilities: This is an unimproved county park which closes at dusk. Facilities consist of picnic tables and two outhouses (one in the upper park and one in the lower park). Air tanks can be filled in Tacoma and Bremerton.

Travel Distance and Directions: Sunrise Beach is located at the south end of Colvos Passage, 4.5 nautical miles north-northwest of the Tacoma Narrows Bridge.

> Mileage from Bellingham = 137 miles
> Mileage from South Seattle = 41 miles
> Mileage from Olympia = 43 miles

From the Tacoma area: drive north on I-5 to the Gig Harbor/Bremerton Exit 132 for Highway 16 West. Exit from I-5, then follow Highway 16 West toward Gig Harbor and across the Tacoma Narrows Bridge. After crossing the Tacoma Narrows Bridge, drive for 3.3 miles before exiting from Highway 16 West at the Gig Harbor/City Center Exit. At the end of the exit ramp, turn right at the stoplight onto Pioneer Way, drive through a second light and down a hill into Gig Harbor. At the bottom of the hill, turn left at a stop sign onto Harborview Drive and follow the roadway around Gig harbor. In 0.5 mile, Harborview Drive will curve to the right and become Stinson Avenue for 0.3 mile. The roadway then curves to the right again (move into right hand turn lane) onto Harborview Drive. Now drive for 0.8 mile, then curve to the right onto Vernhardson Street. Follow Vernhardson Street (which becomes 96th Street) for 0.3 mile to a tee. Turn left onto Crescent Valley Drive NW. Drive 0.6 mile, turn right at the fire station onto Drummond Drive NW and follow the road up a hill for 0.9 mile. At the top of the hill, turn right at a stop sign onto Moller Drive NW. Drive 0.2 mile along Moller Drive NW, then turn left onto Sunrise Beach Drive NW. Follow Sunrise Beach Drive NW for 0.5 mile and turn left into Sunrise Beach Park. Park in the upper parking area.

Current Table: The Narrows
    Look up the daily current predictions for The Narrows. Apply the following time corrections to calculate slack current times:

> Time corrections for Sunrise Beach:
> Minimum inshore current before flood: −90 minutes
> Reverse of inshore flood current: +04 minutes
> Minimum inshore current before ebb: −16 minutes

Telephone Location: None at this site. Drive 3.1 miles back to Gig Harbor. A public phone is located across the street from the grocery store.

Non-Diver Activities: Located 2.4 miles from the entrance to Sunrise Beach Park, between Gig Harbor and Sunrise Beach, is a charming wooded park that has a grass lawn and small adjacent stream. There are two fireplaces in the park (each with a cooking grill), along with picnic tables, a covered eating area, stone rest rooms and a neighboring stone sculpture that you can crawl into to hide. A log play structure offers a tire swing, two slides, a swing bridge to cross and platforms to climb on. There is also a baseball field with abutting tennis courts and swings.

Pacific Octopus

Two species of octopus are commonly seen by divers in the Northwest. One of them, *Octopus dofleini*, is the largest species of octopus in the world. This shy, reclusive octopus may reach a weight exceeding 100 pounds (45 kg), with an arm spread of 13 to 20 feet (4 to 6 meters).

Octopuses have 8 arms, and are able to change color rapidly. They breathe by pumping water through a large bag-like mantle cavity containing gills. Because they do not have skeletons, octopuses can squeeze past openings appearing to be much too small for their size. They usually live singularly in crevices, just visible through narrow openings at the base of rock outcroppings. Often, the area around a den entrance is scattered with clam and crab shells from recent meals. A den opening also may occasionally have a low wall of rocks stacked just inside the entrance, presumably placed as a partial barrier.

Figure 92

Octopuses can change color rapidly by constricting or enlarging specialized color cells called chromatophores. The resulting shades of color provide an effective camouflage used for both defensive and hunting purposes. When an octopus leaves the security of a den, it will often change its skin color, mimicking the color pattern of the surrounding bottom. This camouflage is so effective that it is possible to look right at an octopus without recognizing it, even when the animal is in full view.

Octopuses feed primarily on crab, shellfish and fish. Divers can successfully feed them by slowly approaching an occupied den and offering a crab or fish. If the octopus has not been frightened, it will often reach out a tentacle to touch the food and pull it from the diver's hand (Plates 22-24).

Octopus skin is covered with a layer of mucus that protects the animal from infection. Handling an octopus with nylon covered gloves will injure it by removing patches of this mucous layer and leaving the animal open to infection. The stress from handling further reduces its resistance to infection, so that the combined effect eventually results in the animals death. To avoid injuring an octopus, it is best not to try to grab or hold the animal. Let the octopus do the touching.

Octopuses are intelligent animals possessing reasoning ability that is used for food procurement in the wild. This same intelligence often gets them into tight spots in captivity. Public aquariums must take special precautions to contain octopuses because the animals can easily crawl out of tanks that do not have tightly fitting, locked lids. These active animals also can remove internal drainpipes, thus inadvertently draining their tanks.

Octopuses have well developed eyes. The Seattle Aquarium reported an octopus that would leave its tank at night, apparently crawling across a wall to drop into other tanks for dinner. It then would return to its own tank by morning!

TITLOW BEACH

Habitat and Depth: Two parallel rows of pilings from the old Titlow Ferry Pier still stand, only now they are so thickly covered with sea anemones that they form two white walls beneath the surface. On a sunny day, as the sunlight filters down through the green water and reflects off the shell covered bottom, the anemones seem to be part of an empty stage, quietly waiting for the actors to appear. The abandoned ferry pier, along with an adjacent sunken barge, is only a short swim from shore.

Animals you may see while diving here include shrimp, hermit crabs, kelp crabs, small bottom fish, octopuses, sea urchins, nudibranchs, bullheads, flounder, perch, sea pens and ratfish.

There are wharf pilings and a sandy-cobblestone bottom at this dive site. Bottom depth ranges from 24 feet at the south end of the ferry pier, to 27 feet at the north end of the pier (10 foot tide).

Site Description: Two parallel rows of weathered ferry pier pilings are located immediately in front of the entry point. Walk down onto the beach from the concrete ramp, swim out a short distance and submerge to begin to explore the bottom and pilings. Hundreds of white plumose anemones live on the pilings comprising the old ferry slip.

The remains of a wooden barge rest on the bottom in 31 feet of water (10 foot tide), approximately 50 feet west-southwest of the southwest corner of the ferry slip. For bottle hunters, a field of discarded bottles is located approximately 200 yards southwest of the pilings in 60-70 feet of water.

South of the ferry slip are two pilings with a cross member spanning the distance between their tops. Rocks are rumored to be located offshore from these pilings in approximately 30 feet of water.

Skill Level: Intermediate.

Hazards: Strong current during exchange periods, small boats from a nearby marina, and a long swim out to the bottle field.

White plumose nemones cover the sides of the abandoned peer

Directions of current movement between the rows of pilings (and inshore from the pilings) are opposite that of the main flows in Puget Sound. Flooding currents in Titlow Lagoon (and in the ferry slip) flow northward. Conversely, ebbing currents flow southward. Offshore from the abandoned ferry pier the current runs in the same direction as the main channel flow.

Dive this site only during a period of slack current, so that actual slack occurs during your dive. Display a dive flag, carry a knife and have a great dive.

Facilities: Picnic tables and park benches are mounted on a wood deck, which extends out over a rock bulkhead at the waters edge. A cold shower for rinsing diving equipment is located adjacent to the deck along with two pay phones, and a concrete ramp leading down to a sandy beach. A parking area and walking trail are located immediately across the railroad tracks. Rest rooms are located across the tracks in Titlow Beach Park. Air fills are available in Tacoma and Puyallup. The park closes one-half hour after sunset.

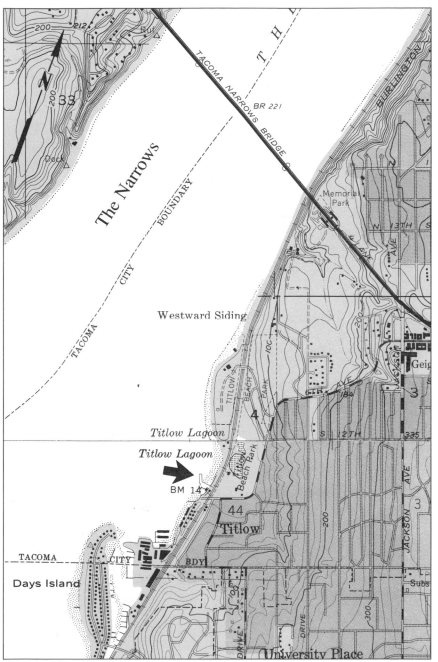

Figure 93

Travel Distance and Directions: Titlow Beach is in Tacoma, approximately 1.2 nautical miles south of the Narrows Bridge.

Mileage from Bellingham = 126 miles
Mileage from South Seattle = 32 miles
Mileage from Olympia = 33 miles

From the Tacoma area: follow I-5 to the Gig Harbor/Bremerton Exit 132 for Highway 16 West. Stay to the right on the exit ramp, following signs for Highway 16 West and Bremerton. Before crossing the Tacoma Narrows Bridge, exit from Highway 16 West at the Jackson Avenue Exit and turn left onto Jackson Avenue. Turn right onto 6th Avenue and follow the road down a hill, past a swimming pool and Titlow Beach Park, then across railroad tracks to a small parking area facing the pilings.

Current Table: The Narrows.
Look up the daily current predictions for The Narrows. Apply the following time corrections to calculate slack current times:

Time corrections for Titlow Beach:
Minimum inshore current before flood: -05 minutes
Minimum inshore current before ebb: +33 minutes

Telephone Location: Across the street at the tavern.

Non-Diver Activities: Titlow Beach Park is on the opposite side of the tracks from the dive site. This large park has a large grass lawn with rest rooms, picnic tables, covered eating areas, a play structure, a duck pond, a baseball field and running trails. Run on the large grass field in Titlow Beach Park, play baseball or tennis, feed the ducks living on Titlow Lagoon or go for a walk or run along a fitness trail that winds past the duck pond and through the trees. The Titlow Pool is within easy walking distance, but is open only during summer months.

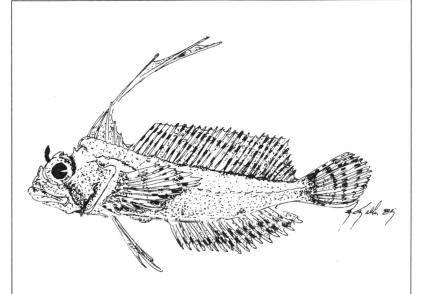

Sailfin Sculpin

The sailfin sculpin, *Nautichthys oculofasciatus*, is a nocturnal fish that is commonly seen during night dives. During daylight hours, the fish is often found on dark ceilings of overhangs and small caves. It grows to 8 inches (20 cm) in length and has a distinguishing tall, sail-like front dorsal fin. A dark stripe extends diagonally through each eye and across each side of the head.

The lateral line is easily recognized along either side of the sailfin sculpin, extending from the head to the base of the tail. Common to all fish, the lateral line is a collection of pressure sensitive nerve endings that are part of a sensory system used to detect small pressure changes caused by other animals. This sensory system warns fish of aggressive or erratic movements made by predators and injured fish.

Figure 94

FOX ISLAND BRIDGE

Habitat and Depth: The intrigue of diving beneath the Fox Island Bridge comes not so much from the fact that you are beneath a bridge, but instead from the realization that your dive is limited to a brief period of time during one of the short intervals between torrential flows of heavy current. Diving this site is both challenging and exciting. During these brief periods, divers can venture out into Hale Passage to catch a glimpse of the rich assortment of colorful animals that live just a short distance from shore.

Along the rock jetty, red and green Christmas sea anemones cling to the rocks, patiently waiting for an animal to fall into their deadly tentacles. Nearby, kelp crabs are moving about, munching on kelp or quarreling over females and living space. In the shallows, between the jetty and pylons, moon snails slide across the bottom in search of a clam meal. Slightly deeper, large sunflower sea stars are often found hunting or digging into the bottom, also looking for their next meal of clam. Other animals, such as red Irish lords, sea perch, flounder and red penpoint gunnels are scattered over the bottom where they feed and reproduce.

On the bridge supports near shore, delicate looking anemones, giant acorn barnacles and small tube worms are attached to the concrete piles. Large white plumose sea anemones live on sections of the deeper rectangular pylons. They stand shoulder to shoulder, like sentries guarding a passage, while their delicate tentacles filter food from the passing water.

The bottom is primarily sandy-cobblestone, with drifts of shell fragments at the base of the shallower pylons and exposed areas of clay ridges. Depths at the bases of the inshore, round concrete piles range from 18 to 28 feet (10 foot tide). The bases of the first, second and third rectangular pylons are at the 32, 38 and 47 foot depths (10 foot tide) respectively. Maximum depth at the center of Hale Passage is 64 feet (10 foot tide).

Site Description: Due to the strong current at this site, timing is important when diving beneath the bridge. Arrive early enough to begin your dive approximately 30 minutes before the calculated

The Fox Island Bridge crosses the west end of Hale Passage.

slack current time. Swim out to the end of the rock jetty and wait for the current to slow. When you are comfortable with the current, swim out underneath the bridge, submerge and begin to explore the pylons. Use a compass while swimming between pylons. Each large rectangular pylon has a concrete ledge part way up its column.

Due to the short slack intervals at this site, begin your return swim as soon as the current changes direction. Do not wait for the current to become uncomfortable or you will be in for a long, hard swim. The rock jetty is also fun to explore. Spending the last part of your dive around the jetty is a safe way to use some of your remaining air after returning from the main current area.

Skill Level: Advanced

Hazards: Strong current and occasional small boats.

The Fox Island Bridge spans a narrow section of Hale Passage. Within the confines of this narrow and shallow section, slack current duration intervals are short and are quickly followed by very strong currents.

During flood exchanges, water moves through the channel to the west, past the lighthouse and toward the bridge. Water striking the east side of the jetty will turn northwards and flow out along the jetty.

During ebb exchanges, water flows eastward from the bridge toward the lighthouse. Water striking the west side of the jetty will turn northward, flowing out along the jetty, before rounding the end of the jetty and turning eastward with the main channel flow.

Facilities: None at the site. Air fills are available in Tacoma, Federal Way, Puyallup and Bremerton.

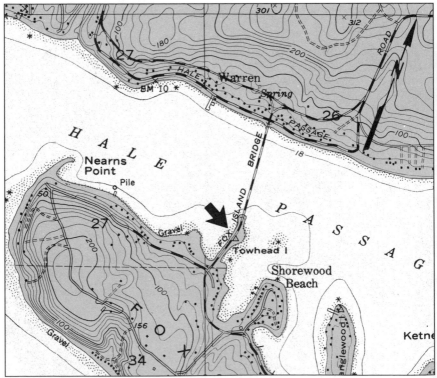

Figure 95   Not Intended For Navigational Use

Travel Distance and Directions: The Fox Island Bridge is located near the north end of Fox Island, 9 miles from the west end of the Tacoma Narrows Bridge.

> Mileage from Bellingham = 136 miles
> Mileage from South Seattle = 40 miles
> Mileage from Olympia = 42 mile.

From Bellingham or Seattle: drive south on I-5 to Exit 132 for Bremerton and Highway 16 West. Exit from I-5 onto Highway 16 west and drive to the Tacoma Narrows Bridge. After crossing the bridge, continue on Highway 16 West for 2.0 miles before exiting at the Olympic Drive NW / Fox Island Exit. Turn left onto Olympic Drive NW from the exit ramp stoplight. Follow Olympic Drive NW over Highway 16, onto 56th Street NW and then onto then Fillmore Drive NW. Turn left at a tee onto Wollochet Drive NW and drive for 1.1 miles before turning right onto 40th Street NW. In 0.7 mile, turn left onto 70th Avenue NW and follow to a tee. Turn right at the tee onto 32nd Street NW (becomes Ford Drive NW) and follow Ford Drive NW to the Fox Island Bridge. Immediately after crossing the bridge, turn right into a parking area for the Fox Island Bridge boat launch and dive site.

From Olympia: drive north on I-5 to Exit 132 for Bremerton and Highway 16 West. Exit onto Highway 16 West and drive to the Tacoma Narrows Bridge. Follow the above directions.

Current Table: The Narrows

Look up the daily current predictions for The Narrows. Apply the following time corrections to calculate slack current times:

> Time corrections beneath the Fox Island Bridge:
> Minimum inshore current before flood: –45 minutes
> Minimum inshore current before ebb: –140 minutes

Telephone Location: None at the immediate site. Drive 1.7 miles to the Fox Island Grocery and Deli. To find the deli from the boat launch parking area, continue onto Fox Island for 1.5 miles. Turn left onto Fox Drive, then take the first left-hand turn onto 6th

Avenue. The Fox Island Grocery and Deli will be on your right-hand side. A phone is on the outside of the store front.

Non-Diver Activities: Visit the Fox Island Historical Museum (open Wednesday and Saturday, 1 to 4 pm) to learn about local history. One display explains the importance the Fox Island Ferry Pier played in the daily lives of residents, between 1914 and 1954, when it was operational. During this time, the ferry "Transit" and the ferry "City of Steilacoom" provided the only means of public access to or from Fox Island.

To drive to the museum from the Fox Island Bridge, follow Island Boulevard for 1.6 miles and turn left onto Fox Drive. Follow Fox Drive past the abandoned ferry pier, on the corner of 9th and Fox Drive, where the roadway makes a sharp turn to the right onto 9th Avenue. Follow 9th Avenue for 0.8 mile to the intersection of 9th and Kamus Drive at the top of the hill. Continue through the intersection (still on 9th Avenue) and past the fire station before turning left to the museum.

Figure 96

Morning Sun Star

The morning sun star, *Solaster dawsoni*, is an aggressive predator that feeds on other sea stars, including its own species. *Solaster dawsoni* has a gray to dark golden-yellow coloration, a large central disc, and a variable number of arms (often 10 to 14). It reaches a diameter of 10 to 16 inches (25 to 46 cm), and is found on sandy and rocky subtidal bottoms that are partially protected from waves. *Solaster dawsoni* is commonly seen by divers in Puget Sound, the Strait of Juan de Fuca and the San Juan Islands.

Solaster dawsoni usually feeds on slow moving sea stars such as *Solaster stimpsoni*, but when a diver places a *Solaster dawsoni* on top of *Pycnopodia* (the sunflower sea star), there is an interesting response. *Pycnopodia* exhibits an escape response that is seemingly "frantic," even though it may have a diameter of over three times the maximum diameter of *Solaster*. The steady gliding movement of *Pycnopodia* suddenly increases to the point where many of its tube feet sweep over the bottom without gaining a firm hold. At the same time, *Solaster dawsoni* responds by pushing the tips of its arms down onto the back of *Pycnopodia*, seemingly in an effort to gain a stronger hold. If not dislodged, *Solaster stimpsoni* will evert its stomach and begin to digest one of the sunflower star's arms.

FOX ISLAND EAST WALL

Habitat and Depth: Looking up to see our exhaust bubbles rising toward the surface, we saw the dark shape of a ledge with kelp silhouetted in the surface light above its rim. From the surface this dive site may misleadingly appear to offer little more than a current-swept cobblestone beach. Beneath the surface there are at least three layered sandstone walls that have been cut by scouring current over time.

In comparison to the large number of animals that are found on rock walls at other sites, there are significantly fewer animals attached to these soft sandstone walls. Most are small, not yet having reached a size large enough to be torn from the surface by the current. Animals living in this area include perch, shrimp, geoduck clams, flounder, slime stars, sunflower stars, red Irish lords, gunnels, hermit crabs, heart crabs, chitons, sponges, tube worms and grunt sculpins.

The beach is cobblestone, changing to a sandy-cobblestone bottom by 15 feet in depth (10 foot tide). Below the ledges, the bottom continues to slope downward past the 110 foot depth (10 foot tide).

Site Description: At least two ledges are located on the south side of the fishing pier, while a third ledge is located north of the fishing pier. Ravines have been cut through the southern ledges like avalanche chutes, which probably are changing from day-to-day as erosion from current continues.

The top of the southern shallower ledge is located in 15 feet of water, directly in front of the trail. Depth at the bottom of this ledge ranges between 40 and 50 feet (10 foot tide). To find a deeper ledge, follow a ravine downward. The bottom of a second ledge is at the 79 foot depth (10 foot tide). Further south, a series of low sculptured sandstone ridges protrude from the sandy-cobblestone bottom at the 80 foot depth (10 foot tide). In the opposite direction, north of the fishing pier, a third sandstone ledge can be found offshore from a large boulder and concrete bulkhead. The bottom of this smaller ledge is in 34 feet of water (10 foot tide).

The Toy Point Fishing Pier has been closed due to disrepair.

Skill Level: Intermediate.

Hazards: Very strong current, occasional small boats and fishing line. Flooding currents move parallel to shore, flowing southward past Fox Point toward the fishing pier on Toy Point, then rounding Toy Point toward Gibson Point. Ebbing currents also move parallel to shore, rounding Toy Point and the fishing pier, then flowing northward toward Fox Point.

When entering at slack before flood, swim northward initially so that your return swim will be with the increasing flood current. Conversely, when entering at slack before ebb, swim southward during the first part of your dive so that your return swim will be with the increasing ebb current.

Facilities: None. Air fills are available in Tacoma.

Travel Distance and Directions: Toy Point is located at the east end of Fox Island, 3.0 nautical miles south of the Tacoma Narrows Bridge.

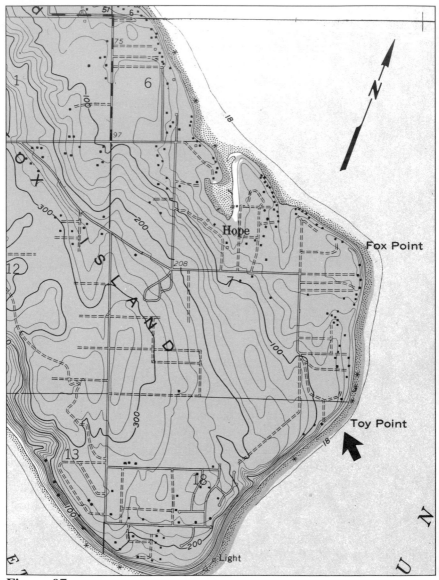

Figure 97

Mileage from Bellingham = 141 miles
Mileage from South Seattle = 45 miles
Mileage from Olympia = 47 miles

From the Tacoma area: follow I-5 to Exit 132 for Gig Harbor, Bremerton and Highway 16 West. Exit from I-5 onto Highway 16 West, then drive to the Tacoma Narrows Bridge. After crossing the bridge, continue on Highway 16 West for 2.0 miles before exiting at the Olympic Drive NW / Fox Island Exit. Turn left onto Olympic Drive NW from the exit ramp stoplight, follow Olympic Drive NW over Highway 16 onto 56th Street NW and then onto Fillmore Drive NW. Turn left at a tee onto Wollochet Drive NW, drive for 1.1 miles and turn right onto 40th Street NW. In 0.7 mile, turn left onto 70th Avenue NW and follow to a tee. Turn right at the tee onto 32nd Street NW (becomes Ford Drive NW) and follow Ford Drive NW to the Fox Island Bridge. Cross the bridge onto Fox Island, drive 3.1 miles from the bridge, then turn right onto 9th Avenue. In 0.2 mile, turn left onto Kamus Drive, then follow the main road around a curve to the right onto Island Boulevard. Island Boulevard soon becomes Mowitch Drive, which in turn will curve to the right onto 14th Avenue. The road ends a short distance from where 14th Avenue becomes Ozette Drive. Park at the end of Ozette Drive and walk down the right-hand trail to the beach.

Current Table: The Narrows.

Look up the daily current predictions for the Narrows. Apply the following time corrections to calculate slack current times:

Time corrections for Toy Point, Fox Island:
Minimum inshore current before flood: −56 minutes
Minimum inshore current before ebb: −65 minutes

Telephone Location: None at the immediate site. Drive back toward the Fox Island bridge to Fox Island Grocery and Deli. Turn right onto 9th Avenue, then left onto Island Boulevard. Follow Island Boulevard for 1.2 miles before turning right onto 6th Avenue and driving the remaining 0.2 mile to the store.

Non-Diver Activities: The fishing pier has been closed due to disrepair. Visitors can fish from shore, catch some sunshine from the beach while enjoying the view of the Tacoma Narrows Bridge or visit the Fox Island Historical Museum (see pages 271-272).

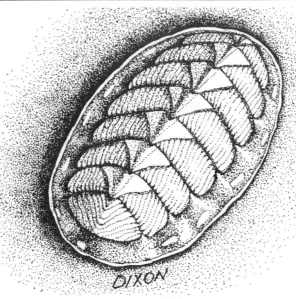

Lined Chiton

Fossil records show that chitons have been competing for survival for more than 500 million years. Their low profile shell and large foot are examples of specialized adaptations that enable this animal to cling to rocks in current swept intertidal areas. The chiton's armor-like shell has eight overlapping plates that cover the animal's body, providing protection from predators and wave action.

Many chitons are light sensitive and hide under rocks during the day. They emerge at night to crawl about while feeding on coralline algae, scraped from rocks with their rasp-like tongue (radula).

The lined chiton, *Tonicella lineata*, is the most colorful chiton in the Pacific Northwest. Dark brown parallel lines wriggle across yellowish shell plates in a distinctive pattern. The center crests of all but the end plates are each marked with a contrasting yellowish triangle. Additionally, the outer edge of the shell is lined with a narrow light colored band.

Figure 98

FOX ISLAND WEST WALL

Habitat and Depth: One excitement of diving is the anticipation of finding a seemingly elusive structure that you heard about from a buddy (or book). Beneath the surface you never know what you will find ... or if you will find anything at all. This sandy bottom slopes downward without sign of a rock ledge or any other type of structure. Then suddenly a slightly darker shape seems to materialize in front of you. As you get closer, the shape becomes more definitive and then materializes into reality. There, where you least expect it, a rock ledge protrudes from the bottom.

A large number of dark purple sand dollars live in the shallow water near the entry point. Other animals living in this area include moon snails, flounders, nudibranchs, hermit crabs, octopuses, blood stars, vermilion stars, sun stars, pink sea stars, sunflower sea stars, rose stars, slime stars, mottled stars, california sea cucumbers, small white sea cucumbers, tube-dwelling anemones, swimming anemones, orange plumose anemones and occasional sea pens.

The cobblestone beach changes abruptly to a sandy bottom by the 10 foot depth (10 foot tide) and then slopes downward past 110 feet. Offshore from the entry point, a rock ledge protrudes from the bottom between the 56 and 64 foot depths (10 foot tide).

Site Description: The southeast section of this crescent shaped rock ledge is oriented parallel to shore, while the opposite northwest end curves to the east-northeast toward the entry point (56 foot depth) and the end of Kamus Drive.

To find the rock ledge, swim out from the end of Kamus Drive on a compass heading between 180 degrees and 215 degrees. Following a heading of 215 degrees south-southwest will lead divers to the approximate center of the ledge. A heading of 180 degrees south will take divers to the southeast end of the ledge.

Skill Level: All divers.

Hazards: Light current and occasional small boats.

The dive site entry is at the end of Kamus Drive.

Facilities: None. This is a residential area. Air fills are available in Tacoma.

Travel Distance and Directions: The west end of Kamus Drive is located on the southwest side of Fox Island, 4.2 nautical miles northwest of Steilacoom.

> Mileage from Bellingham = 140 miles
> Mileage from Seattle = 44 miles
> Mileage from Olympia = 46 miles

From the Tacoma area: follow I-5 to Exit 132 for Gig Harbor, Bremerton and Highway 16 West. Exit and drive to the Tacoma Narrows Bridge. After crossing the bridge, continue on Highway 16 West for 2.0 miles before exiting at the Olympic Drive NW / Fox Island Exit. At the exit ramp stoplight, turn left onto Olympic Drive NW, follow Olympic Drive NW over Highway 16 onto 56th Street NW and then onto Fillmore Drive NW. Turn left at a tee onto Wollochet Drive NW, then drive for 1.1 miles before turning right onto 40th Street NW. In 0.7 mile, turn left onto 70th Avenue NW

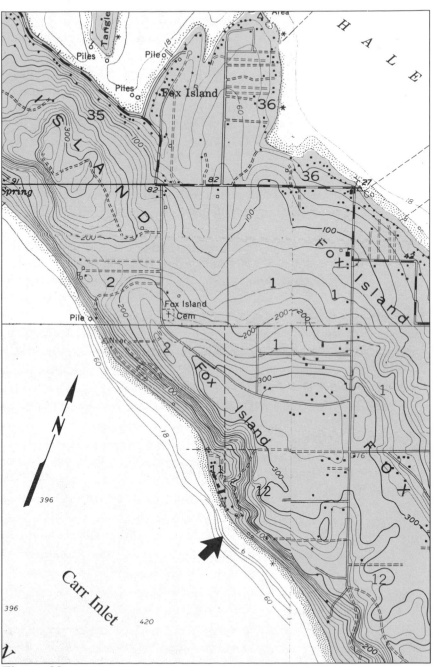

Figure 99   Not Intended For Navigational Use

and follow to a tee. Turn right at the tee onto 32nd Street NW (becomes Ford Drive NW) and follow Ford Drive NW to the Fox Island Bridge.

After crossing the bridge onto Fox Island, drive for 3.1 miles before turning right onto 9th Avenue. In 0.2 mile, turn right onto Kamus Drive and follow Kamus Drive down a steep hill to the water. Please respect the private property located on each side of the public access. Enjoy your dive.

Current Table: The Narrows.

Look up the daily current predictions for the Narrows. Apply the following time corrections to calculate slack current times:

> Time corrections for subordinate station 1280:
> Minimum current before flood: +28 minutes
> Minimum current before ebb: +08 minutes

Telephone Location: None at the immediate site. Drive to the Fox Island Grocery and Deli at the corner of Fox Drive and 6th Avenue. To get there, drive back up the hill and turn left onto 9th Avenue. Follow 9th Avenue to the abandoned ferry pier, where the road curves to the left onto Fox Drive. Continue around the corner onto Fox Drive, then drive the remaining 0.8 mile to the store.

Non-Diver Activities: Bring an art project or a good book. This is an isolated area with private property on either side of the access road. The Fox Island Historical Museum is nearby at the top of the hill (see pages 271-272 for directions).

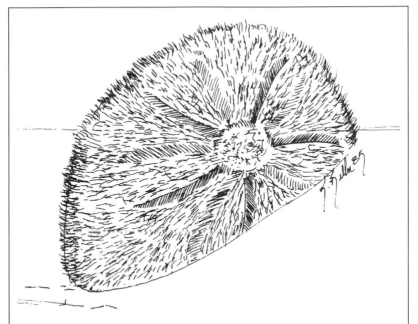

Sand Dollar

The dark purple sand dollar, *Dendraster excentricus*, is a close relative of sea urchins, sea cucumbers and sea stars. All of these animals belong to the family *Echinodermata* (meaning sea urchin skin). They share common structural characteristics such as spines, pedicellariae, tube feet and hydrovascular systems.

Sand dollars are covered with a layer of short, dense spines. The spines function as walking sticks when sand dollars move across the bottom, leaving wide tracks behind them in the sand. When lying flat on the bottom, sand dollars feed on diatoms and detritus, but while standing on end in the sandy bottom, they feed on passing plankton. Particles of food stick to a mucous layer at the base of the spines and are transported to food groves by cilia. Tube feet then take over, pushing the particles along branching grooves to a centrally located mouth.

Figure 100

TOLMIE
UNDERWATER STATE PARK

Habitat and Depth: Swimming over the nearly flat bottom at Tolmie State Park is a wonderful way to see a variety of animals that live in a sandy environment. And yes, the water does finally deepen. In fact, it deepens enough to hide three large barges.

Divers often see different types of animals each time they make this swim. Animals commonly seen include octopuses, perch, sculpins, moon snails, hermit crabs, geoducks, sand dollars and skates.

The bottom slopes gradually downward, reaching 55 feet in depth at the base of the outside wall of the second barge, just outside the red can buoys (10 foot tide). The shallow barge is in 45- to 50 feet of water, while the third barge, to the west-northwest of the can buoys, is in approximately 55 feet of water (10 foot tide).

Site Description: A footbridge crosses over a small estuary to a sand spit that has been formed by erosion material from nearby cliffs, along with a surface layer of stabilizing pebbles that the park service has added. Enter the water in front of this footbridge.

Two of three barges are located near two red & white can buoys and an adjacent white mooring buoy. All of the other buoys are mooring buoys, which do not mark barges.

To reach the shallow barge, swim out from the footbridge to the distant white mooring buoy that is located between the footbridge and west-southwest can buoy. Submerge and swim 50 to 75 feet eastward to the barge (see Figure 102).

The second barge is approximately 30 feet inshore from the east-southeast red & white can buoy (the buoys will change position somewhat as current direction changes). To reach this barge, follow a compass heading of 30 degrees out from the footbridge, or about 210 degrees when swimming from the buoy. The third barge is approximately 150 feet west-northwest of the west-northwest red and white can buoy.

Skill Level: All divers.

A footbridge crosses an estuary to the beach

Hazards: A long swim, small boat traffic and light current during tidal exchanges.

Facilities: Tolmie State Park is closed on Mondays and Tuesdays. During the rest of the week you can enjoy a wooded park with parking, rest rooms, changing rooms, an outside cold shower for washing equipment, picnic tables, barbecue stands, a grass lawn, nature trail and two kitchen shelters with tables and barbecue structures. Air fills are available in Lacey and Olympia.

Travel Distance and Directions: Tolmie State Park is at the south end of Puget Sound, between Johnson Point and the Nisqually Flats.

> Mileage from Bellingham = 148 miles
> Mileage from South Seattle = 52 miles
> Mileage from Olympia = 12 miles

Follow I-5 to the Yelm / Marvin Road Exit 111 for Highway 510 West, located between Tacoma and Olympia. Exit from I-5 onto Marvin Road and drive west 3.7 miles to where the main road

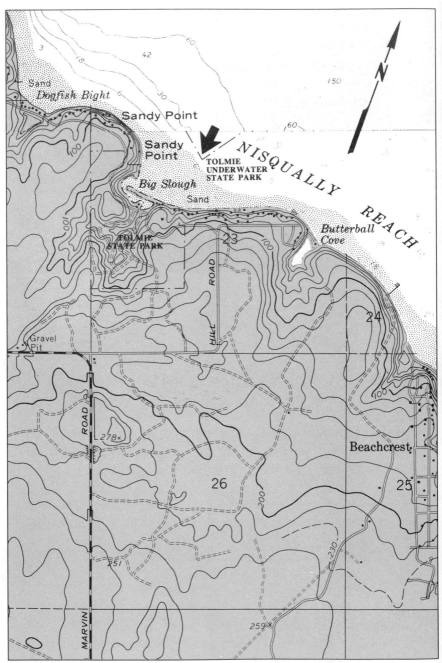

Figure 101

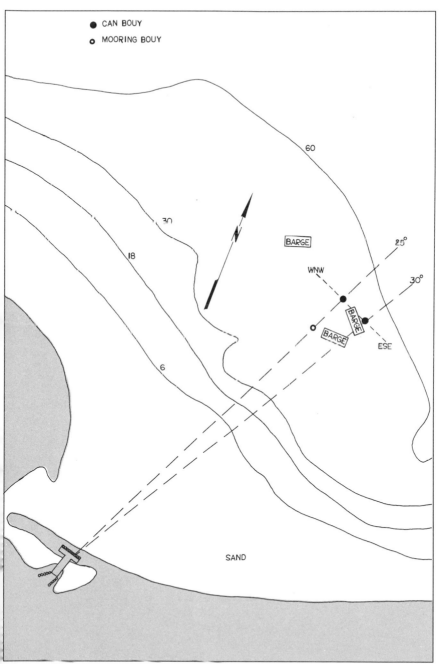

Figure 102 Barge locations at Tolmie Underwater Park

curves sharply to the left. Instead of following the curve, continue straight to where Marvin Road tees into 56th Avenue NE. Turn right onto 56th Avenue NE (dead end) and follow to the park entrance. Just before entering the park, the road will fork. Stay to the left, following the road into the park and down a hill.

Current Table: The Narrows.
   Look up the daily current predictions for the Narrows. Apply the following time corrections to calculate slack current times:

Time corrections for subordinate station 1295:
   Minimum current before flood: +26 minutes
   Minimum current before ebb: +20 minutes

Telephone Location: None at the immediate site. Drive 4.8 miles back toward the freeway to a restaurant and gas stations at the intersection of Marvin Road NE and Hogum Bay Road NE.

Non-Diver Activities: This is a beautiful picturesque wooded park with a view of Anderson Island and the southern end of the Key Peninsula. The shallow bottom is a great place for snorkeling. Bring a picnic lunch, barbecue some hamburgers, play on the grass or go for a hike in the woods along a nature trail. Visitors also can walk out onto the sand spit to watch the birds that live in this estuarine habitat or lie in the sun and read a book. This is a great place to socialize with friends. Other activities might include paddling about the bay in a raft or photographing the plants and animals that you will see here.

Plumose Sea Anemone

The plumose sea anemone, *Metridium senile*, is a common inhabitant of protected Northwest waters wherever there are structures to attach to. Most large individuals are solid white, although varieties of orange and brown also occur. All *Metridium* are presently classified as one species, without further differentiation. *Metridium senile* is a suspension feeder, using many finely branched tentacles to capture plankton and small crustacea from the surrounding water. It typically grows to 16 inches (41 cm) in height and has a life span that will exceed 200 years when individuals are not compromised by pollution or otherwise injured.

Figure 103

PART 10. **HOOD CANAL**

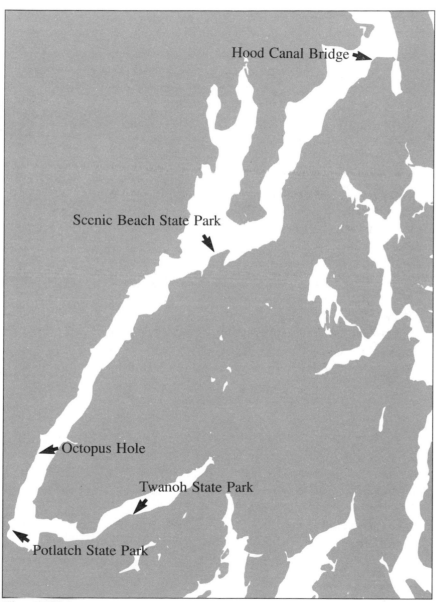

Figure 104

HOOD CANAL BRIDGE
EAST SIDE

Habitat and Depth: Six large concrete pylons anchor the east end of the Hood Canal Floating Bridge. The deeper bases of the fifth and sixth pylons are covered with white plumose anemones, plus a variety of other small animals. This dive is well worth repeating just to see the colorful animals living on these outer two current swept concrete structures.

A variety of nudibranchs live in the area. We saw yellow nudibranchs grazing on sponge, an orange and white clown nudibranch and several frosted nudibranchs. Additional animals included white compound ascidians attached to the side of a concrete pylon, sunflower sea stars, small red sea squirts, morning sun stars, blood stars and a sharp-nosed crab with sponge growing on its back. In shallower water beneath the bridge, colonies of dark purple sand dollars protrude from the bottom as they feed on suspended particles of plankton and organic debris. Other interesting animals, such as jackknife clams and kelp crabs, live on the sandy bottom and in the eelgrass bed between Salsbury Point and the Hood Canal Bridge.

Beneath the bridge, the bottom slope steepens at the base of the 5th pylon. The bottom on the uphill side of this pylon is 15 feet deep, while the bottom on the lower side is at 24 feet (10 foot tide). The base of the sixth pylon is also on a slope, with its uphill side at 33 feet and its deeper side at 43 feet (10 foot tide).

Site Description: Swimming with the current, instead of against it, will make this long swim possible without exhausting yourself in the process. Enter the water from the southern boundary of Salsbury Point County Park, 45 to 60 minutes before a predicted slack before an ebb current. At this time the current will still be flooding toward the bridge, but a reverse inshore current will be flowing in the opposite direction toward Salsbury Point. Swim out from shore until you feel the current shift toward the bridge, then turn and swim to the bridge with the main channel flow.

Flooding midchannel currents flow toward the bridge

After reaching the bridge, submerge on the upstream side of a bridge pylon to avoid being pushed past the bridge by surface current. The outer two pylons each have a ledge part way down their columns that is fun to explore. A compass is useful when swimming between pylons, but is not needed on a sunny day when the dry concrete columns of the third, fourth and fifth pylons are visible from the bottom. When you have finished exploring the bridge pylons, your return swim to the park will be with the newly ebbing current.

The beach south of the park is private and is posted "No Trespassing." Please respect this private property by staying in the water when south of the park.

Skill Level: Intermediate.

Hazards: Current, occasional small boats and up to a half-hour swim over a 0.2 nautical mile distance.

Water movement at mid-channel during a flooding current will be to the south-southwest, past Salsbury Point County Park toward the bridge. Conversely, mid-channel ebb currents move to the north

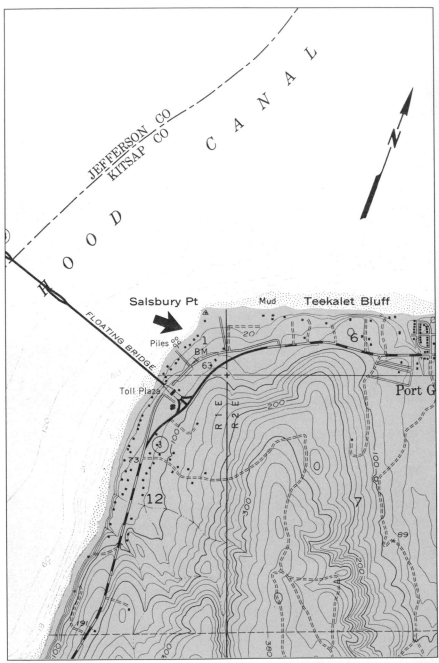

Figure 105

northeast, from the bridge toward the park. There is an inshore reverse current during a flood exchange that begins approximately 2.5 hours into the flood cycle. This current flows along the shoreline from a group of old pilings (located about half-way between the bridge and the boat ramp) toward Salsbury Point.

Facilities: As you might expect, there are no facilities under the bridge, but that is OK because you can swim to Salsbury Point County Park for camping, rest rooms, picnic tables, a covered eating area, barbecue stands, a boat ramp and a grassy play area with a tire swing and slide. Air fills are available in Hadlock, Port Townsend, Bremerton, Edmonds, Lynnwood and Seattle.

Travel Distance and Directions: Salsbury Point County Park is at the north end of Hood Canal, 0.3 nautical mile from the eastern side of the Hood Canal Bridge.

> Mileage from Bellingham = 90 miles
> Mileage from Seattle = 17 miles
> Mileage from Olympia = 83 miles

From Bellingham or Seattle: follow I-5 to north Seattle, then exit from the freeway at Exit 177 for the Edmonds-Kingston Ferry. At the bottom of the exit ramp, turn west onto 244th Street, and follow signs for Highway 104 West and the Kingston Ferry. Board the ferry in Edmonds and ride it across Puget Sound to Kingston. From the Kingston Ferry Dock, follow Highway 104 West for 8.6 miles toward the Hood Canal Floating Bridge. Turn right onto Wheeler Street (posted for Salsbury Point County Park). Continue 0.2 mile, then turn right into Salsbury Point County Park, just past Whitford Road NE. If the park entrance is closed, follow Whitford Road NE to the boat ramp in the park.

From Olympia: drive north on I-5 to Tacoma, then exit onto Highway 16 West (Bremerton Exit 132). Follow Highway 16 West over the Tacoma Narrows Bridge, then north toward Bremerton to the tip of Sinclair Inlet where Highway 16 West becomes Highway 3 North. Continue around Sinclair Inlet to the junction for Highway 3 North and Highway 304 East. Turn left onto Highway 3 North, then drive 16.0 miles to a stoplight at a four-way intersection. Turn left at the intersection and continue on Highway 3 North for 6.9 miles to the Hood Canal Bridge. Continue past the bridge 0.5 mile, turn left onto Wheeler Street (posted for Salsbury Point County Park), drive 0.2 mile, then turn right into Salsbury Point County Park, just past Whitford Road NE.

Current Table: Admiralty Inlet.

Look up the daily current predictions for Admiralty Inlet. Apply the following time corrections to calculate slack current times:

> Time corrections for the Hood Canal Bridge:
> Minimum inshore current before flood: 00 minutes
> Minimum inshore current before ebb: –46 minutes

Telephone Location: None at the immediate site. Drive to the parking area on the eastern side of the Hood Canal Bridge, 0.7 mile from Salsbury Point County Park.

Non-Diver Activities: Barbecue a meal while enjoying the great view of the Hood Canal Bridge and the Olympic Mountains. Walk out onto the Hood Canal Bridge Public Fishing Pier, which is accessed from the northeast side of the bridge by stairs leading down to a concrete float. Camp, photograph the ducks, or drive into the small company town of Port Gamble to visit the Port Gamble Museum (closed during the winter).

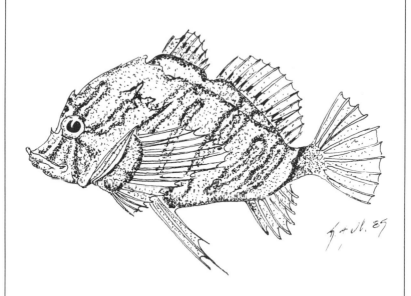

Grunt Sculpin

The grunt sculpin, *Rhamphocottus richardsoni*, is found on rocky and sandy bottoms in both intertidal and subtidal zones. This little fish is cream colored with dark brown bars angling across its sides and radiating from each eye. It grows to 3 inches in length (8 cm), and is easily recognized by its distinctive coloration, long snout, relatively large and broad head, and large pectoral fins. Additionally, the base of the rounded caudal fin is red.

Grunt sculpins are not good swimmers, but instead prefer hopping across the bottom on their large pectoral fins (the lower eight pectoral fin rays do not have webbing between them). When this fish is forced to leave the bottom, it swims slowly with its head held higher than its tail. Grunt sculpins feed on small crustacea and larvae that live on or near the bottom.

Figure 106

SCENIC BEACH STATE PARK

Habitat and Depth: Animal life on protected sandy bottoms, such as the one at Scenic Beach State Park, can be fascinating. Hermit crabs are fun to watch, especially when in the middle of one of their conventions frequently held only a short distance from this sandy-cobblestone beach. When these active animals are not chasing hermit crabs of the opposite sex or eating, they are often searching for a bigger shell or defending their own (Plates 3-4).

At one such convention, thirteen hermit crabs were gathered around a broken moon snail shell that was in sorry need of repair. Much of the shell's outer casing was broken away, revealing a hermit who was tightly curled around the central spiral. A large Bering hermit crab sat nearby, surrounded by a herd of smaller hermits. Off to the side, a small one was being chased by an even smaller one. "Chased" and "Chaser" hunched into their shells as a lone hermit came tearing across the sandy bottom, then slid to a stop between them in a cloud of sand. Finding these shells to be too small, he picked up his shell and was off again, this time toward the broken shell. Pausing only for a brief antennae check of the shell, he mounted the exposed spiral and proceeded to try to dislodge the resident crab with his large pincer. The purpose of this maneuver was not clear. Was the "Lone Hermit" looking for a mate, a bigger shell or just being obnoxious? Springing from his perch, he ran to large Mr. Bering (whose house was in good repair). In went the antennae. Finding this dream shell occupied, the "Lone Hermit" jumped backward, paused, and then returned to the top of the broken shell. But the thought of that big moon snail shell was too much! Down he came again and scurried over to Mr. Bering. In went the antennae again, ... oops ... pause ... yes, this hermie was definitely too big to argue with! The "Lone Hermit" moved off to find that elusive female and even more elusive bigger shell.

Besides possibly swimming upon a hermit crab convention, divers will find many other small animals, such as sea pens, striped nudibranchs, flounder, moon snails, white and orange sea anemones, tube-dwelling anemones, tube worms, comb jellies, sea squirts, sea stars, blackeye gobies, sea cucumbers and shrimp.

Current moves parallel to this long sandy-cobblestone beach

The sandy-cobblestone beach changes by 15 feet in depth (10 foot tide) to a gently sloping sandy bottom with eelgrass. The sandy bottom continues to slope downward past 69 feet (10 foot tide).

Site Description: There are no outstanding structures to see at this site. Entry can be made from any point along the park beach; however, the concrete stairs provide a clear access at a central location.

Skill Level: All divers.

Hazards: Small boats and minimal current.

A boat launch is located on Misery Point, 0.8 nautical mile north-northeast of the cement stairs at Seabeck State Park. Display a dive flag when diving in this area and listen for engine noise before ascending. Due to the long beach and minimal current, this site can be dived during either flood or ebb exchanges.

Facilities: Scenic Beach State Park covers 90 acres and 1600 feet of water front. Facilities include camping, parking, rest rooms, a

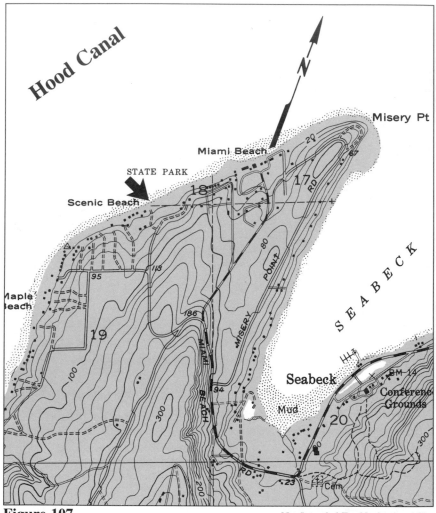

Figure 107   Not Intended For Navigational Use

bathhouse, fire pits, barbecue stands, a covered eating area, picnic tables, horseshoe pits, a volleyball net and a play area with a slide. Air fills are available in Bremerton.

Travel Distance and Directions: Scenic Beach State Park is on the eastern shore of Hood Canal, 1.9 miles from the Town of Seabeck.

Mileage from Bellingham = 110 miles
Mileage from North Seattle = 31 miles
Mileage from Olympia = 74 miles

From Bellingham: drive to Edmonds and ride the ferry across Puget Sound to Kingston. Drive 3.8 miles to the junction of Highway 104 West and NE Bond Road. Turn left onto NE Bond Road, and drive toward Poulsbo and Highway 305. Turn right onto Highway 305 North (4-way stoplight), and drive a short distance to Highway 3. Turn south onto Highway 3, drive 9.4 miles and exit to Scenic Beach State Park. At the bottom of the exit ramp, turn right onto Newberry Hill Road, then continue for 3.0 miles before turning right onto NW Seabeck Highway. Drive 5.1 miles, turn right onto Miami Beach Road NW, and drive the remaining 1.3 miles to Scenic Beach State Park.

From the Seattle waterfront: ride the ferry to Bremerton, then follow Highway 304 West to the Highway 3 junction. Turn right onto Highway 3 North, drive 6.7 miles and exit to Scenic Beach State Park. At the bottom of the exit ramp, turn left onto Newberry Hill Road, continue for 3.0 miles, then turn right onto NW Seabeck Highway. Drive 5.1 miles, turn right onto Miami Beach Road NW, and drive the remaining 1.3 miles to Scenic Beach State Park.

From Tacoma: cross the Tacoma Narrows Bridge and follow Highway 16 west around Sinclair Inlet to Highway 3 North. Turn left onto Highway 3 North, then drive 6.7 miles before exiting to Scenic Beach State Park. At the bottom of the exit ramp, turn left onto Newberry Hill Road. Drive 3.0 miles, turn right onto Seabeck NW Highway, continue for 3.0 miles, then turn right onto NW Seabeck Highway. Drive 5.1 miles, turn right onto Miami Beach Road NW, and drive the remaining 1.3 miles to the park.

Current Table: Admiralty Inlet.
Look up the daily current predictions for Admiralty Inlet. Apply the following time corrections to calculate slack current times:

Time corrections for subordinate station 1040:
Minimum current before flood: −60 minutes
Minimum current before ebb: −15 minutes

Telephone Location: At the park entrance, on the outside of the information hut.

Non-Diver Activities: Toss horseshoes, play volleyball or go for a long walk through the woods or along the beach. Visitors also can dig for clams (check game regulations and red tide first), camp or picnic.

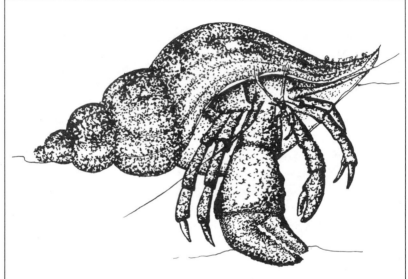

Hermit Crab

There are at least eighteen species of hermit crabs in the Pacific Northwest, but only three are commonly seen by divers. These include the Bering hermit crab, hairy hermit crab and granular hermit crab.

The largest species in the Northwest is found in subtidal and low intertidal areas. The Bering hermit crab, *Pagurus beringanus*, is recognized by its large size and by the orange and white bands on the base of its claws and on the first and second walking legs (juvenile Bering hermit crabs only have red bands on their claws).

Figure 108

The hairy hermit crab, *Pagurus hirsutiusculus*, is recognized by the hairy bristles that cover its legs and claws, and by its banded antennae. This hermit crab is often seen in shells that are too small for the crab to withdraw into completely.

The granular hermit crab, *Pagurus granosimanus*, is recognized by its rough and granular claws, red antennae and spotted legs.

Hermit crabs are comical looking animals that have acquired some interesting habits. Since they are not able to produce their own shells, they protect their soft abdomens by living in empty snail shells. As a hermit crab grows, it becomes too big for the shell that it last backed into. Thus, when not eating or making little hermit crabs, it is off in search of a larger shell. Hermit crabs frequently quarrel with each other over desirable shells that are either empty or occupied by a defending hermit crab (Plate 3). When at last the right shell is found (for that moment anyway) or a shell battle is won, a preliminary inspection is made before the hermit crab moves into its new home. Ed Ricketts described this housewarming event in *Between Pacific Tides, 5th edition* (page 37); "Inspecting a new shell—and every shell or similar object is a prospect—involves an unvarying sacred ritual: touch it, grasp it, rotate it until the orifice is in position to be explored with the antennae, and then if it seems satisfactory, move in." This event is often complicated by the efforts of additional hermit crabs to obtain the same shell at the same time.

Hermit crabs living in areas exposed to tidal surge will rarely abandon their shells unless the move is to a larger one. In contrast, hermit crabs living in the protected waters of Puget Sound often abandon their shells when picked up by a curious diver. These contrasting behavioral characteristics have evolved in different environments, each having a survival advantage within a respective habitat.

OCTOPUS HOLE

Habitat and Depth: Appropriately named for the rock ledge that lies only a few feet from shore, Octopus Hole provides many hiding places for wolf-eel and octopus.

Octopus and wolf-eel populations have decreased over the last six years at Octopus Hole. Unfortunately, a few of the large number of divers visiting this site each year remove animals. The resulting decreased populations mean fewer divers will see an octopus or wolf-eel while diving at this site. As long as animals continue to be removed from the ledge, populations will not recover and the ledge will remain barren. This can still be reversed. If enough divers protect these animals by not removing them, and encourage others to do the same, animal populations will soon begin to recover. A noticeable increase in octopus and wolf-eel populations would be seen within one season, resulting in a richer dive site for all to enjoy. Repopulation of this dive site is up to the people that dive here. If you are one of these divers, then the choice is yours.

Many divers enjoy visiting octopuses and wolf-eels in their natural habitat while observing, feeding or photographing them. Feeding such an animal is a rewarding and exciting experience not easily forgotten. Instead of relying on finding a crab to use for food, divers may wish to stop at a fish store and purchase a few herring or crabs (live crabs are best). Herring are inexpensive, can be easily stored in your freezer until needed, and will easily thaw during the first few minutes of a dive. During a feeding dive, move slowly as you approach an occupied den to avoid frightening the animal. Offer the food to the octopus or wolf-eel, allowing the animal to pull the food from your fingers. When feeding a wolf-eel, keep your fingers clear of the fish's teeth.

Additional animals common to this area include hermit crabs, California sea cucumbers, sunflower sea stars, shrimp, rockfish, ratfish, perch, blackeye gobies, flounder, schools of small fish, and large yellow sponges representing many years of growth.

The sandy-cobblestone beach changes to silty-mud as the depth increases past 15 feet. The top of the ledge ranges between 30 and 35 feet in depth, while the base drops to 60 feet (10 foot tide).

Looking south along Highway 101 toward the dive site

Site Description: To find the rock ledge, enter the water at the base of a short trail, then swim out from shore on a compass heading of 145 degrees. This heading will take you across the north end of the ledge at about the 50 foot depth (10 foot tide). When you reach this depth, turn and swim southward while following the bottom contour at 50 feet. After reaching the ledge, you can explore its base as you swim its length, then return along the rock wall at a shallower level to see parts of it that you missed on your first pass. A light is useful to brighten the dark holes and crevices along the way.

Skill Level: All divers.

Hazards: Minimal current and occasional small boats. This site can be dived during most tidal exchanges.

Facilities: None at the immediate site. Food is available in Hoodsport and hot showers at Potlatch State Park. Air fills are

Figure 109

Not Intended For Navigational Use

available in Hoodsport and at a full service dive store, 5.3 miles south of Octopus Hole on Highway 101.

Travel Distance and Directions: Octopus Hole is located on Hood Canal between the towns of Lilliwaup and Hoodsport.

> Mileage from Bellingham = 124 miles
> Mileage from Seattle = 70 miles
> Mileage from Olympia = 37 miles

From Bellingham: drive to Keystone, then ride the ferry to Port Townsend. From the Port Townsend Ferry Dock, turn left and follow Highway 20 West for 13 miles to the Highway 101 junction. Turn left onto Highway 101 South, then drive through Quilcene to the town of Lilliwaup. Continue 1.2 miles south of the Lilliwaup River Bridge to a turn-out on the left hand side of the road, 0.6 mile past mile marker 328.

From Seattle: either drive to Olympia and follow the directions from Olympia, or drive to Edmonds and ride the Edmonds-Kingston ferry to Kingston. From Kingston, drive 9.0 miles west on Highway 104 to the Hood Canal Bridge. Turn right onto the bridge (still Highway 104 West), drive 11 miles and turn right onto an exit ramp posted for Port Townsend and Quilcene. At the bottom of the ramp, turn right onto the Quilcene-Chimacum Road. Drive 8.1 miles to the Highway 101 junction in Quilcene, then continue south on Highway 101 for 32.9 miles to Lilliwaup. Drive 1.2 miles south of the Lilliwaup River Bridge to Octopus Hole, which is 0.6 mile south of mile marker 328.

From Olympia: drive north on Highway 101 to Hoodsport, then 3.2 miles north of the Finch Creek Bridge to where the road drops down to the water and there are no trees between the road and the water. Park alongside the road.

Current Table: Admiralty Inlet.

Look up the daily current predictions for Admiralty Inlet. Apply the following time corrections to calculate slack current times:

Time corrections for subordinate station 1040:
   Minimum current before flood: 00 minutes
   Minimum current before ebb: −15 minutes

Telephone Location: None at the immediate site. Drive into Hoodsport.

Non-Diver Activities: The drive along Hood Canal, between the water and evergreen trees, is beautiful. Octopus Hole is located only a few feet from Highway 101. There is room for visitors to spread out a towel and sun themselves on this short beach while enjoying the view of Hood Canal. Bring a picnic lunch and a good book.

As an alternate activity, visitors can drive 3.4 miles south into Hoodsport to explore the local winery and shops, and enjoy some ice cream.

The Tacoma City Light Electrical Generating Plant, located 6.0 miles south of Octopus Hole, has a boat launch, picnic area and rest rooms. Visitors can fish from the shore. For a larger grass play area and beach, drive another 0.5 mile south to Potlatch State Park.

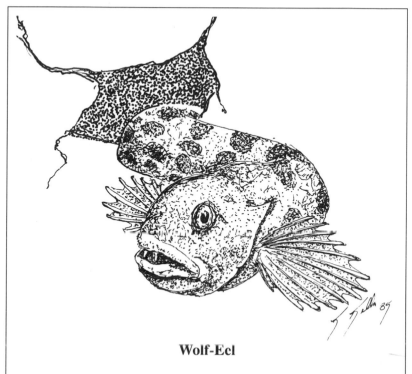

Wolf-Eel

The wolf-eel, *Anarrhichthys ocellatus*, is actually a fish, not an eel. Wolf-eels live in subtidal rocky crevices from 20 feet (6 meters) in depth on down to 738 feet (225 meters). Their color and markings vary. Males are usually slate gray with large black spots, while females and juveniles often have a reddish brown color. A large male may reach 8 feet (2.4 meters) in length; females are slightly smaller. They breathe by pumping water across their gills, opening and closing their mouth as if to show their teeth. They are generally shy animals, but if threatened can inflict a nasty bite with their blunt teeth. They eat crabs, sea urchins, mussels and clams. If hungry, wolf-eels will gladly accept split sea urchins from divers (Plate 21). When feeding a wolf-eel, move slowly so as not to frighten the animal and watch your fingers!

Figure 110

POTLATCH STATE PARK

Habitat and Depth: Potlatch State Park offers a pleasant family park with a dive site that is ideal for divers who are in the process of becoming familiar with their equipment. It is also a good dive site for those who are mainly interested in getting wet. When diving here, look for small animals that inhabit the silty-sand bottom. A few of the animals found on this sparsely populated slope include flounder, hermit crabs, nudibranchs, moon snails, tube worms, burrowing sea anemones and an occasional sea pen.

Potlatch State Park has a long cobblestone beach with a silty-sand bottom that slopes gradually outward to the 30 foot depth. Beyond this depth, the bottom slope steepens and continues downward past the 100 foot mark.

Site Description: Enter the water at any point along the park beach, swim out toward a row of buoys that mark the bottom drop-off, and descend. Divers can explore the sandy bottom above the drop-off or move down the slope to see what can be found on this relatively barren slope. Usually, as you go deeper, the number of animals decrease due to the smaller amount of food available in the darker water.

Skill Level: All divers.

Hazards: Occasional small boats.

Facilities: The day-use area in Potlatch State Park is located next to Hood Canal on the east side of Highway 101. Here, visitors will find a large grass field with swings to play on, picnic tables, a covered eating area, barbecue pits and rest rooms with adjoining outside changing areas. In the upper park, located on the west side of Highway 101, there are rest rooms with hot showers. Fire pits and camping sites have been established along a small stream.

Air fills are available along Hood Canal at three points, the closest being 1.1 miles north of Potlatch State Park. The other two locations are in Hoodsport and 10.3 miles north of Lilliwaup.

The day use area at Potlatch State Park

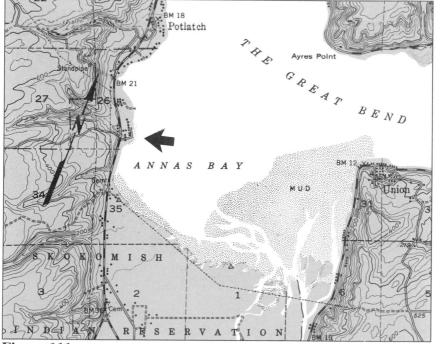

Figure 111   Not Intended For Navigational Use

Travel Distance and Directions: Potlatch State Park is at the southern end of Hood Canal, 3 miles south of Hoodsport.

Mileage from Bellingham = 131 miles
Mileage from Seattle = 86 miles
Mileage from Olympia = 32 miles

From Bellingham: drive to Keystone, then ride the ferry to Port Townsend. Turn left from the ferry dock and follow Highway 20 West for 13 miles to the Highway 101 junction. Turn left onto Highway 101 South and drive to Quilcene, then continue 40 miles past Quilcene to Potlatch State Park.

From Seattle: drive to Edmonds, then ride the ferry across the sound to Kingston. Drive 9.0 miles west from Kingston on Highway 104 to the Hood Canal Bridge. Turn right onto the bridge (still Highway 104 West) and drive 11 miles before turning right onto the Quilcene-Chimacum Road exit ramp. Turn right at the bottom of the ramp onto the Quilcene-Chimacum Road. Drive through Quilcene, then   continue south on Highway 101 to Lilliwaup. From the Lilliwaup River Bridge, drive 7.7 miles south on Highway 101 to Potlatch State Park. Turn left to the day-use area and beach, or right to the camping area and hot showers.

From Olympia: drive north on Highway 101 toward Shelton and Port Angeles. Stay to the right at the Highway 101/Highway 8 Junction, continuing north on Highway 101 for 25.8 miles before turning right into Potlatch State Park.

Current Table: Admiralty Inlet.

Look up the daily current predictions for Admiralty Inlet. Apply the following time corrections to calculate slack current times:

Time corrections for subordinate station 1040:
Minimum current before flood: 00 minutes
Minimum current before ebb: −15 minutes

Telephone Location: In front of the rest rooms at the south end of the day use area.

Non-Diver Activities: Potlatch State Park is a great play area for the entire family. There is a big grass lawn to run and play on, plus a long beach to walk. Spread a towel on the beach and catch some sun while you enjoy the view of Hood Canal. Bring a book, frisbee and picnic lunch, or drive into Hoodsport to explore this small town. The drive along Hood Canal is worth the trip all by itself.

Sunflower Sea Star

The sunflower sea star, *Pycnopodia helianthoides*, is the largest and fastest sea star in the Northwest. An aggressive predator toward many bottom dwelling animals (Plates 11-13), it is commonly seen on rocky, sandy, and muddy subtidal bottoms. This active sea star has a variable number of arms, often 18 to 23, and grows to a diameter of 3 feet (91 cm). Coloration is variable, with individual animals showing a predominant color of orange, light green or light purple.

When a diver touches the back of a sunflower sea star with a gloved hand, the nylon covering on a neoprene glove will seem to snag on the small projections covering the animal's back. These bony projections are actually small pincers, called pedicellariae, that prevent other animals from colonizing on top of this sea star. The glove didn't snag, but instead was pinched by pedicellariae responding to both chemical and physical stimuli. Some pedicellariae may even remain attached to the glove when it is lifted off the sea star. These small pincers (there are two sizes) effectively crush larvae that drift onto the back of sea stars. Still smaller hair-like structures, called cilia, sweep debris from the back of sea stars. As a result, healthy sea stars always have clean backs!

Figure 112

TWANOH STATE PARK

Habitat and Depth: The Great Bend of Hood Canal provides a protected area that is free of strong current and surge. Although currents do exist, they are much more subdued than in northern waters. Because of this, divers can enjoy diving in lower Hood Canal without having to time their dives precisely with the occurrence of slack water.

Although animal life is not as abundant at Twanoh State Park as in northern waters, there are many interesting critters to look for while diving in this game preserve. Here is your chance to feed graceful tube-dwelling anemones by dropping bits of food or small hermit crabs onto their tentacles. Divers also will see large Bering hermit crabs, moon snails, sunflower sea stars, mottled sea stars, flounder, perch, ratfish, threespine sticklebacks, sea cucumbers, sun stars, leather stars, red sea squirts, nudibranchs, jellyfish, sea pens, cockles, mussels, oysters and geoducks.

The pea gravel beach changes to silty sand in the shallows, then slopes gently downward past 70 feet in depth. Eelgrass grows in 14 to 24 feet of water (10 foot tide) between the point and small fishing pier.

Dive Profile: Swim out past the roped swimming area, and submerge. As you pass through the eelgrass, look for small fish that frequent this area, such as blackeye gobies, small perch, tube-snouts, pipefish and threespine sticklebacks. To find tube-dwelling anemones, swim to the 50 foot depth, turn to the southwest, and angle back in to the 40 foot depth while scanning the bottom (Figure 114). Leave enough of an air reserve near the end of your dive so that you can remain submerged until reaching the swimming area or the shallow inshore area where there is no boat traffic.

Skill Level: All divers.

Hazards: Small boats and minimal current.

Use a dive flag, and stay out of the boat launching areas at each end of the park. Listen for engine noise before ascending. When

This kitchen shelter was built in 1937
by the Civilian Conservation Corps.

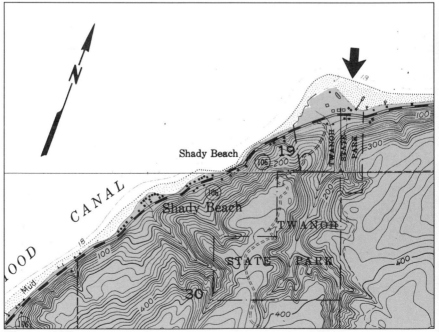

Figure 113

Not Intended For Navigational Use

boats are present, plan your exit point so that you ascend into the roped swimming area, along a piling or in the shallows. Do not remain submerged in depths shallower than 10 feet.

Facilities: The impressive log and stone structures in this park were built by the Civilian Conservation Corps in 1937. They include a pier with a floating dock, a swimming platform, footbridge, concession stand (open Memorial Day weekend through Labor Day weekend), two bathhouses, rest rooms with changing areas, and two huge covered kitchen areas that each have a stove, sink and stone fireplace. Other facilities in the park include camping sites, smaller sheltered kitchen areas, picnic tables, two swing sets, a wading pond and boat launching ramp. Air fills are available in Hoodsport, Bremerton and Olympia.

Travel Distance and Directions: Twanoh State Park is at the south end of Hood Canal, 5.5 nautical miles northeast by east-northeast from Union.

> Mileage from Bellingham = 113 miles
> Mileage from North Seattle = 33 miles
> Mileage from Olympia = 41 miles

From Bellingham and Seattle: drive to the Seattle waterfront and ride the ferry to Bremerton. After leaving the ferry, follow Highway 304 West for 5 miles to the Highway 3 South junction. Turn right onto Highway 3 South toward Belfair and Shelton. In 9.6 miles, turn right onto Highway 106 West and drive 7.7 miles to Twanoh State Park.

From Olympia: drive north on Highway 101, past Shelton to the turn-off for Union. Turn right onto Highway 106 East and drive the remaining 13 miles to Twanoh State Park.

Current Table: Admiralty Inlet.

Look up the daily current predictions for Admiralty Inlet. Apply the following time corrections to calculate slack current times:

Time corrections for subordinate station 1040:
    Minimum current before flood: 00 minutes
    Minimum current before ebb: −15 minutes

Telephone Location: By the park concession stand.

Non-Diver Activities: This is a great park for both divers and non-divers, as there are activities for the entire family. Play tennis or horseshoes, sun yourself on the beach, fish from the pier, play on the swing sets, go wading, walk along the beach, or share a picnic lunch with friends.

Figure 114   Tube-Dwelling Anemone

Tube-Dwelling Anemone

The graceful tube-dwelling anemone, *Pachycerianthus fimbriatus*, lives subtidally in soft mud and silty sand bottoms where it uses a sticky mucus to build a protective tube out of grains of sand, small pieces of broken shells and bits of other available debris. This unusual anemone reaches a height of 12 inches (30 cm), with a tube with a diameter of up to 2 inches (5 cm).

Long, white outer tentacles with dark bands are used to capture small animals as they drift by in the water column. Captured food is passed to a shorter inner ring of tentacles that then relay the food to the mouth. Divers can easily observe this feeding behavior by gently dropping a small animal onto this anemone's oral disc. The large tentacles will immediately begin to bend toward the prey to make contact and paralyze it with stinging barb-like structures called nematocysts. If the small animal is not recognized by the anemone as food (as sometimes happens with a fully retracted hermit crab), it will not be ingested. Instead, the small animal will be passed to the outer ring of tentacles and then dropped back to the bottom.

PART 11. **APPENDIX**

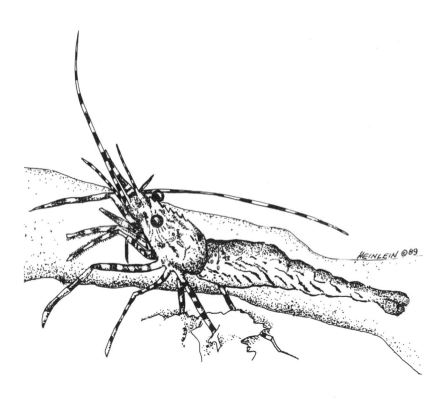

Figure 115   Broken-back Shrimp

DIVING EMERGENCY INFORMATION

Virginia Mason Hospital, Seattle
    Hyperbaric Unit 24-Hour Consultation   (206) 583-6543
    Emergency Room   (206) 583-6433

Divers Alert Network
    May call collect during an emergency.   (919) 684-8111

U.S. Coast Guard Search and Rescue
    Seattle   (206) 442-5880

Canadian Fleet Diving Unit
    Esquimalt, B.C.   (604) 388-2379

OTHER PHONE NUMBERS

Red Tide Hotline   1-800 562-5632

DIVE STORE DIRECTORY

For the "Away From Home" diver!

Dive stores may suddenly change names, business hours or phone numbers. They may also move to new locations or go out of business. Before relying on an unfamiliar dive store for services or air, be sure to call ahead to check on their business hours. The following dive stores are located in western Washington, and are listed by geographical areas.

SAN JUAN ISLAND

Emerald Seas Diving Center
P.O. Box 476
180 First Street
Friday Harbor, WA 98250
(206) 378-2772

Ken's Diving & Towing
Friday Harbor Marina
Friday Harbor, WA 98250
(206) 378-5808
— Air fills only —

STRAIT OF JUAN DE FUCA AREA

Angeles Dive & Sport Center
134 East Lauridsen Blvd.
Port Angeles, WA 98362
(206)452-3483

Herb's Motel & Charters
Box 175
Sekiu, Washington 98381
(206) 963-2346
— Air fills only —

Olympic Divers
509 South Lincoln Street
Port Angeles, WA 98362
(206) 452-5264

Orca Divers
P.O. Box 899
Corner Matheson & Irondale
Hadlock, WA 98339
(206) 385-5688

Scuba Supplies
738 Marine Drive
Port Angeles, WA 98362
(206) 457-3190

Undersea Scuba Adventure
212 Wye Road
Pt Angeles (Joyce), WA 98362
(206)) 928-3044
Call before driving out

NORTH PUGET SOUND AREA

American Sport Diver
Upper Totem Lake Center
12630 - 120th Ave NE
Kirkland, WA 98034
(206) 821-7200

Anacortes Diving & Supply
2502 Commercial Ave
Anacortes, WA 98221
(206) 293-2070

Bellingham Dive n Travel
2720 West Maplewood
Bellingham, WA 98225
(206) 734-1770

Blue Dolphin Diving Center
1375 State Avenue
Marysville, WA 98270
(206) 653-2834

Exotic Aquatics
154 Winslow Way East
Bainbridge Island, WA 98110
(206) 842-1980

Lighthouse Diving Center
5421 196th Street SW, #6
Lynnwood, WA 98036
(206) 771-2679

8215 Lake City Way NE
Seattle, WA 98115
(206) 524-1633

Northwest Sports Divers
8030 NE Bothell Way
Bothell, WA 98011
(206) 487-0624

Puget Sound Dive Enterprises
1921 Wheaton Way
Bremerton, WA 98310
(206) 377-0554

Seattle Skindiving Supply
1661 Harbor Ave SW
Seattle, WA 98126
(206) 937-2550

Silent World Diving, Inc.
13600 NE 20th Street
Bellevue, WA 98005
(206) 747-8842

Silverdale Scuba
2839-A Kitsap Place
Silverdale, WA 98383
(206) 692-1086

Sound Dive Center
990 Sylvan Way
Bremerton, WA 98310
(206) 373-6141

3423 Byron Street
Silverdale, WA 98383
(206) 692-0737

Underwater Sports
Casino Square
205 East Casino Road, #4
Everett, WA 98203-2830
(206) 355-3338

264 Railroad Ave
Edmonds, WA 98020-4133
(206) 771-6322

NORTH PUGET SOUND AREA (continued)

Underwater Sports
  10545 Aurora Avenue North
  Seattle, WA 98133-8811
  (206) 362-3310

  #59 Brierwood Center
  12003 NE 12th Street
  Bellevue, WA 98005-2455
  (206) 454-5168

Washington Divers
  903 North State Street
  Bellingham, WA 98225
  (206) 676-8029

Whidbey Island Dive Center
  9050-D 900th Avenue
  Oak Harbor, WA 98277
  (206) 675-1112

SOUTH PUGET SOUND AREA

A&E Aquatics
  29130 Pacific Hwy South
  Federal Way, WA 98003
  (206) 941-3115

Another World Underwater
  620 Auburn Way South
  Suite L
  Auburn, WA 98002
  (206) 939-7787

Lighthouse Diving Center
  24860 Pacific Hwy South
  Kent, WA 98032
  (206) 839-6881

  3630 South Cedar Street
  Suite A
  Tacoma, WA 98409
  (206) 475-1316

Miller's Dive & Marine
  3005 Harborview Drive
  Gig Harbor, WA 98335
  (206) 858-7989

Northwest Divers
  7824-E River Road
  Puyallup, WA 98371
  (206) 845-5350

Northwest Divers
  4815 North Pearl
  Tacoma, WA 98407
  (206) 752-3973

Pacific Reef
  7516 - 27th West
  Tacoma, WA 98466
  (206) 564-0356

Pro Divers Supply
  9109 Veterans Drive
  Tacoma, WA 98488
  (206) 588-8368

Pro Divers Supply #2
  606 Oxford Street
  Tacoma, WA 98465
  (206) 564-5549

SOUTH PUGET SOUND AREA (continued)

Scuba Sports Expeditions
  241 Sunset Blvd. North
  Renton, WA 98055
  (206) 228-7332

Underwater Sports
  34428 Pacific Hwy South
  Federal Way, WA 98003-7325
  (206) 874-9387

  9608 40th SW
  Tacoma, WA 98499-4302
  (206) 588-6634

Underwater Sports
  9020 Martin Way East
  Olympia, WA 98516-5997
  (206) 493-0322

Underwater Unlimited
  124 Fir Street NE
  Olympia, WA 98501
  (206) 943-8612

HOOD CANAL AREA

Mike's Beach Resort
  North 38470 Highway 101
  Lilliwaup, WA 98555
  (206) 877-5324
  — Air fills only —

Mike's Diving Center
  North 22270 Highway 101
  Shelton, WA 98584
  (206) 877-9568

Sunrise Motel
  P.O. Box 76
  Highway 101
  Hoodsport, WA 98548
  (206) 877-5301
  — Air fills only —

ADDITIONAL READING

Attenborough, David. *Life on Earth: A Natural History*. Boston and Toronto: Little Brown and Company, 1979.

Barnes, Robert D. *Invertebrate Zoology*, Third Edition. Philadelphia, London, and Toronto: W.B. Saunders Company, 1974.

Behrens, David W. *Pacific Coast Nudibranchs: A Guide to the Opisthobranchs of the Northeastern Pacific*. Los Osos, California: Sea Challengers, 1980.

Carefoot, Thomas. *Pacific Seashores: A Guide to Intertidal Ecology*. Seattle and London: University of Washington Press, 1979.

Cousteau, Captain J. Y. with Frederic Dumas. *The Silent World*. New York: Harper and Brothers Publishers, 1953.

Cousteau, Jacques-Yves with James Dugan. *The Living Sea*. New York and Evanston: Harper and Row, Publishers, 1963. Cummings, All and Jo Bailey-Cummings. *Gunkholing in the San Juans*. Edmonds, Washington: Nor'westing, Inc., 1984.

Cousteau, Jacques-Yves and Philippe Diole'. *Octopus and Squid: The Soft Intelligence*. New York: A & W Visual Library, 1973.

Eschmeyer, William N., Earl S. Herald and Howard Hammann. *A Field Guide to Pacific Coast Fishes of North America*. Boston: Houghton Mifflin Company, 1983.

Gotshall, Daniel W. *Fishwatchers' Guide to the Inshore Fishes of the Pacific Coast*. Monterey, California: Sea Challengers, 1977.

Gotshall, Daniel W. and Laurence L. Laurent. *Pacific Coast Subtidal Marine Invertebrates: A Fishwatchers' Guide*. Los Osos, California: Sea Challengers, 1979.

Griffin, Ted. Namu, *Quest for the Killer Whale*. Seattle: Gryphon West Publishers, 1982.

Hart, J.L. *Pacific Fishes of Canada*. Ottawa: Fisheries Research Board of Canada, 1973.

Hoyt, Eric. Orca: *The Whale Called Killer*. Camden East, Ontario: Camden House Publishing Ltd., 1984.

Island Canoe Company. *Current and Tide Tables: For Puget Sound, Deception Pass, the San Juans, Gulf Islands and Strait of Juan de Fuca*. Bainbridge Island, Washington: Island Canoe Company.

Island Canoe Company. *Puget Sound Current Guide*. Bainbridge Island, Washington: Island Canoe Company.

Island Canoe Company. *San Juan Current Guide: Including the Gulf Islands and Strait of Juan De Fuca*. Bainbridge Island, Washington: Island Canoe Company.

Kozloff, Eugene N. *Marine Invertebrates of the Pacific Northwest*. Seattle and London: University of Washington Press, 1987.

Kozloff, Eugene N. *Seashore Life of the Northern Pacific Coast*. Seattle and London: University of Washington Press, 1983.

Krenmayr, Janice. *Exploring Puget Sound by Car*. Seattle: The Writing Works, 1984.

Lamb, Andy and Phil Edgell. *Coastal Fishes Of The Pacific Northwest*. Madeira Park, B.C., Canada: Harbour Publishing Co., LTD., 1986.

Levine, Joseph S. and Jeffrey L. Rotman. *Undersea Life*. New York: Stewart, Tabori & Chang, Publishers, 1985.

McIntyre, Joan. *Mind In The Waters: A Book to Celebrate the Consciousness of Whales and Dolphins*. New York: Charles Scribner's Sons, 1974.

McLachlan, Dan H. and Jak Ayres. *Fieldbook of Pacific Northwest Sea Creatures*. Happy Camp, California: Naturegraph Publishers, Inc., 1979.

Mowat, Farley. *A Whale For The Killing.* Toronto, Ontario: McClelland and Stewart-Bantam Limited, 1972.

Mueller, Marge. *The San Juan Islands, Afoot and Afloat.* Seattle: The Mountaineers, 1979.

Mueller, Marge & Ted. *North Puget Sound, Afoot and Afloat.* Seattle: The Mountaineers, 1988.

Mueller, Marge & Ted. *South Puget Sound, Afoot and Afloat.* Seattle: The Mountaineers, 1983.

Nybakken, James. "Tender Trapper," *Sea Frontiers*, 30-2 (March 1984), 106-110.

Ricketts, Edward F. and Jack Calvin. *Between Pacific Tides*, Fourth Edition, revised by J.W. Hedgpeth. Stanford, California: Stanford University Press, 1968.

Smith, Deboyd L. *A Guide to Marine Coastal Plankton and Marine Invertebrate Larvae.* Dubuque, Iowa: Kendall/Hunt Publishing Company, 1977.

Snively, Gloria. *Exploring the Seashore in British Columbia, Washington and Oregon: A Guide to Shorebirds and Intertidal Plants and Animals.* Vancouver and London: Gordon Soules Book Publishers Ltd.; Seattle: Pacific Search Press, 1978.

Somerton, David and Craig Murray. *Field Guide to the Fish of Puget Sound and the Northwest Coast.* Seattle and London: Washington Sea Grant Program, University of Washington, 1976.

Strickland, Richard M. *The Fertile Fjord: Plankton in Puget Sound.* Seattle and London: Washington Sea Grant Program, University of Washington, 1983.

Wertheim, Anne. *The Intertidal Wilderness.* San Francisco: Sierra Club Books, 1984.

COMMON & SCIENTIFIC ANIMAL NAMES

Common Name	Scientific Name
Basket star	*Gorgonocephalus eucnemis*
Blackeye goby	*Coryphopterns nicholsi*
Blood star	*Henricia leviuscula*
Broken-back shrimp	*Heptacarpus*
C-O sole	*Pleuronichthys coenosus*
Cabezon	*Scorpaenichthys marmoratus*
China rockfish	*Sebastes nebulosus*
Christmas anemone	*Urticina crassicornis*
Festive triton	*Tritonia festiva*
Frosted nudibranch	*Dirona albolineata*
Giant acorn barnacle	*Balanus nubilus*
Giant nudibranch	*Dendronotus rufus*
Grunt sculpin	*Rhamphocottus richardsoni*
Hermit crab	*Pagurus sp.*
Hooded nudibranch	*Melibe leonina*
Kelp crab	*Pugettia producta*
Leather star	*Dermasterias imbricata*
Lined chiton	*Tonicella lineata*
Lion's mane	*Cyanea capillata*
Moon snail	*Polinices lewisii*
Morning sun star	*Solaster dawsoni*
Mosshead warbonnet	*Chirolophis nugator*
Octopus, Pacific	*Octopus dofleini*
Orange peel nudibranch	*Tochuina tetraquetra*
Orange sea cucumber	*Cucumaria miniata*
Pacific sand lance	*Ammodytes hexapterus*
Painted greenling	*Oxylebius pictus*
Piddock clams	*Penitella penita*
Pink scallop	*Chlamys hericia*
Pipefish	*Syngnathus griseolineatus*

COMMON & SCIENTIFIC ANIMAL NAMES

Common Name	Scientific Name
Plumose anemone	*Metridium senile*
Quillback rockfish	*Sebastes maliger*
Ratfish	*Hydrolagus colliei*
Sailfin sculpin	*Nautichthys oculofasciatus*
Sand dollar	*Dendraster excentricus*
Sea urchins	*Strongylocentrotus*
Sea star on barnacles	*Pisaster ochraceus*
Sea lemon nudibranch	*Archidoris montereyensis*
Sea pen	*Ptilosarcus gurneyi*
Sharp-nosed crab	*Scyra acutifrons*
Slime star	*Pteraster tesselatus*
Spiny dogfish, Pacific	*Squalus acanthias*
Striped seaperch	*Embiotoca lateralis*
Striped nudibranch	*Armina californica*
Sturgeon poacher	*Agonus acipenserinus*
Sun Star	*Solaster stimpsoni*
Sunflower sea star	*Pycnopodia helianthoides*
Tiger rockfish	*Sebastes nigrocinctus*
Tube worm, Giant	*Eudistylia vancouveri*
Tube Dwelling Anemone	*Pachycerianthus fimbriatus*
Tube-snout	*Aulorhynchus flavidus*
Vermilion sea star	*Mediaster aequalis*
Wolf eel	*Anarrhichthys ocellatus*

332

INDEX